# HOW THE WORLD

# *REALLY*

## WORKS

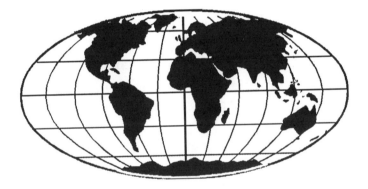

**Alan B. Jones**

ABJ Press

ISBN 0-9640848-1-3

Copyright 1996 by Alan B. Jones

Library of Congress Catalog Card No.  96-94874

ABJ  Press
P.O. Box 2362
Paradise, CA 95967

# CONTENTS

# INTRODUCTION

If it takes you more than a few days to read this book, I have defeated my own purpose. That purpose is to provide a shortcut for politically astute readers to acquire the essential knowledge needed to be effective in the ongoing fight to save for our posterity the great experiment in freedom that was launched 200 years ago by our country's founders.

I have selected and reviewed in this volume a mere handful of the many books which have been written outlining our various problems. Taken together, however, they will correctly spell out who we are really fighting, what their goals are, and what strategies they are utilizing to attain those goals. Once these matters are understood, effective counter-strategies are easy to define. Without this understanding, our efforts will continue to be aimed at symptoms rather than causes, and will continue to be insufficient, misdirected, and ineffective.

These reviews cannot possibly cover all the detail contained in the original books themselves. They can, however, convince you that our problems are interconnected in a way that you probably never guessed, and that very few of even the most politically active people understand. I urge you to acquire these several books yourselves to help you fill in more pieces of the puzzle for yourselves. Many of the actions most needed by our society will then become obvious to you, to the benefit of us all.

Chapter 1

## "A CENTURY OF WAR"

(By F. William Engdahl. Pub. 1993 by Paul & Co., c/o PCS Data Processing, Inc., 360 W. 31st St., New York, NY 10001. Tel. (212)564-3730, Fax (212)971-7200.)

We start with this book because it explicitly defines the mechanics behind the major disruptions which have impacted us all during this last century. These events include World War 1, the 1929 stock market crash and subsequent depression, the rise of Hitler and the subsequent World War 2, the Marshall Plan and subsequent never-ending "foreign aid," the Vietnamese War and LBJ's Great Society, followed in quick order by Nixon's separation of the dollar from gold and the 1974 "Oil Shock," the creation of the massive Third World debt, the buildup of the massive U.S. national debt in the 1980's, and last but not least, George Bush's Gulf War. Omitting Mr. Engdahl's documentation and his gentle entry into his subject, he lays out the following picture:

The wars and other horrors listed above were derived from Great Britain's secret strategies to control gold, the seas, and the world's raw materials, most particularly including, after the turn of the century, petroleum, the new "black gold" which enabled modern warfare to be waged. In the several decades prior to World War 1, the furtherance of this basic policy was in the hands of Cecil Rhodes, Alfred Lord Milner, and others, who formed a secret group called the "Round Table." This group, as recorded in its own writings, was specifically anti-German and pro-Empire. It viewed the economic strengthening of Germany in the late 1800's with alarm, and the German effort after the turn of the century to build a Baghdad-to-Berlin railway as a direct military threat, since it would provide direct German access to the Middle East's oil fields, bypassing the sea routes controlled by the British. Britain had earlier sealed off extension of the railway to the Persian Gulf by the forcible establishment of Kuwait as a "British Protectorate" to be run by the Sabah family, as at present, preventing future Central European (i.e., German) access to the southern oceans. The last northern link of the railway, also of concern, was in Serbia. But before that link could be finished, the Austrian heir-apparent was assassinated by a Serb, to which Austria responded, starting World War 1 by bringing in Germany, France and Russia by treaty with either Serbia or Austria, and also Britain, via a secret treaty which it had signed with France only three months before the assassination.

The war produced between 16 and 20 million deaths, mostly civilians, including a half-million British deaths. Germany was successfully cut off from Russian and Middle-Eastern oil, and the war was essentially won with Rockefeller oil from America. Following the war, Britain and France carved up the Middle East (by prior secret wartime agreement),

Britain obtaining "protectorate" status over Palestine (Israel) and the important oil-producing areas, especially Iraq. Their protectorate over Palestine set the stage for their planned later creation in that area of a Jewish homeland, which intent was proclaimed to British Zionists in a letter from Britain's Foreign Secretary Arthur Balfour to Walter Lord Rothschild, representing the English Federation of Zionists. The letter became known as the Balfour Declaration, which was not implemented until after World War 2. The British intent was to project their control into the oil-laden Middle East by creating a Jewish-dominated Palestine, beholden to Britain for survival, and surrounded by a pack of squabbling, balkanized Arab states.

During the Versailles Treaty talks after the war, Round Table members Lionel Curtis, Balfour, Milner, and others, formed an above-ground group called the Royal Institute of International Affairs for the purpose of coordinating Anglo-American cooperative efforts. They decided also to form an American branch, but gave it a different name in order to obscure its antecedents. Thus was born the Council on Foreign Relations, originally staffed by J.P. Morgan men and financed by Morgan money. The CFR, of course, is still very much with us.

The Rockefeller and British-controlled oil companies struggled after the war over control of world-wide oil resources. Becoming tired of such competition by the late 20's, they sent representatives to a meeting in Achnacarry, Scotland to work out an arrangement for cooperating rather than competing. Out of this came the secret "Achnacarry Agreement" of 1928, defining market shares and geographic divisions and setting world cartel prices. The seven major companies in the cartel, known as the "Seven Sisters," were Esso (Standard of N.J.), Mobil (Standard of N.Y.), Gulf Oil, Texaco, Chevron (Standard of Calif.), and the two British companies Royal Dutch Shell and the Anglo-Persian Oil Company (later named British Petroleum). These folks remain today the *real* cartel, and not the squabbling Arabs in OPEC. They agreed to purchase, or deal even more inhospitably with, any company outside the cartel if it got big enough to be of concern.

Montagu Norman, the Governor of the Bank of England, and without doubt the world's most influential banker, precipitated the U.S. stock market crash by his secret request to George Harrison, the Governor of the New York Federal Reserve Bank, to end the American post-war inflation (which the British had earlier "requested") by raising U.S. interest rates and restricting credit. The stock market crash and the subsequent Great Depression followed. (These financial events are covered in a great deal more detail in "The Creature From Jekyll Island," reviewed below.)

Britain was also largely responsible for saddling Germany with unpayable war debts, and then denying Germany any reasonable possibility of organizing to pay them off. The German reparations debt amounted to 132 billion gold marks, with the unpaid balance to accumulate at 6% annual interest. Germany was prostrate, and even British experts acknowledged the debt to be so huge as to be unpayable. Germany signed the agreement, however, under the pain, if they refused, of the military occupation of the Ruhr, the engine of their economy.

But then Germany's Foreign minister Walther Rathenau worked out, signed, and announced, in April 1922, the bilateral Rapallo Treaty with the Soviet Union, in which the Soviets agreed to forgive reparations payments due it in return for German agreement to sell it industrial technology. The British, fearing the Russian development of the Baku oil fields without them, and to the potential benefit of Germany, protested that the accord had been negotiated "behind their backs." Two months later, Rathenau was mysteriously assassinated, and any hope for German economic stability was lost. The German Mark then began its famous fall. In December 1922, the Mark had fallen to 7,592 to the dollar. Germany was declared in default of her reparations payments on January 9, 1923, and two days later French military forces occupied the Ruhr. By November, the Mark was trading at 750 billion Marks to the dollar, and the savings of the entire German population were destroyed, substantially wiping out their entire middle class.

The political upshot ultimately affected the whole world. The Versailles payment plan was replaced by the Dawes Plan, created by the Anglo-American banking community, which rescheduled the German reparations payments. Then, through a series of political maneuvers and fortuitous accidents and other deaths, a cooperative German banker named Hjalmar Schacht, a long-time correspondent with the Bank of England's Montagu Norman, was elevated to the position of President of the Reichsbank. Reparations continued from 1924 until the 1929 stock market crash, which dried up credit flowing into Germany and then out again in reparation payments. The German economy once again collapsed.

Then, most astonishing of all, after Hitler came to power in 1933, Schacht became Hitler's Minister of Economics and was also reappointed President of the Reichsbank. As soon as Hitler's power was consolidated, credits immediately began to flow from Montagu Norman's Bank of England to Schacht and the Hitler government. Schacht's support of Hitler is shown to go back to around 1926. Many others in the close-knit British ruling class were involved, including Round Table figures, oil executives, and even Edward VIII, King of England, soon to abdicate and become Duke of Windsor. But, I can hear you say, How is it possible? Why in the world...? Years after World War 2, with its millions of deaths and the near demolition of England and the whole British Empire, Mr. Engdahl quotes a conversation with Colonel David Stirling, the founder of Britain's elite Special Air Services, as follows: "The greatest mistake we British made was to think we could play the German Empire against the Russian Empire, and have them bleed one another to death."

The British, finding themselves after the war to be exhausted, broke, and with a worn out industrial system, decided that their salvation lay in long-term support by the U.S. To that end, they set about to convince Americans that a "special relationship" existed between the two countries, justifying such long-term American aid. To help solidify this relationship, and to involve the U.S. in helping to bring about British foreign policy objectives, Britain "helped" the U.S. with the creation of a formal U.S. intelligence network. The CIA which emerged was nothing more than a renamed extension of the wartime OSS, which was itself headquartered in the London offices of the British intelligence services. Two of the many tragic consequences of this secret arrangement are described below, involving the countries of Iran and Italy.

After the war, Iran's leader Mohammed Mossadegh managed to expel wartime troops of Britain and Russia, and then attempted to renegotiate the terms of the British monopoly oil concession which had been in place since 1902. Britain refused, and Mossadegh, becoming Prime Minister in April 1951, got a bill through the Iranian parliament to nationalize, with fair compensation, the Anglo-Iranian Oil Company. In response, Britain sent in their navy and imposed an embargo against all Iranian oil shipments. Feeling the financial impact, Mossadegh took his case first to the UN, which did nothing, and then to the U.S. State Department, which advised him to appoint Britain's Royal Dutch Shell as Iran's oil management company. Getting the message, Mossadegh next took his case to the World Court, which, in July 1952, denied British jurisdiction, which Britain ignored.   Cutting to the chase, British and American intelligence forces (i.e., the CIA) organized a coup in August 1953, forced Mossadegh's arrest, and installed the young Reza Shah Pahlevi in his place.   The sanctions were then lifted, and the British oil monopoly was preserved.   The new Shah was in turn deposed some 25 years later by the same forces that put him in power.

In post-war Italy, the non-communist wartime resistance leader Enrico Mattei rose to the leadership of the moribund oil entity known as AGIP.   He energetically set about to find oil and gas on Italian soil, and was successful.   Success led to further success, until he attracted the negative attention of the Seven Sisters, whose dominance he was determined to avoid. He managed first to negotiate a separate deal with the new Shah of Iran for oil from lands outside of the British concession areas.   Oil was actually delivered under this contract, helping to initiate a viable Italian post-war recovery.   Then came the shocker.   He negotiated another deal with the Soviets for oil from the Baku fields to be paid for with large steel pipe, enabling the Soviets to build a pipeline into Central Europe, threatening the monopoly of the Seven Sisters in that region.   A steel works to roll the pipe was completed in northern Italy, but about a month after it went into operation, in October 1962, Enrico Mattei was killed in a suspicious airplane accident, immediately following which the Rome CIA Station Chief left Italy for the U.S. Italy lost the driving force behind its recovery, and the Seven Sisters again triumphed.

As an epilogue, Engdahl notes that Mattei was at the time of his death planning to meet with President Kennedy, who was then urging the U.S. oil companies to negotiate with Mattei. Kennedy, of course, was himself assassinated about a year later, with trails of evidence also leading to the doors of the CIA. (We'll say much more about that in our review of Final Judgment, by Michael Collins Piper.)

America's present economic decline started in the late 50's as European and Japanese productivity, with their new factories and machinery, began to overtake that of the U.S., whose industrial base dated back to the 40's. The decline was greatly exacerbated by three developments: the flow of investment funds overseas, the start of the Vietnamese War, and LBJ's Great Society. President Kennedy tried to head off the first two of these, and can't really be blamed for the third. Seeing American investment banks channeling funds abroad in response to the higher profits available there, instead of keeping the funds at home to invest in modernized factories and refurbished infrastructure, he pushed for an Interest Equalization Tax on American funds invested abroad. He was assassinated, however, and the version which passed in the following year had been gutted by the Eastern financial community by exempting Canada, through which the investment funds then merrily flowed in the same total amounts as before. JFK was also moving in the direction of ending U.S. involvement in the Vietnam conflict, a policy shift "confirmed by Arthur Schlesinger" says Mr. Engdahl, and in accord with advice given to Kennedy by President de Gaulle of France. President

Kennedy didn't live to bring this about either, and following his death, LBJ expanded Vietnam from a CIA technical advisory operation to a full-scale war. Worse, it was a no-win war, in accordance with the deliberate strategy of LBJ's Pentagon and National Security advisors.    Adding in LBJ's Great Society programs, federal deficits ballooned, mostly financed by printed dollars graciously created by the Federal Reserve.  Our economic decline was thus started down a path from which we have not yet recovered.

The drain on the economy during the 60's decade led to the Fed's reduction of interest rates in an effort to "stimulate" the economy, but it brought instead an outflow of capital for better returns elsewhere, and the increased receipt of foreign dollars for conversion into gold.  Instead of devaluing the dollar to about $70 an ounce, as urged by hard-money proponents such as Jacques Rueff, de Gaulle's former economic advisor, Nixon instead followed the strategy of his own advisors, including budget advisor George Schultz, Treasury's Paul Volcker, and National Security Advisor Henry Kissinger.  Their advice was to stay the course, which he did until the gold outflow became so alarming that, on August 15, 1971, he followed the new advice which they then offered him, which was to terminate the redeemability of foreign dollars into gold.  *This* was the ultimate goal of Edmond de Rothschild, Sir Siegmund Warburg, and the other owners of the London merchant banks, who were, in fact, the real architects of the American policy.  All ties of world currencies to a metallic base were thereby broken, and the fate of such currencies delivered into the hands of central bankers and their prostituted politicians.

After 1971, a White House policy was initiated, under the effective control of Henry Kissinger, to *control* the economies of the nations and to reduce their populations, rather than to facilitate technology transfer and industrial growth. The strategy was to force the price of the cartelized world oil up by about a factor of four, recover the Arab oil receipts back into the British and American central banks, and lend them to the Third World to acquire control over those countries. To this end, the Bilderberg group, containing the world's top financial and political insiders, met privately in Saltsjoebaden, Sweden in May 1973 to discuss how the coming flood of oil dollars was to be handled. Mr. Engdahl lists many of the participants, including Kissinger, George Ball, David Rockefeller, and others. Then in October of that same year, the "Yom Kippur" war broke out, with Syria and Egypt invading Israel, with the U.S. supporting Israel, and the British staying demurely neutral. Kissinger performed his "shuttle diplomacy" among the participants, to assure the war followed the script previously worked out in Sweden. The Arab OPEC countries declared an embargo on all oil shipments to the U.S. and mainland Europe (but not Britain), and started cranking up the price, which rose by the scheduled factor of four by the end of the year. Nixon, drowning in the Watergate affair, tried to get the Treasury to find a way to get the Arabs to reduce their prices, but was rebuffed, and advised to support the "recycling" of the oil dollars at the current prices. Nixon agreed, and the deed was done. The great bulk of the petro-dollars were repatriated in purchasing U.S. government debt and in deposit accounts in Chase Manhattan, Citibank, et al. From there they were loaned to the Third World, which could not otherwise buy the fuel they needed to survive, whence many of those countries became enslaved to the bankers, and forced to follow their edicts on how to run their countries. Engdahl supplies lots more of the ghastly details.

Next to hit the economies of the world was the "Green" movement, or, as known in the U.S., environmentalism. Was it all one of those natural, spontaneous events in history, like an asteroid collision? Hardly. The movement on limiting industrial growth and responding to environmental threats was orchestrated by the same Anglo-American oil and financial interests that produced the oil shock. (But why? Stay with us.) For example, Robert Anderson, head of Atlantic Richfield Oil Co., and Bilderberg participant, helped fund Friends of the Earth, which, among other things, helped bring about the fall of the Australian government of Gough Whitlam in order to stop an Australian contract for supplying uranium to Japan for their nuclear power program. Anderson also created the Aspen Institute, which worked diligently to stop the developing nuclear power program in the U.S. The institute's board was peopled with board members from most if not all of the Seven Sisters. Another actor was McGeorge Bundy's Ford Foundation, whose operatives extended their reach into Germany to try to stop Germany's attempt to attain energy independence via nuclear power.

But why the effort to slow industrial growth? Engdahl says that American officials in the mid 70's openly claimed in news conferences that they were "neo-Malthusians." Malthus, says Engdahl, was an English clergyman who, in 1798, wrote an essay claiming that human populations expanded geometrically, while their means of subsistence expanded only linearly. Hence, populations must be limited, and, if necessary, governments should enhance the operations of nature to produce the needed mortality. Consistent with such pseudo-science, Henry Kissinger produced, in April 1974, the classified National Security Council Study Memorandum 200 (NSSM 200), directed to Washington high officialdom, defining a program aimed at population reduction in Third World countries possessing needed raw materials, since growing populations with aspirations for a better standard of living give rise to high prices for such materials. Kissinger named 13 target countries for population control, including Brazil, India, Egypt, Mexico, Ethiopia, Columbia, and others. (But what was the *real* reason for playing God in this way? You'll have to stay tuned just a little longer.)

The new "petro-dollar order" proceeded apace during the remainder of the 70's decade, but not without recognition and resistance by those most impacted, and the suppression of that resistance by the oil and banking elites. Most of the Third World, including the bulk of South America, Africa, and the Asian underbelly, unable to afford the oil they needed, found not only their industrial development stopped, but even food purchases curtailed, and starvation threatening. Far from living standards continuing the growth begun during the 50's and 60's, many of these countries were being pushed back to a condition of bare subsistence. A coalition of "Unaligned Countries" attempted to break free and deal independently with OPEC, with the help of Central European countries showing a willingness to help, including Italy and West Germany. Kissinger and company managed to isolate and pick them off one by one, however. Bonn was allegedly threatened with the pullout of U.S. troops if it persisted, and it backed off. Italy thereupon did likewise. Indira Gandhi in India was faced with political defections and a new opposition party and lost her next election. Mrs. Bandaranaike of Sri Lanka, one of the leaders of the coalition, encountered a wave of strikes and riots by a "Trotskyite" party having reported intimate ties to the Anglo-American intelligence services, and was forced out of office. Kissinger and company momentarily remained ascendant.

In 1978, the European Community, led by Germany and France, created the beginnings of the EMS, the European Monetary System, as a result of policy disagreements with the Anglo-Americans. The EC and the EMS sought independent ties with the Arab countries, offering them help in establishing nuclear power facilities and other technology, in return for long-term oil supply agreements. London opposed these efforts at every turn, refused to join or cooperate with the EMS, and decided that more shocks were needed to assure the ongoing primacy of the petro-dollar system. This time, President Carter, at the behest of advisors George Ball and Zbigniew Brzezin-ski, dropped U.S. support of the Shah of Iran, who was negotiating with the EC countries for nuclear power plants. Support was transferred to the Islamic funda-mentalist Ayatollah Khomeini, and a coup was mounted deposing the Shah, whom the same CIA and related intelligence forces had installed by coup some 25 years earlier. The Khomeini regime canceled the nuclear development plans, and cut off oil exports to the world. World prices skyrocketed to around $40 per barrel, and the second great oil shock of the 70's was underway.

Immediately thereafter, Paul Volcker, Nixon's 1971 architect of closing the gold window, was ap-pointed Federal Reserve Chairman by President Carter. Gold was then changing hands at about $400 per ounce, and rising rapidly. To stop the world from dumping their dollars to buy gold, and to restore the dollar to its post-war status as the world's most sought after currency, Volcker started cranking up U.S. interest rates, reaching an incredible 20% in just a few weeks. Gold prices peaked at about $800 per ounce, and then retreated toward present levels. Interest rates stayed high for a short time, and then were gradually reduced over a period of years to more normal levels. The Anglo-American Establishment had momentarily won again.

The cost, however, was incredible, particularly to the Third World. But even in the U.S. any invest-ment which took more than four or five years to complete was financially impossible with interest rates at 17 to 20 percent.    Thus long-term government-funded infrastructure was deeply cut, as were similar long-term private projects, most particularly including nuclear power plant construction.    Dozens of such contracts were canceled, and no new domestic contracts have been signed since.    In the Third World, however, not only did the purchase of nuclear power plants become out of the question, but bare survival was in doubt.    Those countries had been suckered into floating interest rate contracts on their Eurodollar loans, and those interest rates had now gone out of sight.    Oil costs were up 140% after the Iran Oil Shock, and the U.S. dollar itself, mandatorily required for making oil purchases, was now becoming more expensive against other currencies.    The great bulk of the Third World was essentially instantaneously bankrupted.    The Anglo-American banks magnanimously agreed to reschedule the debt owed them, provided target countries would agree to accept the terms laid down for their future economic operation by the International Monetary Fund, which became the collection agency for the big banks.    Engdahl supplies lots of detail about this matter, in the process bringing in again such familiar names as George Schultz, Henry Kissinger, Citicorp, Chase Manhattan, Manufacturers Hanover, Lloyds Bank, etc.    The IMF's terms were uniformly Malthusian to the core.    By 1987, the amount then owed in principal and interest amounted in total to some $1.3 trillion dollars, a sum virtually impossible ever to repay, even under healthy economic conditions.

Engdahl concludes with a brief but fascinating look at the Reagan and Bush years, with its massive deficits, S&L bailouts, leveraged buyouts, etc., ending with the Saddam Hussein episode, about which much more will undoubtedly be written as more and more facts are uncovered by future historians.  He does, however, outline some of the economic pressures that were brought to bear on Iraq following Saddam's refusal to denationalize Iraq's oil, pressures which eventually led to the Gulf War and the destruction of Iraq's infrastructure, including its rail system.

Chapter 2

## "TRAGEDY AND HOPE"

(By Professor Carroll Quigley. Pub. 1966 by Macmillan, NY. Available from American Opinion Books, PO Box 8040, Appleton, WI 54913, 414-749-3783.)

This book is subtitled *A History of The World in Our Time*. It runs over 1300 pages, and is Professor Quigley's *magnum opus*. The book is establishmentarian to the core, and I don't really recommend that you seek out a copy (its publication run was truncated, and library copies have disappeared), since I can steer you instead to a much shorter book devoted solely to a detailed review of Quigley's book from an anti-elitist viewpoint.

Quigley and his book are highly important for our purpose, however, for one very good reason. While his establishmentarian credentials are impeccable, and while he acknowledges his agreement with the broad goals of the international elites, he states that he disagrees with them in one primary particular, namely that they insist on preserving their behind-the-scenes secrecy. They have been too important an element in Western history, he says, to remain unknown and unacknowledged. Having been granted access to their secret files for a period of time, he says, he has decided to provide some historical illumination, not only on some of their unknown works, but also on a number of their individual faces. His was the first book by an "Insider" which acknowledges the existence of an organized but heretofore secret "international Anglophile network" (p. 950) which has, since the late 1800's, been controlling much of our world's history. His book clearly went much too far for the liking of the elites, however, and they did their best to push the book down their (incompletely constructed) memory hole.

We'll discuss first a few of the lesser matters Quigley covers, just to give you the flavor of what it's about, and to substantiate several points made in Engdahl's book. First, he acknowledges (pp. 50-53) the existence and identity of the British merchant bankers who took advantage of the capital accumulated during their industrial revolution, and their skills in manipulating its use, to "take the old disorganized and localized methods of handling money and credit and organize them into an integrated system, on an international basis, which worked with incredible and well-oiled facility for many decades. The center of that system was in London, with major offshoots in New York and Paris.... The men who did this ... aspired to establish dynasties of international bankers, and were at least as successful at this as were many of the dynastic political rulers. The greatest of these dynasties, of course, were the descendants of Meyer Amschel Rothschild (1743-1812) of Frankfort...." He then lists the names of the important banking families: "They include Baring, Lazard, Erlanger, Warburg, Schroder, Seligman, the Speyers, Mirabaud, Mallet, Fould, and above all Rothschild and Morgan." Concerning the latter name, he notes that J.P. Morgan and Company was "originally founded in London as George Peabody and Company in 1838." More will be said about the subservience of Morgan to the British bankers in a review yet to come. Quigley, however, makes no bones about their joint power. It reached its peak in the period 1919-1931, he says, "when Montagu Norman and J.P. Morgan dominated not only the financial world but international relations and other matters as well." Concerning the thrust of the bankers' control, Quigley notes, as a preview generalization (p. 62), "The history of the last century shows, as we shall later see, that the advice given to governments by bankers, like the advice they gave to industrialists, was consistently good for bankers, but was often disastrous for governments, businessmen, and the people generally."

The closest Quigley gets to going out on a limb and identifying underlying causes of World War 1, rather than just the public diplomatic maneuvers of the participating European powers, is to state (p. 224) that: "[I]nternational economic competition was, in the period before 1914, requiring increasing political support [from such groups as] British gold and diamond miners in South Africa, German railroad builders in the Near East, ... British oil prospectors in the Near East" and others. Elsewhere, however, he does talk more specifically (pp. 120-121) about the threat perceived by the British in Germany's growing internationalist outlook, most particularly in its effort to complete a "Berlin to Baghdad" rail link: "After 1889 the situation was different. Economically, the Ger-

mans began to invade Anatolia [i.e., Turkey] by establishing trading agencies and banking facilities…. Most
important, perhaps, was the projected 'Berlin to Baghdad' railway scheme…. This project was of the greatest economic, strategic, and political importance not
only to the Ottoman Empire and the Near East but to
the whole of Europe. Economically, it tapped a region
of great mineral and agricultural resources, including
the world's greatest petroleum reserves." Best of all
from the German viewpoint, says Quigley, these ties to
raw materials needed by Germany "were beyond the
reach of the British Navy" and therefore solved a
"crucial problem" which would face the Germans in
time of war. Then, starting about 1900, "for more then
ten years, Russia, Britain, and France showed violent
disapproval, and did all they could to obstruct the
project." He outlines many of these efforts, but then
concludes that it had nothing to do with starting the
war because, about a month before the war started,
Britain "withdrew her opposition" to the railway.
Suspicious people might conceivably treat that procla-
mation with some doubt.

The only mention that Quigley makes of the
Seven Sisters cartel is as something of a footnote to his
discussion of the overthrow of Prime Minister Mossadegh of Iran by the CIA for the benefit of the cartel,
which Mossadegh was trying to oust. Concerning the
cartel formation, he says only: "The world oil cartel
had developed from a tripartite agreement signed on
September 17, 1928 by Royal Dutch-Shell, Anglo-
Iranian, and Standard Oil. The three signers were Sir
Henri Deterding of Shell, Sir John (later Lord) Cadman

of AIOC [Anglo-Iranian Oil Co., later BP], and Walter C. Teagle of ESSO [Standard of N.J.]. These agreed to manage oil prices on the world market by charging an agreed fixed price plus freight costs, and to store surplus oil which might weaken the fixed price level. By 1949 the cartel had as members the seven greatest oil companies of the world...." which he then names, the same as did Engdahl.

Concerning the Mossadegh overthrow, Quigley expounds at considerable length about the negotiations between Iran on one side and Britain and the AIOC on the other concerning terms of oil extraction rights. The negotiations ended, says Quigley, as follows: "The British, the AIOC, the world petroleum cartel, the American government, and the older Iranian elite led by the Shah combined to crush Mossadegh. The chief effort came from the American supersecret intelligence agency (CIA) under the personal direction of its director, Allen W. Dulles, brother of the Secretary of State." He goes into a fair amount of detail about how the coup was managed by Dulles, following which the Shah was returned to power and Iranian oil exploitation returned to the Seven Sisters.

We come now to the two matters comprising the unique importance of this book. The first has to do with the existence, organization, and personnel of the elite group ruling us. The second has to do with the historical origins of World War 2, with its 20 million deaths and worldwide disruption and misery.

The concept behind the movement that produced the elitist control structure, the core of which
remains hidden today, was elucidated, says Quigley (p.
130), by John Ruskin, who was appointed to the fine
arts professorship at Oxford in 1870. He made an
immense impact on the undergraduates, all of them
members of the privileged, ruling class in England.
"He told them that they were the possessors of a
magnificent tradition of education, beauty, rule of law,
freedom, decency, and self discipline, but that this
tradition could not be saved ... unless it could be
extended to the lower classes in England itself and to
the non-English masses throughout the world. If this
precious tradition were not extended to these two great
majorities, the minority of upper-class Englishmen
would ultimately be submerged by these majorities and
the tradition lost."

Listening transfixed in his audience was Cecil
Rhodes, later to be the prime exploiter of the diamond
(De Beers Consolidated Mines) and gold (Consolidated Gold Fields) resources in South Africa, who,
with the help of financing by Lord Rothschild, attained
an annual income in the middle 1890's of "at least a
million pounds sterling a year (then about five million
dollars) which was spent so freely for his mysterious
purposes that he was usually overdrawn on his
account. These purposes centered on his desire to
*federate the English-speaking peoples and to bring all
the habitable portions of the world under their control.*
For this purpose Rhodes left part of his great fortune to
found the Rhodes Scholarships at Oxford in order to
spread the English ruling class tradition throughout the

English-speaking world as Ruskin had wanted." The most recent American big name to have gone through this training is our current President, Bill Clinton.

Among Rhodes' fellow students who became Ruskin adherents were Arnold Toynbee, Alfred (later Lord) Milner, and others named by Quigley. A similar group appeared in Cambridge, including Reginald Brett (Lord Esher) and Albert (Lord) Grey. The two groups were brought together in 1891, says Quigley, by William T. Stead, England's most successful journalist, ardent social reformer, and imperialist, whereupon "Rhodes and Stead organized a secret society of which Rhodes had been dreaming for sixteen years. In this secret society Rhodes was to be leader; Stead, Brett (Lord Esher), and Milner were to form an executive committee; Arthur (Lord) Balfour, (Sir) Harry Johnston, Lord Rothschild, Albert (Lord) Grey, and others were listed as potential members of a 'Circle of Initiates'; while there was to be an outer circle known as the 'Association of Helpers' (later organized by Milner as the Round Table organization).... Thus the central part of the secret society was established by March 1891."

Rhodes died in 1902, but the secret society retained control of his fortune, which was added to by funds of other supporters, including Alfred Beit and Sir Abe Bailey. Milner became the chief Rhodes trustee, and, during his governorship in South Africa (1897-1905) he recruited young men from Oxford, etc., to assist him, men whom he later helped "into positions of influence in government and international finance, and [who] became the dominant influence in British imperial and foreign affairs up to 1939." Originally known as Milner's Kindergarten, "In 1909-1913 they organized semisecret groups, known as Round Table Groups, in the chief British dependencies and the United States. These still function in eight countries.... In 1919 they founded the Royal Institute of International Affairs (Chatham House) for which the chief financial supporters were Sir Abe Bailey and the Astor family (owners of *The Times*). Similar Institutes of International Affairs were established in the chief British dominions and in the United States (where it is known as the Council on Foreign Relations) in the period 1919-1927. After 1925 a somewhat similar structure of organizations, known as the Institute of Pacific Relations, was set up in twelve countries holding territory in the Pacific area, the units in each British dominion existing on an interlocking basis with the Round Table Group and the Royal Institute of International Affairs in the same country."

Quigley then identifies Round Table leaders in Canada, South Africa, India, and elsewhere. Concerning the effectiveness of the group he says, "The power and influence of this Rhodes-Milner group in British Imperial Affairs and in foreign policy since 1889, although not widely recognized, can hardly be exaggerated. We might mention as an example that this group dominated *The Times* from 1890 to 1912 and has controlled it completely since 1912 (except for the years 1919-1922). Because *The Times* has been owned by the Astor family since 1922, this Rhodes-Milner group was sometimes spoken of as the "Cliveden Set," named after the Astor country house where they sometimes assembled."

In a later chapter which Quigley calls "American Confusions, 1945-1950," he updates the personnel, policies, and methodologies of the American branch of the Rhodes-Milner creation. It is a fascinating chapter, providing an explanation, for example, of the frequently asked question, Why do we so often see capitalists and their tax-exempt foundations supporting left-wing entities who have vowed to destroy capitalism? Quigley says (p. 938): "More than fifty years ago the Morgan firm decided to infiltrate the Left-wing political movements in the United States. This was relatively easy to do, since these groups were starved for funds and eager for a voice to reach the people. Wall Street supplied both." Another example that he gives is the creation of *The New Republic* magazine using Payne-Whitney money, Whitney being derived from the New York utility millionaire William C. Whitney, and Payne from Oliver Payne of the Standard Oil "trust." Quigley continues, "The original purpose for establishing the paper was to provide an outlet for the progressive Left and to guide it quietly in an Anglophile direction. This latter task was entrusted to a young man, only four years out of Harvard, but already a member of the mysterious Round Table group, which has played a major role in directing England's foreign policy since its formal establishment in 1909. This new recruit, Walter Lippmann, has been, from 1914 to the present, the authentic spokesman in American journalism for the Establishments on both sides of the Atlantic in international affairs."

Quigley puts an establishment spin on the communist infiltration into its several organizations (like the Institute of Pacific Relations), and its deleterious effects on world history, such as Chinese history. He is then led, however, into revealing the hidden workings of the big tax-exempt foundations. Behind the "unfortunate situation" concerning the IPR, he says (p. 936), "lies another more profound relationship which influences matters much broader than Far Eastern policy. It involves the organization of tax-exempt fortunes of international financiers into foundations to be used for educational, scientific, 'and other public purposes.'" He further explains (p. 938), that these Wall Street elites "had to adjust to a good many government actions thoroughly distasteful to the group. The chief of these were in taxation law, ... above all else, in the inheritance tax. These tax laws drove the great private fortunes dominated by Wall Street into tax-exempt foundations, which became a major link in the Establishment network between Wall Street, the Ivy League, and the federal government." Quigley describes in a fair amount of detail (p. 937) how the foundations managed to acquire control over the primary Ivy League colleges, including Harvard, Yale, Columbia, and Princeton, and then briefly notes a little later (pp. 954-955) the unwelcome effort by the anti-Communist 1953 Congress to shed some light on foundation activities: "A congressional committee, following backward to their source the threads which led from admitted Communists like Whittaker Chambers, through Alger Hiss and the Carnegie Endowment to Thomas Lamont and the Morgan Bank, fell into the whole complicated network of the interlocking tax-exempt foundations.  The Eighty-third Congress in July 1953 set up a Special Committee to Investigate Tax-Exempt Foundations, with Representative B. Carroll Reece of Tennessee as chairman.   It soon became clear that people of immense wealth would be unhappy if the investigation went too far" and it was duly emasculated.  We will later review a book specifically devoted to what that investigation uncovered.

The second of the two matters referred to above which comprise the unique importance of this book has to do with the origins of World War 2.   Quigley's concentration in this area is not so much on the mechanics of Hitler's rise within Germany as it is on the British secret policies during the 10 years or so before the war broke out (in September 1939) of encouraging and assisting Hitler's rise to political and military dominance over Europe.

One fact which Quigley relates (p. 433) which appears also in Engdahl's book is that the deal which made Hitler the Chancellor of the German Reich was negotiated in Cologne at the home of Baron Kurt von Schroder on Jan. 4, 1933. (Historian / correspondent William A. Shirer in his *Rise and Fall of the Third Reich* further notes on page 179 that Hitler's meeting with Schroder also promised Hitler that "West German business interests" would take over the debts of the Nazi Party, and that ten days later Joseph Goebbels announced that the financial position of the party had "fundamentally improved overnight.") Baron von Schroder is the same Schroder that Quigley lists as

among the major world banking families (p. 52).
Quigley, however, leaves the matter there, whereas
Engdahl describes the close relationship between
Baron von Schroder and Montagu Norman's friend
Hjalmar Schacht, which bore fruit for Schacht when,
after consolidating his power and receiving Bank of
England credits from Montagu Norman, Hitler made
Schacht his Minister of Economics as well as President
of the Reichsbank, the latter being a position he held
until 1939.

Quigley relates a great deal of detail concerning
the many actions taken by Great Britain during the
1930's in support of Hitler. A short way into his tale,
he decides to lay out the motivations, as he saw them,
of the several groups within the British government
that were making and administering its foreign policy.
He says (p. 580) that by 1938, "the motives of the
government were clearly not the same as the motives
of the people, and in no country has secrecy and
anonymity been carried so far or been so well preserved as in Britain." From the outermost circles of
government to the central inner circles, motives
became more and more secret. There were four
circles: "(1) the anti-Bolsheviks at the center, (2) the
'three-bloc-world' supporters close to the center, (3) the
supporters of 'appeasement', and (4) the 'peace at any
price' group in a peripheral group." In the years before
World War 2, the latter two groups were, says
Quigley, "remote from the real instruments of government," but were used by the two inner groups to sway
public opinion toward actions which were in support
of their secret policies.

The policies of the anti-Bolshevik group were (p. 581): "to destroy reparations, permit German rearmament, and tear down what they called 'French militarism.'" That is, they proposed to rearm Germany, let it dominate Europe (particularly including France), and then let it (and perhaps help it) destroy the Soviet Union.

On the other hand, the three-bloc-world group, says Quigley, sought not to destroy the Soviet Union, but to "contain" it between a German-dominated Europe and an English-speaking bloc.  More specifically (p. 582), it "sought to weaken the League of Nations and destroy all possibility of collective security [i.e., of protecting France from Germany] in order to strengthen Germany in respect to both France and the Soviet Union, and above all to free Britain from Europe in order to build up an 'Atlantic bloc' of Great Britain, the British Dominions, and the United States."

This latter policy thus coincided with that of the anti-Bolshevik group up to and including the domination of Europe by Germany, a configuration which they regarded as stable, producing peace for many years into the future.  It involved, however, a number of sacrifices to be made by a number of other countries.  They believed that their three-bloc system, once set up (p. 582), "could force Germany to keep the peace (after it absorbed Europe) because it would be squeezed between the Atlantic bloc and the Soviet Union, while the Soviet Union could be forced to keep the peace because it would be squeezed between Japan and Germany.  This plan would work only if Germany and the Soviet Union could be brought into contact with each other by abandoning Austria, Czechoslovakia, and the Polish Corridor to Germany.  This became the aim of both the anti-Bolsheviks and the three-bloc people from the early part of 1937 to the end of 1939 (or even early 1940).  These two [groups] cooperated and dominated the government in that period."

The three-bloc-world policy belonged precisely to the Milner Group / Round Table Group / Cliveden Set described earlier in this review.  Quigley repeats the same familiar set of names (p. 581).  He also lists a few names in the anti-Bolshevik group, somewhat less familiar, but including General Jan Smuts and Prime Minister Neville Chamberlain.  Quigley notes that relations between the two groups were cordial, with some members in both groups, such as General Smuts.

Quigley goes into great detail about how Britain secretly maneuvered to strengthen Hitler's Germany at the expense of France and all of the other weaker countries in Europe.  He devotes a whole chapter to discussing Britain's publicly "neutral" role in the Spanish Civil War, and concludes (p. 602): "Britain's attitude was so devious that it can hardly be untangled, although the results are clear enough.  The chief result [of the war] was that in Spain a Left government friendly to France was replaced by a Right government [General Franco's] unfriendly to France and deeply obligated to Italy and Germany.  The evidence is clear that the real sympathies of the London government favored the rebels, although it had to conceal the fact from public opinion in Britain."

Quigley then proceeds to Britain's involvement in the acquisition by Hitler of Austria, then Czechoslovakia, and then Danzig, the "free" city in the Polish Corridor.   Britain's policies with respect to these matters, he says, were spelled out in a seven-point policy secretly delivered to Germany, since "the British government could not publicly admit to its own people these 'seven points' because they were not acceptable to British public opinion."   The seven points were (p. 619):

1. Hitler's Germany was the chief defense against the spread of communism in Europe.

2. A four-power pact of Britain, France, Germany and Italy, consolidating the Anglo-French Entente and the Rome-Berlin Axis, and excluding all Russian influence, was the goal to be sought as the foundation of a stable Europe.

3. Britain would not object to German acquisition of Austria, Czechoslovakia, and Danzig.

4. Germany must not use force to achieve these aims, as this would start a war which public opinion would force Britain into.

5. An agreement with Germany restricting the number and use of bombing planes was desired.

6. Britain would give Germany certain (Portuguese and Belgian) African colonies, given German cooperation with the above.

7. Britain would pressure Czechoslovakia and Poland to negotiate with Germany on its desires.

Quigley then notes that Germany's professional diplomats and soldiers were perfectly willing to gain European domination without going to war, but that the leaders of the Nazi Party were not, "especially Hitler, Ribbentrop, and Himmler, who were too impatient and who wanted to prove to themselves and the world that Germany was powerful enough to take what it wanted without waiting for anybody's permission." It was this lack of understanding between the British elites and the Nazi leaders which ultimately brought on the horror of World War 2.

Activities in support of Point 3 then proceeded apace. The substantially bloodless takeover of Austria was accomplished in March 1938, with no significant response from the British public. Czechoslovakia was carved up by Britain, France, Germany, and Italy on September 29, 1938, with incredible prior pressures exerted on France and Czechoslovakia by Britain, in accordance with Point 7 above, as described in detail by Quigley. The British public had been prepared to welcome this result as the great lifting of the fear of war with Germany, a fear that had been driven into them by several years worth of propagandizing by the British elites as to the overwhelming military superiority of the Germans, a superiority which Quigley exposes as being entirely fraudulent (p. 633 ff.).

The continuation of the seven-point policy with respect to Poland suffered two new setbacks, however. First, says Quigley, Hitler had not made up his mind whether to attack France or Poland next. British diplomats in Europe smelled this out in January 1939 (p. 642) and "began to bombard London with rumors of a forthcoming attack on the Netherlands and France." Appeasement as a policy suddenly appeared to many Britishers to be unrealistic and personally dangerous. Second, on March 15 Chamberlain told the House of Commons "that he accepted the seizure of Czechoslovakia, and refused to accuse Hitler of bad faith." The howls of rage from Commons changed his mind as to what he could say and do in public, and two days later he denounced the seizure to his constituency in Birmingham. The reality of underlying policy did not change, however, though a second policy effort was mounted to satisfy the British public about ending "appeasement." Of the two policies, says Quigley, "One policy was public; the other was secret. Since the Foreign Office knew of both, it tried to build up the 'peace front' against Germany so that it would look sufficiently imposing to satisfy public opinion in England, and to drive Hitler to seek his desires by negotiation rather than by force, so that public opinion in England would not force the government to declare a war that they did not want in order to remain in office."

Hitler, however, was determined to have his war, and notwithstanding additional British efforts, including first a threat to come to Poland's aid if it were attacked, and then a secret offer to make a non-aggression pact with Germany along the lines of the three-bloc-world plan of the Round Tablers (p. 653), Hitler did finally act. He signed a non-aggression pact with the USSR on August 23, 1939, including a secret protocol defining how Poland was to be divided up, and on September 1 invaded Poland. For two more days, France and England begged Hitler to withdraw his forces from Poland and open negotiations. When the British public and the government's supporters in Parliament began to grumble, Britain reluctantly declared war on September 3, followed by similar French action a few hours later.

Even after being forced into a war that he did not want, Chamberlain did not give up his anti-Bolshevik policy of using Germany to destroy the USSR. According to Quigley (p. 668), the conflict during the period from September 1939 to May 1940 was referred to as "the 'Sitzkrieg' (sitting war) or even the 'phony war' because the Western Powers made no real effort to fight Germany." He noted, for example, that the British air force was ordered to refrain from bombing any German land forces, to the air force's considerable dismay. Quigley attributes this policy to Chamberlain's continued effort to make peace with Germany, so he could get on with his original plan. Now hating Hitler because of Hitler's insistence upon war, Chamberlain felt that "the best way to reach peace would be to encourage some anti-Hitler movement within Germany itself." The only action of any significance taken against Germany during this period was a weak-kneed blockade, mounted primarily as a sop to public opinion.

Chamberlain during this period had the secret support of France, whose government was well aware of Hitler's vacillation as to whether to attack France or

Poland first.    Thus, when the Soviet Union made demands upon Finland and then invaded on November 29, 1939, the British and French (p. 679) "regarded it as a heaven-sent opportunity to change the declared but unfought war with Germany, which they did not want, into an undeclared but fighting war against the Soviet Union." They took their case to the moribund League of Nations, reawakened it, and obtained a condemnation of Russia in just 11 days.  More importantly, they got up an expeditionary force of 100,000 troops to aid Finland, and tried to get Swedish and Norwegian permission to transit their territory to get to Finland.  Under pressure from Germany and Russia, Sweden and Norway refused.  Finland made peace on March 12, 1940, but even then the British did not give up their efforts.  They kept their expeditionary force at the ready, issued threats to Norway and Sweden to cooperate, and ordered the French General Weygand to carry out a bombing raid on Russia's Caucasus oil fields from their bases in Syria.  However, Hitler invaded Denmark and Norway on April 9, cutting off British access to the Russians via that route, thereby assuring Russian quiescence while he dealt with western Europe.  Weygand could not mount his attack on the Caucasus until the end of June, but Hitler invaded France and the lowlands on May 10, 1940, obviating that possibility, and the issue was forever settled.

The British anti-Bolshevik and three-bloc-world circles finally got what they wanted - the hegemony of Germany over Europe - but not without military force, as they had wished.    They consequently lost their public support, and in a violent debate in Parliament from May 7 to May 10, Chamberlain, still feebly trying to defend his policies, was attacked from all sides. He was the appointed fall guy, however, and the recipient of the famous words (p. 684): "Depart, I say. Let us have done with you. In the name of God, go!" These words were delivered by Leopold Amery, "the shadow of Lord Milner" says Quigley (582), he who, Quigley says, as one of the three-bloc-world leaders, led his circle into an increasingly anti-German posture, and into a split with the anti-Bolsheviks. Chamberlain resigned on May 10, as France was being invaded, and was replaced by Winston Churchill, the old war-horse previously known as "The best-hated man in the House of Commons," to prosecute the war against Germany.

Quigley reveals nothing concerning any involvement by Churchill in helping Roosevelt maneuver the United States into the war, enabling the war to finally be brought to a conclusion. His prose does, however, elucidate facts of great interest regarding the mind-set of British leadership – the same leadership which today reaches across the ocean to execute its policies through the offices of the Council on Foreign Relations, the U.S. branch office of the Round Table group. That mind-set led them to find a German villain as bad as Stalin, secretly support and build him up, and hand him all of Europe, all of which policies were obviously against the best interests of millions of Europeans, and would of course have been violently opposed by the British electorate had those policies been publicly revealed.

It should further be noted that the financial assistance leading to Hitler's buildup derived from the actions of Montagu Norman at the Bank of England and Hjalmar Schacht, protégé of Baron von Schroder, at the Reichsbank. It is impossible to believe, however, that Hitler was not raised up without the approval of the major banking families which run this world, for, as Quigley points out (pp. 326-327): "It must not be felt that these heads of the world's chief central banks were themselves substantive powers in world finance. They were not. Rather, they were the technicians and agents of the dominant investment bankers of their own countries, who had raised them up and were perfectly capable of throwing them down. The substantive powers of the world were in the hands of these investment bankers ... who remained largely behind the scenes in their own unincorporated private banks. These formed a system of international cooperation and national dominance which was more private, more powerful, and more secret than that of their agents in the central banks."

It therefore becomes extremely hard to believe that these major banking families which run our world, listed at the beginning of this review, were not themselves culpable in the origination of World War 2. It is said that power corrupts, and that absolute power, close to being realized in both Britain and Germany of the 20's and 30's, did in fact corrupt close to absolutely, to the great sorrow of millions around the world during that greatest single human conflagration that our world has yet seen.

Chapter 3

## "THE NAKED CAPITALIST"

(By W. Cleon Skousen. Pub. 1970 by Mr. Skousen. Presently available from Reviewer, 9137 Edenbrook Way, West Jordan, UT 84088.)

This short book (121 pages of text) was the first anti-establishment review of *Tragedy and Hope* of which I am aware, but certainly was not the last. Mr. Skousen's credentials stem from a law degree at George Washington University, his service in the FBI from 1935 to 1951, and a career thereafter involving four years as Police Chief of Salt Lake City, the editorship of the police magazine *Law and Order*, a teaching position at Brigham Young University, and many years on lecture circuits in the United States and abroad. His work in the FBI was heavy into investigations of communism, and resulted in his earlier book *The Naked Communist* which reached the best seller list in 1961.

Quigley's book, appearing in 1966, was a revelation for which Mr. Skousen was already primed, and he took immediate advantage of it. He aimed for the core of the matter on his page 1, on which he related a conversation he had with Dr. Bella Dodd, "a former member of the National Committee of the U.S. Communist Party," as saying: "I think the Communist

conspiracy is merely a branch of a much bigger conspiracy!" Skousen then explains:

"Dr. Dodd said she first became aware of some
mysterious super-leadership right after World War 2
when the U.S. Communist Party had difficulty getting
instructions from Moscow on several vital matters
requiring immediate attention.  The American Communist hierarchy was told that any time they had an
emergency of this kind they should contact any one of
three designated persons at the Waldorf Towers.  Dr.
Dodd noted that whenever the party obtained instructions from any of these three men, Moscow always
ratified them.  What puzzled Dr. Dodd was the fact
that not one of these three contacts was a Russian.  Nor
were any of them Communists.  In fact, all three were
extremely wealthy American capitalists!  Dr. Dodd
said, 'I would certainly like to find out who is really
running things.'"

Skousen relates the many similar puzzlements
he has had during his years of investigation, and how
he had "waited for thirty years for somebody on the
inside of the modern political power structure to talk"
as he had long expected that someone ultimately
would.  When Quigley's book appeared, he sought
from it clues as to Quigley's motivation to publish.  He
quotes (p. 5) Quigley's single disagreement with the
elites concerning his feeling that their historical impact
has been so great that history should be permitted to
properly record that impact, but further notes that
Quigley "feels that the forces of total global control are
now sufficiently entrenched so that they can reveal

their true identity without fear of being successfully overturned." Quigley's sympathy with the secret goals of the elites is demonstrated, says Skousen, in the title of the book, "Hope" referring to the men composing the elite group, and "Tragedy" the men opposing that group.

Skousen then goes directly to Quigley's description of the apex of the secret control structure. Quigley, he says (p. 7), "points out that during the past two centuries when the peoples of the world were gradually winning their political freedom from the dynastic monarchies, the major banking families of Europe and America were actually reversing the trend by setting up new dynasties of political control through the formation of international financial combines. Dr. Quigley points out that these banking dynasties had learned that all governments must have sources of revenue from which to borrow in times of emergency. They had also learned that by providing such funds from their own private resources, they could make both kings and democratic leaders tremendously subservient to their will. It had proven to be a most effective means of controlling political appointments and deciding political issues."

Skousen then proceeds with a critique and elucidation of Quigley's account of the development by these major dynastic banking families and their minions of secret control over much of the political and economic life of Europe, the United States, and much of the rest of the world. He quotes Quigley's account of how commercial and savings banks and insurance companies were drawn into the web, strengthening its influence over both government and industry, and then repeats Quigley's list of the major banking families (p. 7), i.e., "Baring, Lazard, Erlanger, Warburg, Schroder, Seligman, the Speyers, Mirabaud, Mallet, Fould, and above all Rothschild and Morgan." He digresses briefly (p. 8) to assure his readers that the banking conspiracy is not a "Jewish Conspiracy" as alleged by the well-known and fraudulent document called "The Protocols of the Learned Elders of Zion," a document that we might label today an exercise in disinformation, aimed at discrediting the conspiracy's opponents. Skousen then quotes Quigley's description of how the "international" (or "merchant" or "private" or "investment") bankers differ from legitimate commercial or savings bankers, particularly regarding the former's preoccupation with handling government debt, and its efforts to convince both government and business that the bankers could manage government debt better than government could. Quigley's narrative is then presented concerning the setting up of the Bank of England, and the overwhelming political power which it secretly acquired and exercised.

Skousen then quotes Quigley's description of the development in the United States of the Morgan and Rockefeller financial dynasties, and then goes to a summarization of their secret machinations which produced our Federal Reserve System. (Skousen's summary is fascinating, but we'll cover this subject much more thoroughly in a later review.) Skousen does set out to ask and then answer, Who controls the Fed? What are the goals of the Fed and the other central banks? What are the goals of the international banking families who control the central banks?

As to 'Who controls?' Skousen first explains (p. 15) who does *not*, namely, the government: "As we have previously noted, the dynastic 'banker families' in England had established their monopoly control over finance by setting up the Bank of England as a privately controlled institution which had the *appearance* of an official government institution. Similar centers of financial control had been set up in France, Germany, Italy and Switzerland." Moving then to our Federal Reserve System, he says (p. 21), "The system consists of 12 'National Banks' but the only one of any significance is the one in New York. The New York bank has always been managed by someone completely congenial to the interests of the international bankers." He then notes Quigley's description of Benjamin Strong, the first governor of the New York Federal Reserve Bank (p. 23): "Strong owed his career to the favor of the Morgan Bank.... He became governor of the Federal Reserve Bank of New York as the joint nominee of Morgan and of Kuhn, Loeb and Company in 1914. Two years later, Strong met [Montagu] Norman for the first time, and they at once made an agreement to work in cooperation for the financial practices they both revered." (Quigley, p. 326)

And just what were these "revered" financial practices and goals of the Fed and the other central banks? Skousen (p. 22) quotes Quigley as saying that the international bankers intended to use the financial power of Britain and the United States to force all the major countries to operate "through central banks free from all political control, with all questions of international finance to be settled by agreements by such central banks without interference from governments." (Quigley, p. 326) He continues by quoting Quigley concerning the higher-level goals of the dynastic bankers as being "nothing less than to create a world system of financial control in private hands able to dominate the POLITICAL SYSTEM of each country and the ECONOMY of the world as a whole. This system was to be controlled in a feudalistic fashion by the central banks of the world acting in concert, by secret agreements arrived at in frequent private meetings and conferences. The apex of the system was to be the Bank for International Settlements in Basle, Switzerland, a private bank owned and controlled by the world's central banks which were themselves private corporations. Each central bank, in the hands of men like Montagu Norman of the Bank of England, Benjamin Strong of the New York Federal Reserve Bank, Charles Rist of the Bank of France, and Hjalmar Schacht of the Reichsbank, sought to dominate its government by its ability to control Treasury loans, to manipulate foreign exchanges, to influence the level of economic activity in the country, and to influence cooperative politicians by subsequent economic rewards in the business world." (Quigley, p. 324, emphasis added)

And the goals of the dynastic banking families themselves? Mr. Skousen concludes the following (p. 24): "There is a growing volume of evidence that the highest centers of political and economic power have been forcing the entire human race toward a global, socialist, dictatorial-oriented society. And what has been most baffling about it has been the fact that this drift toward dictatorship with its inevitable obliteration of a thousand years of struggle toward human freedom, is being plotted, promoted, and implemented by the leaders of free nations and the super-rich of those nations whose positions of affluence would seem to make them the foremost beneficiaries of the free-enterprise, property-oriented, open society in which so much progress has been made. Certainly they, above all men, should know that in order for this system to survive, freedom of action and the integrity of property rights must be preserved. Then why are the super-capitalists trying to destroy them?

"Dr. Quigley provides an answer to this question but it is so startling that at first it seems virtually inconceivable. It becomes rational only as his scattered references to it are collected and digested point by point. In a nutshell, Dr. Quigley has undertaken to expose what every insider like himself has known all along – that the world hierarchy of the dynastic super-rich is out to take over the entire planet, doing it with Socialistic legislation where possible, but having no reluctance to use Communist revolution where necessary."

Having thus derived an understanding of the underlying causality pervading our recent political and economic lives, permitting many heretofore inexplicable events to suddenly become rationally understandable, Mr. Skousen proceeds forward with Dr. Quigley's wish to let history record who some of the major actors really are, and what they did.    He thus follows Quigley's revelations concerning Ruskin, Cecil Rhodes, Milner's Round Table groups, the formation of the RIIA, the CFR, and the IPR, and their invasion of the media and the Ivy League colleges.    Much of this was discussed in our own review of *Tragedy and Hope*.

But then Mr. Skousen arrives at and expresses what seems to us to be another highly cogent insight. We, in our review, discussed at some length Quigley's revelation concerning the insiders' buildup of Hitler during the decade before World War 2.    Mr. Skousen spends much of the latter part of his book discussing the corresponding buildup by these same elites of Lenin and Stalin in the USSR and Mao Tse-tung in China.    What is to be made of the fact that the elites were instrumental in building up the three most bloodthirsty dictators of the twentieth century – Hitler, Stalin, and Chairman Mao, the first two of whom ended up in a violent war with each other?    Some hard-core conspiracy buffs have suggested that the banking elites were in complete control of these dictators and their actions.    The elites themselves of course publicly insist that no tie at all existed to such evil personages. Mr. Skousen, in contrast to both of these views, suggests that the real relationship was very much like the simple risk that a person will take to gain large rewards rapidly [perhaps like speculating in penny stocks].    He explains (p. 38):

"Power from any source tends to create an appetite for additional power.   Power coming from wealth tends to create an appetite for political power, and vice versa.  It was almost inevitable that the super-rich would one day aspire to control not only their own wealth, but the wealth of the whole world.  To achieve this, they were perfectly willing to feed the ambitions of the power-hungry political conspirators who were committed to the overthrow of all existing governments, and the establishment of a central world-wide dictatorship along socialist lines.

"This, of course, was a *risky business* for the Anglo-American secret society.  The super-rich were gambling on the expectation that when the violence and reconstruction had been completed by the political conspirators, the super-rich would then take over ... to guide mankind hopefully and compulsively into a whole new era of universal peace and universal prosperity.

"To *take such a risk*, the cadre of the super-rich had to ignore the most elementary aspects of the ferocity of the left-wing conspiratorial mentality.  Mao Tse-tung has articulated the basic Communist conviction that political power comes from the barrel of a gun, and once they seize control it is their expressed intention to use the gun to prevent the super-rich or anyone else from taking that control away from them. [Similarly, Hitler repeatedly told Britain that he intended to realize his goals by going to war, not by diplomatic negotiation.]

"Nevertheless, the secret society of the London-Wall Street axis elected to *take this risk*.  The master-planners have attempted to control the global conspiratorial groups by feeding them vast quantities of money for their revolutionary work, and then financing their opposition if they seemed to be getting out of control."

He then quotes Quigley's defense for the elites' support of such ruthless psychopaths, claiming that their own altruistic ends justified such means: "The chief aims of this elaborate, semi-secret organization were largely commendable: to coordinate the international activities and outlooks of the English-speaking world into one (which would largely, it is true, be that of the London group); to work to maintain peace; to help backward, colonial, and underdeveloped areas to advance toward stability, law and order, and prosperity *along lines somewhat similar to those taught at Oxford and the University of London (especially the School of Economics and the Schools of African and Oriental Studies*)." (p. 954) Mr. Skousen adds that his emphasis was inserted so that readers wouldn't miss the intent of the elites that their remade world be organized along the socialist lines taught by the listed British educational institutions.

Mr. Skousen then goes into Quigley's revelations concerning why the elites ventured into supporting left-wing organizations. Having spent a good part of his career in investigating domestic communist activities, he is in a remarkable position to compare his knowledge of those activities to Quigley's bland assertions. He quotes Quigley at length concerning the bankers' efforts, mostly by Morgan men, to control political parties and movements, naming which men infiltrated the Republicans, the Democrats, the extreme right, and the extreme left. He further quotes Quigley concerning the communist front groups set up by the Morgans, their efforts to block investigation by Congress, their support of the Institute of Pacific Relations and its infiltration by communist agents, and then a lengthy section concerning the Council on Foreign Relations, complete with names of major actors up to the time of publishing his book (e.g., Alger Hiss, Harry Dexter White, Owen Lattimore, Christian Herter, John and Allen Dulles, Nelson Rockefeller, George Ball, Henry Kissinger, and many others).

Skousen then gets to the matter of the tax-exempt foundations, and their investigation by the Reece Committee of the U.S. House of Representatives, a matter which Quigley himself had discussed in connection with congressional probing into IPR policies and actions. Skousen goes a little beyond our own review of Quigley's observations in that he also attempts to summarize the findings of Rene Wormser's book, *Foundations: Their Power and Influence*, which Quigley had noted and then dismissed as perhaps shocking to Wormser but not to him. Wormser's summarization (reproduced by Skousen, p. 60) of the efforts of the foundations to dominate U.S. education, for example, reads as follows:

"7. Foundations use their funds to subvert and control American education.

a. 'Conform or no grant!' (p. 140)

b. The birth of Educational Radicalism. (pp. 143-145)

c. Carnegie finances a socialist charter for education. (pp. 146-152)

d. The radical educators. (pp. 152-155)

e. The Progressive Education Association. (pp. 155-156)

f. Financing and promoting socialist textbooks. (pp. 156-167)

g. Financing Left-wing reference works. (pp. 167-171)

h. The National Education Association not designed to advance 'American' education. (pp. 142, 145, 160, 164-165, 216-217)"

Noting next that Wormser's book then spends 79 pages exclusively on the Ford Foundation, Skousen proceeds to combine his own and Wormser's knowledge concerning the personnel and works of that organization. Following the death of Henry Ford, Sr. in 1947, the scramble for control of the foundation was won by Paul G. Hoffman, who, says Skousen (p. 62), "was not only a member of the London-Wall Street nexus, but had been director of the principal propaganda arm of the Council on Foreign Relations and also a trustee for the Institute of Pacific Relations." Hoffman then brought in "the well-known global collectivist, Robert Hutchins" as his associate director, and through their joint efforts, "By 1956 the Ford Foundation had spent more than one billion dollars in contributions to 'education' and had thereby become a well-nigh all-encompassing influence over hundreds of colleges and universities."

The directorship of the foundation was handed in 1966 to McGeorge Bundy, shortly after he was hounded out of L. B. Johnson's administration by

Congress because of his apparent efforts to support a communist coup attempt in the Dominican Republic. Skousen describes a number of Bundy's grantees and various of their activities, and then summarizes (p. 66): "Official Ford Foundation reports show that millions upon millions are being poured into revolutionary, communist-dominated or global collectivist organizations under the direction of McGeorge Bundy." Skousen lists a dozen or so of such organizations supported by the Ford Foundation, and then concludes, "So much for the activities of the major foundations which 'insider' Carroll Quigley says were 'not shocking' to him at all."

Mr. Skousen, after first noting the establishment's continually felt fear of exposure frequently alluded to by Dr. Quigley, then describes in some detail several attempts at such exposure following World War 2, some of which he was personally involved with. Included are: (1) revelations by Major Racey Jordan (*From Major Jordan's Diaries*, N.Y., Harcourt, Brace Co., 1952) concerning shipments to Russia, ordered in 1943 by Harry Hopkins under the Russian lend-lease program, of refined uranium and atomic bomb research documentation; (2) the U.S. involvement in disarming Chiang Kai-shek and the resulting conquest of China by the Chinese communists, to the anger and disgust of Americans when they began to find out about it; (3) the exposure in 1948 of the State Department's Alger Hiss as a communist spy; (4) the firing of General MacArthur during the Korean War for revealing to Congress that he was now fighting Chinese communist "volunteers" after essentially defeating the North Korean army; (5) the publication in July 1953 of the Senate Judiciary Committee's famous Jenner Report, entitled "Interlocking Subversion in Government Departments"; (6) the public stir raised by Senator Joe McCarthy in the early 1950's concerning communist infiltration into the State Department and elsewhere, activities which evoked paroxysms of rage and malevolence from Carroll Quigley (pp. 928 ff.); (7) the flood of anti-communist literature from such as J. Edgar Hoover, W. Cleon Skousen, Dean Manion, Dan Smoot, Robert Welch, Billy James Hargis and others, and the beginning of televised mass meetings and radio broadcasts concerning the communist menace, responded to by the establishment elites with the Reuther Memorandum proposing government measures to curb these activities, one of which was the FCC's "Fairness Doctrine," which required radio and TV stations to give free rebuttal time to anyone criticized within another purchased program; and (8) the rise of Senator Barry Goldwater as a presidential candidate challenging the establishment, an effort which again evoked a vitriolic diatribe from Quigley, and which the well-oiled establishment handled with a fair degree of ease.

Mr. Skousen ends the development of his narrative with a description, as of knowledge available to him in 1970, of the Bilderberg Group. Their conferences, he says (p. 108), "are held each year as an international master planning conclave. They are secret and attendance is restricted to invited 'guests.' These turn out to be about 100 men from the top inner circle representing the four major dimensions of power: the international banking dynasties, their corporations involved in vast, international enterprises, the American tax-exempt foundations, and the establishment representatives who have gained high offices in government, especially the United States government. These conferences always have the same chairman – his royal highness Prince Bernhard of the Netherlands, who, with his family, owns a massive fortune in the Royal Dutch Shell Oil Corporation. Then, close at hand, will always be David Rockefeller representing his family and especially Standard Oil of New Jersey which is one of the largest corporate structures in existence. It is interesting that in the past two decades when political revolutions have occurred in various parts of the world, these two companies usually end up with all of the oil and natural gas concessions. This has been largely true in Africa, the Middle East, South America, and the Far East. These are also the companies whose installations seem to be virtually off limits to the bombers in both sides of any recent war. We mention this simply to demonstrate the fact that Dr. Quigley does seem to be correct in alleging that the political and economic forces of the earth are being woven into a gigantic monolith of total global power."

Skousen identifies the first meeting as being held in May 1954 at the Bilderberg Hotel in Oosterbeek, Netherlands. After each of their annual meetings, he says, the conferees "depart to the four corners of the earth to carry out their adopted goals, but the world is never given the slightest hint as to what has been decided. This is particularly frustrating to Congress, which has tried several times to ferret out the activities of these Bilderberg conferences. Even when top government officials such as Navy Secretary Paul Nitze were placed under oath and interrogated, it became virtually impossible to learn anything of significance." Trusted members of the major media are invited, but also never report on the substance of the proceedings. Skousen names such personages representing the New York Times, the Atlanta Constitution, Look magazine, and Life magazine. Similar personages continue to represent the major newspapers and TV networks as this is being written in 1995. (The list of 1995 attendees was printed in the Washington weekly *The Spotlight* for 10/23/95. Call 800-522-6292. A few familiar names on that list were Lloyd Bentsen, Tom Foley, David Gergen, Richard Holbrooke, Peter Jennings, Henry Kissinger, and David Rockefeller.)

Mr. Skousen summarizes that the elites who wish to set up their world dictatorship recognize their main enemy to be the great middle class of the United States, which, being made up of individuals who have acquired a little education, property, and independence, will fight strenuously to keep them. The strategy of the elites is to squeeze the middle class to death by creating or exacerbating the major problems facing the society, including class warfare, crime, education, moral decay, etc., and then creating in response spurious governmental programs to "cure" the problems that they just created. He describes (p. 115) the enmity which Dr. Quigley holds toward the middle class: "The middle class is to be identified as the 'petty bourgeoisie,' the 'neo-isolationists' ... who are described by Dr. Quigley as 'often very insecure, envious, filled with hatreds, and are generally the chief recruits for any Radical Right, fascist, or hate campaign against any group that is different or which refuses to conform to middle class values.' (p. 1243)"

Mr. Skousen finally thanks Dr. Quigley for gratuitously giving us a peek behind the curtain, helping us to identify our real enemy and thus better aim our arrows of reform. Our future task, he says (p. 117), is political in nature, and should be aimed at "throwing the rascals out. Every Democrat, Republican, or Independent from the top of the federal government right down to the lowest official on the local level, who has been consistently supporting the collectivist policies and tactics of the global network, should be summarily replaced as fast as the electoral process will permit."

Truly a daunting job, but possible. Mr. Skousen then concludes, "It is time we got on with the task."

# Chapter 4

# "THE TAX-EXEMPT FOUNDATIONS"

(By William H. McIlhany, II. Pub. 1980 by Arlington House, Westport, CT.)
(Subsidiary reference: "The Dodd Report to the Reece Committee on Foundations," by Norman Dodd. Pub. 1954 by Long House, New Canaan, CT.)

We take up this book next to flesh out the brief exposition concerning the tax-exempt foundations that appeared in *The Naked Capitalist*. McIlhany's book, appearing ten years later, and devoted to its one single topic, gives startling illumination to the scope of "un-American" activities undertaken by the major American tax-exempt foundations and the satellite organizations which they financially support.

McIlhany's incentive for writing this book stemmed from the abortive 1954 hearings of the House of Representatives' Special Committee to Investigate Tax Exempt Foundations, chaired by Rep. Carroll Reece. Both Carroll Quigley and Cleon Skousen have discussed the Reece hearings in their respective books, as we have reviewed above. McIlhany's approach was to obtain an extensive interview with Norman Dodd, the Research Director of the Reece Committee, to get his account of the history of that investigation, and follow it up with his own investigations and interviews with officials in the primary foundations and "accessory agencies" (as Dodd labels them) that were under investigation.  We will go immediately to the major new revelations transmitted to McIlhany by Mr. Dodd.

Following his appointment and prior to the hearings, Dodd prepared a list of questions and sent them to the major foundations.  One reply he received was a call from the Carnegie Endowment for International Peace, which resulted in an appointment with Dr. Joseph Johnson, its recently appointed president (replacing the former president, Alger Hiss).  Johnson said he couldn't take the time to research and answer Dodd's questions about the organization, but would make the minute books of the foundation available to one of Dodd's staffers in their library.  Dodd swiftly agreed, believing that Johnson probably did not know what might be in those records.

He sent Kathryn Casey, the legal analyst for the Reece Committee, to examine those records, asking her to concentrate on the first years of the Endowment after 1910, and the years from 1917 to 1920.  She came back shocked and upset, but having transcribed enough material for Dodd to reconstruct what she had found.  In his words (pp. 60-61):

"[In the minutes, about 1911] the trustees raised a question.  And they discussed the question and the question was specific, 'Is there any means known to man more effective than war, assuming you wish to alter the life of an entire people?'  And they discussed this and at the end of a year they came to the conclusion that there was no more effective means to that end known to man.  So, they raised question number two, and the question was, *'How do we involve the United States in a war?'*

"And then they raised the question, 'How do we control the diplomatic machinery of the United States?' And the answer came out, 'We' must control the State Department.  At this point we catch up with what we had already found out, and that was that through an agency set up by the Carnegie Endowment every high appointment in the State Department was cleared.

"Finally, we were in a war.  These trustees in a meeting about 1917 had the brashness to congratulate themselves on the wisdom *of their original decision because already the impact of war had indicated that it would alter life and can alter life in this country.*  This was the date of our entry in the war; we were involved.  They even had the brashness to dispatch a telegram to [President] Wilson, cautioning him to see that the war did not end too quickly.

"The war was over.  Then the concern became, as expressed by the trustees, seeing to it that there was no reversion to life in this country as it existed prior to 1914.  And they came to the conclusion that, to prevent a reversion, *they must control education.*  And then they approached the Rockefeller Foundation and they said, 'Will you take on the acquisition of control of education as it involves subjects that are domestic in significance?  We'll take it on the basis of subjects that have an international significance.'  And it was agreed.

"Then, together, they decided the key to it is the teaching of American history and *they must change that.* So, they then approached the most prominent of what we might call American historians at that time with the idea of getting them to alter the manner in which they presented the subject."

The minutes further showed, says Dodd (pp. 61-62), that the Carnegie trustees, upon encountering resistance from established historians, set about "to build their own stable of kept historians, and they even got a working agreement with the Guggenheim Foundation to grant scholarships to their selected candidates who were seeking graduate degrees.... The extent to which the Carnegie trustees were able to build their stable of submissive historians is significant.... Though encountering resistance at first, this group succeeded gradually in capturing more influence in the American Historical Association and affiliated circles."

McIlhany continues (p. 62), "It is important to remember that the [Carnegie] endowment supported U.S. entry into the war, not for any patriotic purpose, but so that the war would provide an excuse for, if not necessitate, Andrew Carnegie's goal of British-American regional government." He supports this allegation by quoting much earlier words from Andrew Carnegie himself, dating back to 1893 (p. 21): "Time may dispel many pleasing illusions and destroy many noble dreams, but it shall never shake my belief that the wound caused by the wholly unlooked-for and undesired separation of the mother from her child is not to bleed forever. Let men say what the will, therefore, I say that as surely as the sun in the heavens once shown upon Britain and America united, so surely is it one morning to rise, shine upon, and greet again the re-united state, the British-American union." It is thus easy to see how close Carnegie's intellectual outlook was to that of the Rhodes-Milner group, whose secret society had already been established, according to Carroll Quigley, by March, 1891.

The foundation minutes of around 1911 ex-pressing the need to control the State Department, as noted above, were apparently written during the tenure of the first president of the endowment, Elihu Root. Mr. Root had himself just finished a term as Teddy Roosevelt's Secretary of State from 1905 to 1908, so he was in a position to know what control of the State Department could accomplish. Later, says McIlhany (p. 61), "as a U.S. Senator and Nobel Peace Prize recipient, Root was probably the most influential trustee at this time." On August 16, 1918, he wrote to Colonel Edward Mandell House, President Wilson's advisor and alter ego, discussing the need for "an international community system" to enforce World War 1 settlement terms which were soon to be negoti-ated. In response, "Colonel House wrote back on August 23, telling Root that he had discussed his letter with Wilson, and that he did 'not believe there would be much difficulty in bringing our minds in harmony upon some plan' for a 'Community of Nations.'"

This interest in the control of international relations is especially interesting in light of the second major revelation which Dodd related to McIlhany. Dodd said that in response to his request for information prior to the Reece hearings, he sought and was extended an invitation to visit Rowan Gaither, the president of the Ford Foundation. The visit took place in December 1953. Dodd said that Gaither opened the conversation with an unforgettable admission (p. 63):

"'Of course, [Mr. Dodd,] you know that we at the executive level here were, at one time or another, active in either the OSS, the State Department, or the European Economic Administration. During those times, and without exception, we operated under directives issued by the White House. We are continuing to be guided by just such directives. Would you like to know the substance of these directives?'

"And I said, 'Yes, Mr. Gaither, I'd like to know.'

"'The substance was to the effect that *we should make every effort to so alter life in the United States as to make possible a comfortable merger with the Soviet Union.*'"

Shocked by this confession, Dodd recalls responding that, in the light of those directives, he was no longer surprised at the record of left-wing grants made by the Ford Foundation. He suggested that Mr. Gaither make those directives public, a suggestion which Gaither brushed aside, indicating that, for public consumption, his foundation was guided by the Ten Commandments, The Sermon on the Mount, the Declaration of Independence, and the U.S. Constitution.

Thus, the thrust of the major foundations to alter life in the United States toward internationalism, expressed first in 1911 in the minutes of the Carnegie Foundation, is found substantially unchanged 42 years later as a guiding principle of the relatively new (but much wealthier) Ford Foundation.

Dodd also related to McIlhany that about a month earlier, in November 1953, after having given a speech at the Mayflower Hotel in Washington, he had been approached by Mr. Herman Edelsberg, who identified himself as an Anti-Defamation League lobbyist. Over a drink in the hotel bar, Dodd says he got the man to open up, whereupon "he spoke of a very powerful group of men whom he represented," but implying that the ADL was only an agency for those men. McIlhany continues Dodd's story (p. 64):

"Edelsberg said the men had some very serious problems. They had amassed so much power that it would destroy them. They should dissolve their associations, but he was sure they would not be willing to do so. Dodd well recollects what [Edelsberg] said, continuing: 'We will exercise our power and it will destroy us, but it will destroy everything else in the process.... As we exercise our power from here on out, we're going to get closer and closer to the surface, and somebody's going to get very curious and pick up the end of the string and follow the string and he's going to find himself at our door.'

"It was obvious that Edelsberg was claiming to represent an elite far more powerful than anyone active in the ADL. He told Dodd that the strength of the group was their secrecy and their understanding of the nature of a free society. And their Achilles heel was the possibility that their efforts to cloud public understanding in these areas might fail."

Dodd related that, following the first day of the hearings, he was again contacted by Mr. Edelsberg, who said that he had been ordered to deliver a threat against Dodd's life. No such attempt was apparently made, however, though Dodd says that his phone was subsequently tapped, he was crudely followed, and he was subjected to a verbal attack in the October 1954 *A.D.L. Bulletin.*

Before going to a discussion of the hearings themselves, let us detour to pick up a valuable supposition spotted by Mr. McIlhany regarding the motivations of the Rhodes-Milner group. McIlhany notes (p. 19) that Cecil Rhodes attached to his will a "Confession of Faith" which contained the following:

"The idea gliding and dancing before our eyes like a willow – a wish at last frames itself into a plan. Why should we not join [or 'form' as other writers have interpreted Rhodes' handwriting] a secret society with but one object: the furtherance of the British Empire, for the bringing of the whole uncivilized world under British rule, for the recovery of the United States, for the making the Anglo-Saxon race but one Empire."

Though sounding remarkably like the sentiments voiced by Andrew Carnegie, it seems a contradiction that Rhodes would attach to a public document, i.e., his will, the purposes of a *secret* society. The contradiction is further explored by McIlhany (p. 18):

"This goal [of merging Great Britain and the United States] was put forth by their public organization, the Round Table Groups, organized and led by Milner after Rhodes' death in 1902. In spite of Milner's public declarations of fidelity to the interests of the British Empire, much controversy has arisen from the fact that Milner's agents were instrumental both in provoking hostilities with Germany in 1904 through the Jameson Raid in South Africa, and in assisting with the financing of the 1917 Bolshevik takeover of Russia. [E.g., see Skousen, pp. 40-41.] That the Round Table leadership in the British government and press after 1919 spearheaded the drive not only for socialism at home but also for the dismantling of the Empire around the globe has caused researchers to question what the goals of the Rhodes-Milner group really were."

McIlhany supplies copious references to the works of these other researchers. He is clearly suggesting that the Pan-British oratory is little more than a cover for the real (and really secret) objective, which is to reorganize the world by socializing its governments and then merging them into one, by, for example, "altering life in the United States such as to make possible a comfortable merger with the Soviet Union," as revealed above by Rowan Gaither. This secret objective is exactly that described by Mr. Skousen in our previous review, which he summarized as follows:

"[The] world hierarchy of the dynastic super-rich is out to take over the entire planet, doing it with socialistic legislation where possible, but having no reluctance to use Communist revolution where necessary."

McIlhany then proceeds to describe the two attempts of Congress to investigate the foundations – first by the special committee of the House run by Democrat Congressman Eugene Cox of Georgia, and second by a similar committee chaired by Republican Congressman Carroll Reece of Tennessee.

The Cox committee was formed April 4, 1952, and was required to complete its work by January 1, 1953, i.e., at the start of the next congressional session. It's motivation centered on the concern raised by the immediately preceding work of the Senate Internal Security Subcommittee which found, as McIlhany puts it (p. 35) "that much of the Roosevelt-Truman foreign policy that led to the fall of mainland China to the Communists was deliberately calculated to produce that result. The private organization which influenced or supplied so many of the State Department personnel responsible for shaping Far East policy was the American Council of the Institute of Pacific Relations. The IPR, founded in 1925, was by far the most influential source for all information about China in this country. It has already been mentioned that the Rhodes-Milner Round Table Groups supported and used the IPR as an extension of their strategy for global power. But the Senate subcommittee concluded, 'The IPR has been considered by the American Communist Party and by Soviet officials as an instrument of Communist policy,

... [and] was a vehicle used by the Communists to orientate American far eastern policies toward Communist objectives.'"

The Senate report then identified the main sources of IPR funding, the American IPR receiving, in the 26 years from 1925 through 1950, 50 percent of its total income from foundations (chiefly Rockefeller and Carnegie groups), and the International IPR receiving in the same period 77 percent of its total income from the Rockefeller and Carnegie groups and the American IPR. These funds included grants as late as 1950 of $50,000 and $60,000 from the Rockefeller Foundation to the American and the International IPR, respectively. Further, the temporary chairman of the Carnegie Foundation, John Foster Dulles, recommended in 1946 that the foundation's presidency be given to the upcoming State Department figure Alger Hiss. The board so acted in December 1946. Though evidence concerning Hiss's role as a Soviet spy was made available to Dulles a few weeks later, and though Hiss was publicly identified as a spy by Whittaker Chambers in December 1948, Hiss was not removed as the foundation president until 1950.

These several revelations provided the momentum for forming the Cox committee to investigate the foundations and their apparent promotion of Communist objectives. McIlhany quotes from the House Resolution authorizing the committee study (p. 37): "The committee is authorized and directed to conduct a full and complete investigation and study of educational and philanthropic foundations and other comparable organizations which are exempt from federal income taxation ... to determine which such foundations and organizations are using their resources for un-American and subversive activities or for purposes not in the interest or tradition of the United States."

The hearings then proceeded apace, with selected testimony described by McIlhany in some detail. The time was short, however, and compilation of a report was interrupted by the unexpected death of Chairman Cox. The job was given to another, and the final report which emerged consisted of just 15 pages, lacking any significant, supported conclusions or generalizations concerning the thrust of foundation activities and grants. As McIlhany puts it (p. 49):

"The issues discussed in the hearings were summarized for the report in the form of twelve questions. Several of these focused generally on the grants made to subversive organizations and individuals with Communist affiliations, but the report, perhaps due to the impossibility of in-depth analysis, concluded that the foundations had overwhelmingly lived up to their respective reputations as public trusts." However, he continues, "there was one angry member of the Cox committee who was disappointed by the outcome of the hearings and the very limited nature of the report. Representative B. Carroll Reece of Tennessee knew that another investigation would be necessary to tell the whole story. And, if he could help it, he was determined that the foundations were not going to get away with a whitewash."

Carroll Reece got the continuing investigation he wanted by a House resolution passed in July 1953. The best single thing that he did in furtherance of his goal was to hire Norman Dodd as research director. Dodd's background and mentality matched the task at hand, as McIlhany makes clear in his thumb-nail biography of Dodd. McIlhany relates the following exchange in January 1954, shortly after Dodd's hiring:

"'Norm, would you accept the premise that this country is the victim of a conspiracy?' Dodd remembers thinking for a moment and saying, 'Yes, Carroll, I'll accept that.' Then [Reece] said, 'Can you conduct this investigation in a manner which will expose it with proof?' .... Dodd agreed to conduct the research on the suggested basis of proving what they both knew was true – what had been demonstrated in the Cox Committee hearings but not stated in its report – that some of the foundations were part of a totalitarian conspiracy."

The roadblocks that were erected to first prevent, and then sidetrack, and finally to stop the Reece Committee hearings make as good a story as ever came out of Hollywood. As related by Dodd to McIlhany, Dodd received a call in February 1954, from Bob Humphreys, an officer of the Republican National Committee, who as much as ordered him to stop what he was doing. At about the same time, Rep. Wayne Hays, a Democrat minority member of the Reece Committee, told Dodd he had been contacted by President Eisenhower's congressional liaison, General Jerry Persons, who asked Hays to "throw as much of a

monkey wrench into the investigation as possible."
Hays said that he refused, though he had told Dodd
several months earlier that he thought the investigation
was nothing more than a publicity stunt on the part of
Carroll Reece.

Then when Reece called the committee mem-
bers and staff to his office to discuss when the hearings
should start, Rene Wormser, the committee counsel,
proposed (p. 57), "Gentlemen, I recommend that the
committee hold no hearings, but that you permit me to
write a report and we'll let the foundations do anything
they want."  Reece said no, but Wormser's suggestion
was consistent with the prior expressed concern felt by
both Dodd and Reece that Wormser did not share their
premise of a foundation conspiracy.  Dodd then offered to write, and did write, a report to the committee
setting out the basis upon which the committee would
proceed with its work.  We'll discuss that report more
fully in a moment.

On May 10, just after the first public hearing,
Dodd received a death threat via Mr. Edelsberg, as
previously related.  Then, during the one month or so
of actual hearings, Dodd and his witnesses were
continuously interrupted for harangues by Wayne
Hays, delaying the hearings and preventing adequate
time for development of coherent causal relationships.
Hays exploded on June 17 into a tirade of obscenities
directed at Reece and the committee staff, immediately
following which the hearings were postponed and then
finally called off entirely.

Hays subsequently apologized to Reece, but Reece did not reinstate the hearings. Dodd related to McIlhany that he was later informed that Reece did not do so because of blackmail pressure brought against Reece relating to a prior recorded charge by Washington police of his homosexual behavior in a public washroom. Dodd believed the charges to be a frame-up, but whether true or false, the hearings were discontinued, and Dodd was prevented from bringing up the content of the Carnegie Foundation minutes which Kathryn Casey had transcribed, or the conversation he had had with Rowan Gaither of the Ford Foundation, both of which would have gotten damning evidence on the record in support of his thesis.

McIlhany devotes about two pages (pp. 66-68) to a discussion of the Dodd Report to the Reece Committee, which we referred to above, and which we also identified as a "subsidiary reference" at the beginning of this chapter. For our purposes, the Dodd Report provides us with a highly important insight into the scope and power of the forces seeking to socialize our society. As the report points out, the implementation of socialization actions by government, and the aggrandizement of Executive branch power, went through a revolutionary increase during FDR's first term, but with the wide acceptance of the electorate. This led to additional studies by the Reece Committee staff which indicated that such a revolution could not have been publicly accepted "unless education in the United States had been prepared in advance to endorse it." It was therefore reasonable to hypothesize that educational grants by the foundations would reflect

such preparation.  On this basis, the staff was directed
(Dodd Report, p. 7) "to explore Foundation practices,
educational procedures, and the operations of the
Executive branch of the federal government since 1903
for reasonable evidence of a purposeful relationship
between them."  The Dodd Report continues:

"Its ensuing studies disclosed such a relationship, and that it had existed continuously since the
beginning of this 50-year period.  In addition, these
studies seem to give evidence of a response to our
involvement in international affairs.  Likewise, they
seemed to reveal that grants had been made by Foundations (chiefly by Carnegie and Rockefeller) which
were used to further this purpose by:

"Directing education in the United States toward an international viewpoint and discrediting
the traditions to which it [formerly] had been
dedicated.

"Training individuals and servicing agencies to
render advice to the Executive branch of the
federal government.

"Decreasing the dependency of education upon
the resources of the local community and freeing it from many of the natural safeguards inherent in this American tradition.

"Changing both school and college curricula to
the point where they sometimes denied the
principles underlying the American way of life.

"Financing experiments designed to determine the most effective means by which education could be pressed into service of a political nature.

"At this point the staff became concerned with ... identifying all the elements comprising the operational relationship between Foundations, education, and government, and determining the objective to which this relationship had been dedicated and the functions performed by each of its parts.... To insure these determinations being made on the basis of impersonal facts, I directed the staff to make a study of the development of American education since the turn of the century and of the trends in techniques of teaching and of development of curricula since that time. As a result, it became quite evident that this study would have to be enlarged to include the accessory agencies to which these developments and trends had been traced.

"The work of the staff was then expanded to include an investigation of such agencies as:

"The American Council of Learned Societies, the National Research Council, the Social Science Research Council, the American Council on Education, the National Education Association, the League for Industrial Democracy, the Progressive Education Association, the American Historical Association, the John Dewey Society, and the Anti-Defamation League."

Dodd then proceeds to provide a sketch of each of these organizations (excepting only the ADL). The scope of their activities is awesome. Here, somewhat abbreviated, is how he describes them:

"The *American Council of Learned Societies* was founded in 1919 to encourage humanistic studies, including some which today are regarded as social sciences. It is comprised of 24 constituent member associations. In its entirety, it appears to dominate this division of scholarship in the United States.

"The *National Research Council* was established in 1916, originally as a preparedness measure in connection with World War 1.... [Since 1919,] on behalf of its 8 member associations, it has been devoted to the promotion of research within the most essential areas ordinarily referred to as the exact and applied sciences.

"The *Social Science Research Council* was established in 1923 to advance research in the social sciences. It acts as spokesman for 7 constituent member associations representing all of the subdivisions of this new field of knowledge, i.e., history, economics, sociology, psychology, political science, statistics, and anthropology.

"The *American Council on Education* was founded in 1918 'to coordinate the services which educational institutions and organizations could contribute to the Government in the national crisis brought about by World War 1.' Starting with 14 constituent or founding organizations, this formidable and influential agency has steadily expanded until today its membership is reported to consist of:

> 79 constituent members (national and regional educational associations),

> 64 associate members (national organizations in fields related to education), and

> 954 institutional members (universities, colleges, selected private school systems, educational departments of industrial concerns, voluntary associations of colleges and universities within the states, large public libraries, etc.)

"The *National Education Association* was established in 1857 to elevate character, advance the interests of the teaching profession, and to promote the cause of popular education in the United States. Broadly speaking, this powerful entity concentrates on primary and secondary schools. Its membership is reported to consist of 520,000 individuals who include in addition to teachers – superintendents, school administrators and school secretaries. It boasts that it is 'the only organization that represents or has the possibility of representing the great body of teachers in the United States,' thus inferring a monopolistic aim.

"The *League for Industrial Democracy* came into being in 1905, when it was known as the *Intercollegiate Socialist Society*, for the purpose of awakening the intellectuals of this country to the ideas and benefits of socialism.  This organization might be compared to the Fabian Society of England, which was established in 1884 to spread socialism by peaceful means.

"The *Progressive Education Association* was established around 1880.  Since then it has been active in introducing radical ideas to education which are now being questioned by many. They include the idea that the individual must be adjusted to the group as a result of his or her educational experience, and that democracy is little more than a system for cooperative living.

"The *American Historical Association* was established in 1889 to promote historical studies. It is interesting to note that after giving careful consideration, in 1926, to the social sciences, a report was published under its auspices in 1934 which concluded that the day of the individual in the United States had come to an end and that the future would be characterized, inevitably, by some form of collectivism and an increase in the authority of the State.

"The *John Dewey Society* was formed in February 1936, apparently for the two-fold purpose of conducting research in the field of education and promoting the educational philosophy of John Dewey.... He held that ideas were instruments, and that their truth or falsity depended upon whether or not they worked successfully."

Dodd concludes: "The broad study which called our attention to the activities of these [accessory] organizations has revealed not only their support by Foundations, but has disclosed a degree of cooperation between them which *they* have referred to as 'an interlock,' thus indicating a concentration of influence and power.  By this phrase they indicate they are bound by a *common interest* rather than a dependency upon a single source for capital funds.  It is difficult to study their relationship without confirming this. Likewise, it is difficult to avoid the feeling that their common interest ... lies in the planning and control of certain aspects of American life through a combination of the federal government and education....  In summary, our study of these entities and their relationship to each other seems to warrant the inference that they constitute a highly efficient, functioning whole.  Its product is apparently an educational curriculum designed to indoctrinate the American student from matriculation to the consummation of his education.  It contrasts sharply with the freedom of the individual as the cornerstone of our social structure.  For this freedom, it seems to substitute the group, the will of the majority, and a centralized power to enforce this will – presumably in the interest of all."

Dodd finishes off his report with observations, first, about the potentially pernicious effects of new government-sponsored foundations, such as the National Science Foundation, moneys to which "are so large that they dwarf Foundation contributions," and second, about the unprecedented funding and activities of the relatively new Ford Foundation, in the light of which he suggests "that the Committee give special consideration to the Ford Foundation."

Given the insights that Dodd displayed in his report, and his intention to make them public and dig for documentary evidence backing them up, is it any wonder that those directing this targeted monolith of educational brainwashing would find ways, fair or foul, to subvert and quash the Reece Committee hearings?

The remaining portion of McIlhany's book, comprising about two-thirds of the total book, is devoted to updating information on the activities of, primarily, the three major foundations that the Cox and Reece Committees had sought to investigate, namely those of Carnegie, Rockefeller, and Ford. He starts off his chapter on Carnegie by referring back to Dodd's most critical finding:

"The reader will recall the minutes of the trustees of the endowment during its first decade and the reason they so shocked an unsuspecting staff member of the Reece Committee. Here were very powerful men, the likes of Secretary of State Elihu Root and Professor James T. Shotwell, planning in secret to push the United States into a European war so they would have the excuse of heralding the 'solution' to such conflicts in the form of a postwar League of Nations. They also began trying to influence American history teachers to push public opinion eventually in the direction of what Nicholas Murray Butler [long-time president of the endowment] called 'the international mind.'"

McIlhany then updates the Carnegie Foundation's history and major involvements through the early 70's. He finishes the Carnegie chapter with an interview he recorded in June of 1976 with David Robinson, "the Carnegie Corporation's congenial vice-president." The conversation is fascinating, replete with key-words such as Look-Say, New Math, Day Care Council, OSHA, Teacher Tenure, Chelation, Laetrile, FDA, NAACP, Howard Roark, Gunnar Myrdal, Corp. for Public Broadcasting, Education Vouchers, Bussing, Ralph Nader, National Lawyers Guild, ACLU, CFR, and more. It's like a questioning expedition through the multitudinous shoals and tribulations which ever more tightly surround and press upon our body politic as the months and years roll by.

Next is the Rockefeller group. A large part of McIlhany's treatment consists of a 1976 interview with John M. Knowles, MD, the then current president of the Rockefeller Foundation. Subjects covered included medicine, nutrition, child welfare, public health services, public education, planned parenthood, Austrian economics, and many other matters. His responses were rather more evasive than Mr. Robinson's, and McIlhany noted: "The overriding impression Knowles left with me was a tremendous lack of credibility." He backs this up by analyzing at some length the panegyric entitled *China Diary* which Knowles authored and had printed in 1976 as a Rockefeller Foundation Working Paper, following his 1975 visit to Red China in the company of a huge phalanx of CFR members and other insider elites (whom McIlhany lists), led by Cyrus Vance, at that time a Rockefeller Foundation trustee and vice chairman of the Council on Foreign Relations, and soon to be Secretary of State.

McIlhany's last major target is the Ford Foundation. His interviewee there turned out to be Mr. Richard Magat, the director of the Office of Reports, and a 20-year employee of the foundation. Magat started off by effectively implicating a couple of the high ranking "accessory agencies" identified by Norman Dodd:

"One of [our ways of supporting researchers] is the general support of a discipline or field…. For example … we have, as you probably know, given a very, very large amount of money to the Woodrow Wilson Fellowship Foundation…. We do not select the individuals. So that immediately eliminates any skewing in one direction or another. Now that's true of a lot of the research we support. In fact, in terms of the numbers of individuals, that probably accounts for the great majority. So that, for example, we give funds to the Social Science Research Council and the American Council of Learned Societies, who support a very large amount of research in the social sciences. They make the selection and they are, you know, beyond question, reputable, even-handed...."

The interview goes on at length, the basic matter under discussion being the paucity of grants to study free enterprise-based solutions to social problems. The fields of psychology, economics, public broadcasting, education, political advocacy, property rights, and law enforcement are among those which came under the microscope. Mr. Magat weaseled his way expertly through the bulk of these matters, admitting little that would cast a significant shadow on his employer.

McIlhany finishes his examination of the Ford Foundation by listing and describing the immense range of causes and studies it has supported up through the mid-70's (pp. 175-187). If there is one common thread running through this massive outpouring of money and energy, it is that the federal government is therewith encouraged or enabled to expand its involvement with every problem that is brought up about which something should be done. This guiding principle is demonstrated in each of McIlhany's many listed examples, including lastly the emphasis on governmental control over environmental and energy use issues. McIlhany's concluding summation (p. 217) is:

"That portion of the record which we have reviewed is only a small fraction of the total evidence that could be presented.  Further study will surely establish not only the degree of consistency with which the foundations we have examined have promoted the growth of big government and the objective of world government, but also the fact that there are no foundations successfully promoting to any similar degree an individualist goal of limited government."

Though written in 1980, that statement undoubtedly remains true today (1996).  Though a few such Constitutionalist foundations do now indeed exist, it can hardly be said that their influence yet is anywhere near comparable to those which have been in existence for the last 80 years or so.  Truth, however, is on our side.  The question is, do we have enough time to get enough of it out to enable a return to a Constitutionalist society without the major train wreck which, as Mr. Edelsberg told Norman Dodd, "will destroy everything else in the process."

Chapter 5

## "THE CREATURE FROM JEKYLL ISLAND"

(By G. Edward Griffin. Pub. 1994 by American Media, PO Box 4646, Westlake Village, CA 91359. Tel. (800) 282-2873.)

We move now to a discussion of the agencies which are more directly the initiators of the frightful world events which so distress us, as compared to the institutions described in the previous chapter which are devoted to a long-term educational effort to socialize both our personal outlooks and our political institutions. The agencies to be discussed in this chapter are the world's central banks, but more specifically, America's own Federal Reserve System.

Many books have been written about the Federal Reserve, but Griffin's is a new one and, in my opinion, by far the best. Further, of all the books reviewed in this, our own book, Griffin's is the one we most urgently suggest you acquire and absorb, since corrective actions on our part will otherwise most surely be misdirected and ineffective over the long term.

Griffin organizes his book into six parts. First is a section describing how and where the banking elites secretly met and agreed to push for the formation of a central bank, what their real motivations were as opposed to what their public pronouncements were, and to what extent those secret purposes were in fact accomplished over the next eighty years or so. The second section deals with the technical aspects of how banking, and in particular *central* banking, works. It's a little complex, but not at all beyond the capabilities of reasonably ordinary mortals. It is mandatory foundation material for those who would represent us in political arenas. The third section discusses how the first central bank, the Bank of England, was formed to finance a war, and how central banks since then have utilized and promoted wars for their own profit, starting with the Rothschild involvement with the Napoleonic wars, and continuing up to the present day the use of that same "Rothschild Formula." The fourth section outlines the three encounters prior to the Federal Reserve that America has had with fiat currency systems, and why we managed to resist such a system for so long. The fifth section describes the ties between the London and the American financial elites, how the American political system was subverted and the Congress hornswoggled into passing the Federal Reserve System, and some illuminating detail about the immediately following financial roller coaster of the roaring twenties expansion and the stock market crash and great depression. The sixth and last section devotes itself to looking into the future concerning what the elites have in store for us, and what we might be able to do to avoid that scenario and build one of our own.

The banking conspirators met secretly for nine days in November of 1910 at a vacation estate belonging to J.P. Morgan on Jekyll Island, off the coast of Georgia.   The participants were, as identified by Griffin (p. 5):

"1. Nelson W. Aldrich, Republican 'whip' of the Senate, Chairman of the National Monetary Commission, business associate of J.P. Morgan, father-in-law to John D. Rockefeller, Jr.;
2. Abraham Piatt Andrew, Assistant Secretary of the U.S. Treasury;
3. Frank A. Vanderlip, president of the National City Bank of New York, the most powerful of the banks at that time, representing William Rockefeller and the international investment banking house of Kuhn, Loeb & Company;
4. Henry P. Davison, senior partner of the J.P. Morgan Company;
5. Charles D. Norton, president of J.P. Morgan's First National Bank of New York;
6. Benjamin Strong, head of J.P. Morgan's Bankers Trust Company; and
7. Paul M. Warburg, a partner of Kuhn, Loeb & Company, a representative of the Rothschild banking dynasty in England and France, and brother of Max Warburg, who was head of the Warburg banking consortium in Germany and the Netherlands."

The representation thus included the banking houses of Morgan, Rockefeller, Rothschild, Warburg, and Kuhn-Loeb, representing around one-fourth of the total wealth of the entire world.   Griffin presents evidence showing that the intellectual leader of the group, indeed, the "cartel's mastermind," was Paul Warburg, the "Daddy Warbucks" of the Little Orphan Annie comic strip. Representing the Rothschilds of Europe, he was the only one of the Jekyll Island conferees with expert knowledge on the construction, policies, and mechanics of the European central banks.

A brief statement of their purpose, Griffin says, was to form a cartel aimed at increasing profits by reducing competition, and with the policies of the cartel enforced by the police power of the government. The solution, the participants knew, was to create a copy of the European model of a central bank. The problems which led them to consider this were that their big-city banks were rapidly losing business to the many smaller country banks being formed around the interior of the country, and also to corporations financing their growth out of profits rather than the relatively high-interest banking loans. The cartel structure would permit pooling the reserves of the big banks (i.e., those included in the cartel), thereby permitting them to safely make loans at a higher multiple of their metallic assets without instigating bank runs, in turn permitting them to make lower-interest loans than their smaller competitors. But considering the other things that such a cartel was also capable of, the conspirators in the end came to an agreement having five objectives:

1. Reduce the growing competition from the smaller banks.
2. Make the money supply more "elastic" by making loans less dependent upon gold reserves, i.e.,

permitting money for a loan to be created out of nothing, and therefore at lower interest rates.

3. Pool and control member bank reserves to reduce the risk of bank runs on a member bank guilty of reckless lending.

4. Get Congress to agree to bail out member banks (with taxpayer funds, of course) if major losses did nevertheless occur.

5. In order to get the scheme through Congress, convince Congress and the public that the objectives of the system were only to lower interest rates, better fund industrial growth, and protect the public by eliminating boom-and-bust economic cycles and bank runs brought on by irresponsible private banking.

Succeeding years showed the economy to be anything but stabilized, whereas the secret purposes of the Federal Reserve were all very successfully realized. The system, says Griffin (p. 21), "is incapable of achieving its stated objectives" because those objectives "never were its true objectives." In actuality, the Fed "is merely a cartel with a government facade," and whenever its interests run up against the interests of the taxpaying public, "the public will be sacrificed."

Griffin next considers how well the system has been able to meet the fourth of the true objectives listed above. Here are the steps that a member bank may now take to protect itself from losses due to non-performing loans:

1. If a major borrower (like a South American country) can't manage to repay its loan principal when it becomes due, the bank (let's pretend for a moment that *you* are the banker) will happily *roll over* the loan, i.e., re-loan the owed amount to pay off the old loan, and keep the interest flowing in from the new. (The United States has been doing this for years.)

2. When the borrower becomes unable even to pay the interest on his loan, make him a new loan to supply him with the money needed to pay the interest on both the old loan and the current new loan.

3. When he again figures out that he can't pay, make him another new loan, but this time sweetened by adding *additional* money beyond that needed for all the interest payments, so he will be able to spend some new money on himself, like for projects which will earn some money to get him out of his financial jam.

4. When next he realizes that taking on new debt to pay off old debt is a losing strategy, and he still can't pay but doesn't want to take on more debt, offer to *extend* his debt for a longer period, and therefore with lower periodic payments. The loan thereby will remain "performing" for a little longer.

5. When he soon thereafter finds that he can't make even these lowered payments, and starts to call you dirty names, go to Congress and let those folks know that it is in the best interests of the country (for lots of reasons you can come up with) for Congress to supply the needed money. The taxpayers need not be

asked about it, since the money can be created out of
nothing by the Fed, and the public will never know
why the prices they have to pay for everything some-
how have gone up a little bit more.

6.  If the above ploy doesn't work, you may well be
able to get Congress to *guarantee* payment to you if
your borrower defaults, and then likely use conduits
such as the World Bank and the IMF to deliver subsi-
dies, development loans, foreign aid, etc., directly to
your distressed borrower to assure that he avoids
default, i.e., keeps making payments to you.   Our
generous taxpayers have a hard time keeping track of
all these details.

7.  If you can't get Congress to help, you still have
a chance with the Fed.  Go to them and ask them, as
the *lender of last resort*, to bail you out.  Since they
can create as much money as anyone will ever need
out of nothing at all, they will be happy to accommo-
date you, provided they can see some hope for your
ultimate survival.  But if you're not a TBTF bank (Too
Big To Fail), they'll probably say, "Don't call us; we'll
call you."

8.  If all of the above ultimately fails, and you see
that your bad loans are about to sink you, you and your
management friends should sell your stock before the
public and the other stockholders find out about it, and
then declare bankruptcy.  The FDIC will be there to
pay your depositors' losses, and if the FDIC runs out of
money, the Congress will, out of fear of the consequences, resupply the FDIC with the needed funds,

created of course by the Federal Reserve out of nothing. The taxpayers *still* won't have figured out why prices for everything seem to continue going up.

Griffin then devotes an entire chapter to illustrating how these principles have been applied over the years, by detailing the bailout maneuvers involving, as debtors, the Penn Central Railroad, the Lockheed Corporation, New York City, and the Chrysler Corporation, and then involving, as bankrupt banks, the Unity Bank and Trust Company of Boston, the Commonwealth Bank of Detroit, the First Pennsylvania Bank of Philadelphia, and the Continental Illinois Bank of Chicago, the last two being TBTF banks. In each case, in one way or another, the taxpayers ended up paying for the losses, justifying Griffin's characterization of the Fed's real objective, which was not to *protect* the public, but rather to *sacrifice* the public to the interests of the banking cartel.

Griffin goes next to the S&L bailout, which piled an unprecedented additional financial debt on our bewildered public. Whereas Fed chairman Alan Greenspan recently estimated that total bailout costs would run to $500 billion (p. 76), Griffin himself estimates that, including additional taxes and inflation, the total cost will be over one *trillion* dollars (p. 84). Even the $500 billion is a monster figure, which Congress and the Federal Reserve were successful in loading onto a relatively uncomplaining public because of its ignorance about how big debts can be secretly financed via inflating the currency. A few of the defining milestones in the S&L fiasco were:

1. Following the stock market crash of 1929, the Fed's instigation of which will shortly be discussed, the Federal Savings and Loan Insurance Corporation (FSLIC) was created to insure depositors against losses, thereby relieving S&L managers of the burden of being careful to protect their depositors' money.

2. The Federal Housing Authority (FHA) was then created to subsidize home loans, thereby permitting S&L's to make loans at under-market interest rates.

3. The Federal Reserve then issued regulations requiring that interest rates offered by banks to depositors must be lower than corresponding S&L rates, thereby causing money to stream from banks to S&L's.

4. Years later, another unexpected financial jolt occurred, this time involving the Fed raising interest rates in 1979 to as high as 20% in order to stop the world from dumping the now purely fiat dollars to buy gold, which was then on the way up to $800 per ounce. (See our review of "A Century of War" by Engdahl.)

5. The high interest rates in the following decade, which only slowly abated following the "gold shock," drove S&L depositor interest much higher than the long-term interest return on existing mortgages, sealing the financial doom of the S&L industry. However, since deposits were guaranteed, depositors flocked to the S&L's to take advantage of the safe, high interest that the government effectively made available.

6. With FSLIC money nowhere near that required to pay S&L depositors if massive bankruptcies were declared, FSLIC reversed the requirement that S&L loans be restricted to home mortgages, and *encouraged* S&L's to lend to all comers, at risky high interest rates, to attempt to "save themselves." The shady operators then emerged from the woodwork, and lots of them got rich on building projects which were riddled with fraud.

7. The S&L's then started failing en masse, but failures were, for a time, covered up by Congress and the regulators, which let the S&L's use phony accounting practices to make their books show that they were still solvent.

8. When the above game was finally up, FSLIC was abolished, and a new agency reporting to the FDIC was created to oversee the liquidation of the failed S&L's. The necessary taxpayer funds were of course appropriated by a much abashed Congress, contributing mightily to the historically high deficits of the 80's. The high interest rates during these years permitted the deficits to be largely funded by selling bonds to the public, however, with little additional funds required from the Fed, so that price inflation was kept reasonably under control during this period.

Griffin describes (p. 83) what the S&L system had become as "a cartel within a cartel," the outer cartel being the Federal Reserve System, which ultimately funded the inner cartel of S&L's. Whereas the Federal Reserve System was put together by bankers with 200 years of successful cartel operating experience, the S&L system was amateurishly put together by committees of socialist interns in our own Congress, who perhaps truly believed that they could manage things better than the free market. The failure of that effort is surely one of the things that has brought about the recent change of heart that we see evidence of in our current (1995-1996) Congress.

Griffin goes next to describing how the bailout game is played with third-world countries (and U.S. taxpayers) being the victims. The operative agencies set in place to play the game were the International Monetary Fund (IMF), which was to act as a sort of World Federal Reserve System, and the World Bank, which was to act as the IMF's lending agency to the world.

The IMF and the World Bank were created in July 1944 at a UN-sponsored monetary conference in Bretton Woods, New Hampshire. Griffin observes (p. 87): "The theoreticians who drafted this plan were the well-known Fabian Socialist from England, John Maynard Keynes, and the Assistant Secretary of the U.S. Treasury, Harry Dexter White." White, who became the first Executive Director for the U.S. at the IMF, was also a member of the CFR, and, as was later shown, a member of a communist espionage ring in Washington. Being intellectually led by a Fabian Socialist and a Communist, who differed only in *how* the world was to be socialized, it isn't surprising that the Bretton Woods conference produced agencies which have in fact been highly active in bringing about world socialism.

Whereas the announced plan of the Bretton Woods system was to help rebuild the war-torn world and to promote the economic growth of underdeveloped countries, the real goals of the IMF and the World Bank, as Griffin convincingly demonstrates, were to:

1. Separate the dollar from gold backing, and reduce the economic dominance of both the dollar and gold around the world.
2. Replace the dollar and all other currencies with a world currency which the IMF, acting as the world's central bank, would create out of nothing.
3. Socialize the countries of the world, one by one, by transferring money to their governments to be used for governmental aggrandizement, producing the simultaneous destruction of individual independence and free enterprise.

The dollar was separated from gold by spreading dollars around the world in post-war rebuilding, and then in post-war war-making, while keeping the price of gold at $35 per ounce, which became much lower than its market value. Foreign dollar holders finally began a "run" on America's gold, and Nixon, in 1971, seeing that it was probably better to have *some* gold remaining rather than none at all, "closed the gold window," i.e., defaulted on America's promise to foreign holders to redeem their dollars in gold. (He could have performed a lesser default by keeping the gold backing, but setting its price closer to its then-current market value, about $400 per ounce).  Dollars could now be spread around the world with much greater abandon, and they were. Griffin discusses our burgeoning trade deficits, and the progressive weakening of the dollar as perceived around the world. A good part of Objective #1 listed above has already been accomplished.

The IMF has been working diligently on Objective #2, creating a piece of paper called a "Special Drawing Right," or SDR. It doesn't yet have the backing of a negotiable government bond, as a Federal Reserve Note has, and so is lacking the status of the FRN or of any other major national currency. It is a start, however, and has as its backing a "credit," which is a promise by an IMF member nation that it will tax its citizens and come up with the amount of the "credit" when and if the IMF needs it.

Concerning Objective #3, the world elites are proceeding apace, not waiting for the development and acceptance of usable SDR's, but utilizing as many dollars, pounds, francs, marks, and yen as they are able to get individual countries to donate to the IMF, or to supply to the World Bank for them to "invest." To repeat, those "investments" are *not* to promote capital-building enterprises, but the opposite. (In World Bank Newspeak, a "Sectoral Loan" is one for a specific socialistic project, such as a government hydro-electric project, a government oil refinery, a government lumber mill, or a government steel mill. On the other hand, a "Structural-Adjustment Loan" requires that certain structural changes be made in order to get the money, such as the government assuming price-control or wage-control power, so that it can hold down or otherwise manipulate prices or wages.)  The economic plights of Argentina, Brazil, and Mexico under the advancing onslaught of such socialization financed by the World Bank and other world elites are described in some detail.

In addition, Griffin describes many of the supported activities by despotic rulers, such as the genocidal relocation plans and other inhumanities of brutal dictators in countries such as Tanzania, Zimbabwe, Ethiopia, Laos, Syria, and lots more.  These various efforts of the IMF/World Bank to socialize the Third World could not exist without its flow of American dollars, supplied ultimately by the Federal Reserve.  The role of the Fed in supporting anti-democratic regimes around the world is one of the several reasons that the Fed should be abolished, says Griffin, since "*It is an instrument of totalitarianism.*" (p. 101)

Griffin then completes his description of the "bailout" game, and simultaneously answers the question as to the purpose served by socializing the various countries of the world, as listed above as purpose #3 of the Bretton Woods system.  In a few words, that ultimate purpose is to create a world government ruled by the banking elites, using the United Nations as the core of a political structure and the IMF as the world central bank, issuing and controlling the world's only important currency.  That picture is entirely consistent with the allegations made by Carroll Quigley (cf. our Chapter 2) as to the ultimate purposes of the banking elites, but Griffin, in his development, relies on more recent evidence.   The picture which he paints is as follows:

The elites understand that they will never be able to consolidate and hold their power by means of a gradualist program unless and until they are able to complete Purpose #2 listed above, i.e., make the IMF the sole issuer of the world's only important currency. Individual countries can then easily be turned into vassal states dependent upon UN/IMF dictates.   The big problem is that strong, independent countries with their own currencies, histories, and nationalist prides are not likely to succumb easily, and exhortations, trickery, and any other pressure which works may fairly be used to produce the desired result.   Griffin quotes Harvard professor Richard Cooper, a CFR member and Under Secretary of State for Economic Affairs in the Carter administration, writing in 1984 in the CFR's house organ *Foreign Affairs*:

"I suggest a radical alternative scheme for the next century: the creation of a common currency for all the industrial democracies, with a common monetary policy and a joint Bank of Issue to determine that monetary policy.... How can independent states accomplish that? They need to turn over the determination of monetary policy to a supranational body....

It is highly doubtful whether the American public, to take just one example, could ever accept that countries with oppressive autocratic regimes should vote on the monetary policy that would affect monetary conditions in the United States....   For such a bold step to work at all, it presupposes a certain convergence of political values...."

The drive to "convergence" noted above of course leads us to recall from our Chapter 4 the words of Rowan Gaither, the president of the Ford Foundation, directed to Norman Dodd, the Research Director of the Reece Committee, saying that secret White House directives to the Ford Foundation and to its various predecessors were to the effect that "we should make every effort to so alter life in the United States as to make possible a comfortable merger with the Soviet Union."

Griffin quotes John Foster Dulles, in 1939: "Some dilution or leveling off of the sovereignty system as it prevails in the world today must take place ... to the immediate disadvantage of those nations which now possess the preponderance of power.... The establishment of a common money ... would deprive our government of exclusive control over a national money.... The United States must be prepared to make sacrifices afterward in setting up a world politico-economic order which would level off inequalities of economic opportunity with respect to nations."

Next is Zbigniew Brzezinski, in 1970: "... some international cooperation has already been achieved, but further progress will require greater American sacrifices. More intensive efforts to shape a new world monetary structure will have to be undertaken, with some consequent risk to the present relatively favorable American position."

Then Carter advisor Richard Gardener, in 1974: "In short, the 'house of world order' will have to be built from the bottom up.... An end run around national sovereignty, eroding it piece by piece, will accomplish much more than the old-fashioned frontal assault."

And finally, Paul Volcker, in 1979: "The standard of living of the average American has to decline.... I don't think you can escape that."

Griffin has much more, but how much convincing does one need? The gist of the game of bailout is to simultaneously (1) deliver into the clutches of the New World Order both the Third World countries, whose leaders are to be the recipients of riches from the taxpayers of the developed countries, riches that they are expected to squander and never pay back, but thereby remain in thrall to the bankers forever, and (2) drag down the economies and comforts of the strong countries to the point, for example, of economic collapse and a breakdown in civil order, perhaps exacerbated by widespread "terrorist" bombings, following which the countries' citizens will be grateful to yield their sovereignty and receive in return the support, acceptance, and protection of an economically and militarily strong central organization claiming to be ready and able to provide such support. Such a capitulation might be made easier to accept if it could be previously arranged for Russia to disappear as an external threat, and to appear to be in just as much economic and social difficulty as the United States.

Griffin reviews the bailout activities of several of the major Third World countries to see how the blueprint which he has outlined fits those individual actions. It fits. He throws in for good measure a discussion of the recent creations of NAFTA and the World Trade Organization, and shows how they fit into the effort to chip away at sovereignty, "eroding it piece by piece." He quotes a description of the WTO appearing in a full-page ad in the New York Times taken out by its originators: "The World Trade Organization – the third pillar of the New World Order, along with the United Nations and the International Monetary Fund."

Another development that few are aware of is that Congress granted to the Fed a major new power in the Monetary Control Act of 1980, giving it the power to "monetize foreign debt." This means that the Fed could henceforth create new Federal Reserve Notes and give them away to *foreign* governments, or, to be formal, "loan" them, receiving as collateral debt instruments (bonds, etc.) held by those foreign governments. With the power to create dollars not only for the American governments, but now for any foreign government as well, the Fed has become very close to becoming a central bank for the entire world.

Another major development in very recent years has been the large-scale extension of funding by the same "bailout" routes to China, to Russia and its previous component states, and to Russia's previous client states in Eastern Europe. Griffin makes a case for the view that the sudden demise of "Communism" is a ploy agreed upon between the banking elites and the Soviet leaders to enable bailout funds to flow to those states, further eroding the American economy, while terminating, at least for now, the militarily threatening posture of the USSR. The communist leaders would mostly remain in power, though re-named Social Democrats, or something similar. They and the elites would continue to work together for one socialist world.

Griffin's case is logical, with lots of evidence, but all circumstantial. (It would be nice to have another insider confession, like that of Carroll Quigley's.) Recalling Cleon Skousen's suggested relationship between the totalitarian leaders and the elites, it may be that the elites are simply taking the *risk* that the Communists, who insist that all power emerges from the barrel of a gun, can in the long run be controlled by the power of money. The Communists, on the other hand, may still believe that they can have both the capitalists' money for now, and also all their property and lives later on.

You, the reader, may perceive a more satisfactory outcome. Whereas we all may have viewed the Third World's indebtedness and socialization as just one of the many bad problems around the world, and our own loss of economic vigor an independent but very troubling and puzzling problem, Griffin has tied them together and defined why *both* are happening, to the great discomfort of both U.S. and Third World citizens. We therefore now have a new action choice – to remove the Fed's money creation authority, forcing Congress to live within its budgets, and terminating the use of American dollars to socialize the world (and maybe even our own society as well – e.g., the $4 trillion or so we have spent fruitlessly on the War on Poverty). We may even get back to an honest gold standard, using gold-backed currency created by a multitude of independent commercial banks in support of our own American economy. Once we've gotten our own house back in order, we may be of some real use to the Third World as a model of how it can be done, absent the existence of conspiratorial control by the dynastic banking elites.

We'll include just a few words about Griffin's second section, which anyone interested in following the Fed's manipulation of debits and credits in creating our fiat currency will find fascinating. The scheme mimics that used by a cabal of English aristocrats and bankers to create the Bank of England in 1694. King William, in need of money to fight a certain war, money which he couldn't raise by taxing or borrowing, granted a charter to a favored group of intriguers to form a bank which would be given a monopoly on issuing English bank notes, i.e., English paper money, which would be created out of nothing and credited to the government in return for a government IOU, the only "backing" that would be required. The government would pay interest on this "loan," making it look legitimate to the public, but the bank's even larger payback was that it was empowered to make additional

commercial loans, at interest, using the same government IOU's as "backing," just as though the IOU's were
hard, metallic gold.  The banks, by receiving interest
on money they could create and lend out at will, were
thereby going to get rich, the king was going to be able
to raise any amount of "money" he wanted, and the
public, remaining ignorant of what was going on, was
going to pay for it all by having their savings devalued
by the expansion of the currency.  (Our Federal Reserve does essentially the same thing, with added
refinements which greatly increase its leverage over
commercial credit.)  Griffin labels this process the
"Mandrake Mechanism," a magician's way of creating
something out of nothing.

Immediately upon issuing the charter, the King
and his fellow conspirators rushed to become shareholders in this money manufacturing monopoly they
had just created, shares which their upper-class heirs
still hold.  Griffin makes clear that this system, widely
copied first in Europe and then in the United States,
substantially guarantees boom and bust cycles, and
enables the government to surreptitiously steal the
wealth of its citizens by the hidden, most cruel tax of
all – inflation.

In Griffin's third section, he generalizes the
world outlook of the international financiers, as he sees
them, starting with the motivations of the founders of
the Bank of England described above.  Their success
depends upon a pattern of character traits including
"cold objectivity, immunity to patriotism, and indiffer-
ence to the human condition."  That profile gives rise

to a strategy he labels the Rothschild Formula, which motivates these financiers "to propel governments into war for the profits they yield."  To drive a country to go into debt because of war or the threat of war, the strategy is to assure that the country has enemies with credible military might.  If only weak enemies exist, give them money to strengthen their military;  if no enemy exists, create one.  Don't let any one nation stay predominant, since that may bring on peace and a reduction of debt.  Griffin then lists seven European wars fought since the founding of the Bank of England, in all of which the operation of this Rothschild Formula was apparent.

Concerning the major military events of this century, we have reviewed how Carroll Quigley revealed the help given by Montagu Norman of the Bank of England in building up Hitler.  Griffin, in his book, spends two chapters discussing how the bankers arranged the Bolshevik coup in Russia in 1917, and then supported the regime thereafter, both for the profit involved and, presumably, to build up a "credible enemy."  He also goes into considerable detail concerning the role of the bankers in applying the Rothschild Formula to World War 1, which we will summarize in the next few paragraphs.

Let's put a few items we have previously reviewed into chronological order with several which Griffin brings up.  First, we note that the "Rothschild Formula" defined by Griffin had been in successful operation for over 100 years.  Second, we recall what Norman Dodd found in the 1911 minutes of the

Carnegie Foundation, with the trustees noting that there was nothing more effective than war to alter the life of an entire people, and wondering how to involve the United States in a war. Third, Engdahl spelled out in considerable detail (see our Chapter 1) the preparations for war that the several European countries were making during the two or three decades prior to the start of World War 1, including the secret treaty signed between Britain and France just three months prior to the start of the war, guaranteeing Britain's entry following the assassination of Austrian Archduke Ferdinand on July 28, 1914.

Next, Griffin describes the arrangement J.P. Morgan made with the British and French to raise borrowed money for them, and to act as their agent in purchasing war materiel and shipping it off to them, collecting commissions both when the money was raised (by selling bonds) and when it was spent. The first such purchase contract was signed in January 1915. Griffin then quotes a congressman who described how Morgan got together leaders in the newspaper business and essentially "bought" their editorial policy-making function regarding "questions of preparedness, militarism, financial policies, and other things ... considered vital to the interests of the purchasers." Morgan then set about drumming up support for the war.

Next in line was the Lusitania affair. It was a British liner, built to military specifications, being used as a passenger liner, but secretly carrying munitions which Morgan was responsible for procuring and shipping. The German embassy, being aware of what was being shipped, and not wanting to provoke an incident which would bring the U.S. into the war, submitted an ad to go in 50 East Coast newspapers a week prior to the sailing date, warning U.S. citizens of the dangers of traveling on British ships in a war zone. Morgan, however, managed to prevent nearly all of these ads from being run as requested, and the ship sailed on May 1, 1915, with 195 Americans on board.

Across the ocean, Winston Churchill, then the First Lord of the Admiralty, was arranging for the deadly encounter. He recalled the destroyer escort that had been planned to protect the Lusitania upon its reaching U-boat waters. He further ordered it to proceed at three-fourths speed in order to "conserve coal." It made an easy target. One torpedo on the starboard quarter detonated munitions stored below, blowing off most of the bottom of the bow, and the ship sank in less than eighteen minutes. Griffin quotes sources indicating that even King George V was aware and was following the progress of the Lusitania. The official inquiry some time later put the blame on the ship's captain, though Lord Mersey, the director of the inquiry, resigned from the British Justice system immediately thereafter, and years later commented, "The Lusitania case was a damned dirty business."

Back in the U.S., Morgan turned up the tempo of the editorial drumbeat to convince Americans to stand on the side of civilized behavior and support the Allies, a chant that was echoed and re-echoed until the Congress finally declared war. But before that, in

March of 1916, President Wilson signed a secret treaty with Britain, negotiated by his alter ego Colonel Edward Mandell House, without the knowledge or consent of the United States Senate. The treaty amounted to a diplomatic plot to bring the U.S. into the war against Germany. It was never implemented, but reveals the strength of the pressures on House/Wilson to get the United States into the war. The public at that time was still opposed, as shown by Wilson's decision to run his reelection campaign in the fall of 1916 on a pacifist platform with the slogan "He kept us out of war!" The honesty of such political declarations has not changed much to the present day (1996).

Early in 1917, the British came to fear that they were on the verge of having to capitulate to Germany, since the U-boat blockade had successfully reduced Britain's food reserve to just a few weeks' supply. It then became impossible for Morgan to find buyers of British war bonds, since they would become worthless upon British surrender, and without more bonds, war materiel supply would halt, ensuring the loss of the war. Current bondholders, including Morgan and various of his friends, would, of course, also suffer. Intense pressure was then brought upon the Congress to supply the needed money to keep the war going. But that would necessarily require the Congress to declare war, since such help would be a violation of neutrality treaties. The pressure from both the President and the press was more than the Congress could withstand, and war was officially declared on April 15, 1917, to the delight formerly described (Chapter 4) of

Elihu Root and the other trustees of the Carnegie Endowment for International Peace.

The British and the French both started placing massive orders for war goods with Morgan, who, when the British and French accounts became well overdrawn, approached the U.S. Treasury to come up with the needed funds. The Treasury said they didn't have that kind of cash on hand, but the Federal Reserve under Benjamin Strong showed up in the nick of time saying maybe they could help. Which they did, via the same Mandrake Mechanism which Griffin described in his Section 2. By the time the war ended, the Treasury had loaned out about $9.5 billion. Morgan's investments in British bonds were saved, but Morgan made very much more than bond interest, having directed the larger part of British war orders to companies which he and other insiders controlled. Griffin points out that total U.S. war expenditures between April 15, 1917 and October 31, 1919, when the last U.S. soldiers arrived back home, amounted to some $35 billion. During the war years, the money supply approximately doubled (from $20 to $40 billion), and the purchasing power of the dollar was about halved. The people thus paid via the hidden tax of inflation, while the banks received interest on the money they had created out of nothing, just as the Mandrake Mechanism intended. The same process was repeated during World War 2 and during the corporate bailout operations of the 80's and 90's.

The fourth section of Griffin's book relates the financial history of the United States with respect to the use of paper bank notes, from colonial times through the era of Civil War greenbacks.  The early experiments with fiat currencies invariably produced civil distress and were therefore fairly short-lived, since the elites pressing these schemes on the people were not politically powerful or astute enough to sustain their operations.  Griffin brings this history back with a clarity which, had it been available to Congress in the early 1900's, would probably have prevented the passage in 1913 of the Federal Reserve Act.  Knowledge of this history should be particularly useful to those today seeking to replace the Federal Reserve with an honest banking system.

As a last effort, we'll highlight the portion of Griffin's fifth section which deals with the connection of our banking elites to their counterparts in Britain, and two of the major fallouts of that connection: the roaring twenties' expansion, and the subsequent crash leading to the Great Depression.

The J.P. Morgan Company, the American agent of the British during World War 1, was also the prime backer of the Council on Foreign Relations, the American branch of the British Round Table organization, whose secret core was established by Cecil Rhodes to bring about the worldwide dominance of the British Empire.  No surprise, says Griffin, since Morgan's antecedents went back to the Boston merchant Junius Morgan who was accepted into the London investment firm of George Peabody, moved to London in 1854, and became a full partner in the firm, which later became known as Peabody, Morgan & Co.

The firm peddled bonds in London for American states and commercial ventures, but became wildly successful as the London agent for the Union government during the Civil War.  Peabody retired in 1864, and the firm was renamed J. S. Morgan & Co.

Junius Morgan enrolled his son, John Pierpont Morgan, in European schools and otherwise immersed him in the British tradition.  In 1857 he set him up in business in America, and in several years had him running the American branch of Junius' business, first called Dabney, Morgan & Co., and finally settling on J.P. Morgan & Co. in 1895.  Junius died soon thereafter, and J.P. Morgan sent his son, J.P. Morgan, Jr., to London to learn British ways and, more importantly, to remodel Junius' company into a clearly British one. This was done by taking into Junius' company as a new partner a Bank of England director named Edward Grenfell, and renaming the company Morgan, Grenfell & Co.  The idea was to make J.P. Morgan & Co. look more like an independent American entity rather than an American branch of a British firm, though the reality was that both firms remained highly attuned to British financial and political objectives.

Griffin then addresses the question discussed by many others, namely the nature of the relationship between the Morgans and the Rothschilds.  He presents his references and evidences, drawing a picture which includes early secret cooperation between George Peabody and Nathan Mayer Rothschild in London, the Rothschild effort to set up a "front" in the United States using the person and name of August

Belmont (which shortly became common knowledge and thus ineffective), the large loan from the Bank of England saving Peabody & Co. but no one else during the panic of 1857, the staunch public anti-Semitism of J.P. Morgan, Jr., which attracted business from borrowers not wishing to deal with Rothschild or any other Jewish firm, the repeated private financial cooperation reported by many sources between Morgan and Rothschild entities, and finally the meager financial estates left by both J.P. Morgan and his son, suggesting that the entirety of their operations were more in the nature of acting as agents for others rather than serving their own personal self-interest. Griffin concludes by noting that the degree of subservience that actually existed between Morgan and Rothschild might be historically interesting, but was nevertheless quite immaterial, the only important matter being that they always managed to cooperate in business matters that were profitable to them both.

We touched, in our review of Engdahl's book (Chapter 1), upon the creation of the speculative bubble during the 20's that was pricked in 1929 producing the stock market crash and the great depression. Griffin spells that out here in considerable detail, with lots of documentation. In short, Britain inflated during WW1 much more than did the U.S., and thus entered the 20's with higher prices, wages, and interest rates than the U.S., accompanied by an increasing trade deficit and loss of gold reserves. Britain wished to correct this relationship, not by deflating its economy, which would entail politically dangerous wage cuts, but rather by convincing the United States to further *inflate* the U.S. economy, to equalize prices and interest rates.

The plan was organized primarily between Benjamin Strong, the Governor of the Federal Reserve System, and Montagu Norman, the Governor of the Bank of England. The need for so doing was spelled out in a letter written in May 1924 from Strong to Andrew Mellon, the Secretary of the Treasury. Implementation began in 1924 with the monetization by the Fed of about $1.3 billion, followed by another $0.5 billion in 1927. The former expansion was accompanied by a reduction of the discount rate from 4 to 3.5 percent, making it easier for the banks to borrow additional "reserves" from the Fed to enable more loans to be made. With the commercial banks able to create around 5 times more fiat dollars than the Fed creates, the total currency infusion amounted to ($1.3 + $0.5) x (5+1) which is equal to about $11 billion from 1924 through 1929.

Benjamin Strong indicated in early 1929 his pleasure with how well the scheme worked out, enabling the successful reorganization of the European monetary system, though with the unavoidable hazards of credit expansion and speculation. J.P. Morgan, Jr. concurred with the speculative threat, but was attributed to declare that such speculation "is the price we must pay for helping Europe." This latter quote, says Griffin, comes from a man "who was imbued with English tradition from the earliest age, whose financial empire had its roots in London, whose family business was saved by the Bank of England, who had openly insisted that his junior partners demonstrate a 'loyalty to Britain,' and who directed the Council on Foreign Relations, the American branch of a secret society dedicated to the supremacy of British tradition and political power. It is only with that background that one can fully appreciate [his] willingness to sacrifice American interests."

Early in 1929, with the bubble of stock market speculation fully inflated, an abrupt change in policy occurred. In February, Montagu Norman arrived in the U.S., conferred privately with Federal Reserve officials, and then with Andrew Mellon. Griffin suggests that it was in these meetings that decisions were made, or orders transmitted, to reverse the expansion, making it appear, of course, that it was just happening by itself. He quotes Galbraith: "How much better, as seen from the Federal Reserve, to let nature take its course and thus allow nature to take the blame." He further quotes Herbert Hoover's description of Mellon's views: "Mr. Mellon had only one formula: 'Liquidate labor, liquidate stocks, liquidate the farmers, liquidate real estate.' He insisted that, when the people get an inflation brainstorm, the only way to get it out of their blood is to let it collapse. He held that even a panic was not altogether a bad thing. He said, 'It will purge the rottenness out of the system. Values will be adjusted, and enterprising people will pick up the wrecks from less competent people.'"

But before the fleecing of the public could begin, the insider worker bees had to be gotten out whole. The financial fraternity was warned to get out of the market, the Fed on February 6 issued instructions to its member banks to sell their stock market holdings, and Paul Warburg similarly advised the stockholders of his International Acceptance Bank. The lists of preferred customers of Kuhn, Loeb & Co. and of J.P. Morgan & Co. were similarly warned. History shows that the Wall Street biggies came through very well indeed, including John D. Rockefeller, J.P. Morgan, Joseph P. Kennedy, Bernard Baruch, Henry Morgenthau, Douglas Dillon, etc. As Griffin puts it, "Virtually all of the inner club was rescued. There is no record of any member of the interlocking directorate between the Federal Reserve, the major New York banks, and their prime customers having been caught by surprise."

It was a different matter with the public, of course. Public assurances were forthcoming from the likes of President Coolidge, Treasury Secretary Mellon, the socialist economist John Maynard Keynes from London, and Benjamin Strong, from his offices in the New York Federal Reserve Bank. But then on August 9, 1929 the pin was inserted into the bubble. On that date, the Federal Reserve raised its discount rate to six percent and simultaneously began to sell securities on the open market. Both actions acted to shrink bank reserves and therefore the money supply, in a reverse application of the Mandrake Mechanism. The market reached its peak on September 19, then started its slide downward. On October 24 the slide became a torrent, and on October 29, the market collapsed.

While the uninformed were in the process of loosing their shirts, the insiders who had sold out before the crash were now to be found, with cash at the ready, on the buying side. Companies whose stock had dropped to a fraction of their value were still basically viable, but their ownership, in large measure, had been shifted from, to use Andrew Mellon's phrase, the "less competent people," who had been sucked into the speculative maelstrom created by the Fed's easy credit, to the financial elites, who had been made privy to the crash that was around the corner. Great fortunes were made or added to by the latter, as Griffin briefly outlines. So why, again, should the Federal Reserve be abolished? Griffin's Second Reason was: "Far from being a protector of the public [as it claims], *it is a cartel operating against the public interest.*"

Griffin has shown in his absolutely magnificent book how the banking elites have managed to obtain and today exercise economic control over all of our lives, whereas McIlhany has shown us in his book on the tax-exempt foundations how they have been molding our minds to accept international socialism. In the final section of Griffin's book, he paints a picture of the world society that the elites seek, and describes alternate methodologies that the elites are considering to get to that point. He then outlines what a counter-effort will have to accomplish to at least bring about a return to honest money and the abolition of the Federal Reserve. We will deal with all these same issues, however, by first reviewing two books which Griffin references, both devoted specifically to revealing the elites' plans for our future, and later

reviewing our own book on what political and legislative changes we must accomplish to reverse the political tide which is destroying our free society.

# Chapter 6

## "1984"

(By George Orwell. Orig. pub. by Harcourt Brace Jovanovich, 1949; presently available from Laissez Faire Books, tel. 800-326-0996)

George Orwell, the pen name for the English socialist Eric Blair, presented in this book a very dark picture of what our world's society might come to in the hands of an irresistibly powerful secret elite which controlled the life or death, the economic status, and every significant movement, word, and thought of every member of the society. We can't presume to know what the author's motivation was for writing this widely read classic, though various establishment figures have labeled it a warning of sorts, particularly in view of our recent experiences with totalitarianisms of one kind or another. We shall choose for our review, however, not to try to analyze Orwell's motives, or those of establishment reviewers. Instead, because of the significant and obvious parallels between the development and maintenance of collectivist control in Orwell's fictional world and the similar development proceeding apace in our own world, we shall operate under the hypothesis that his work is a description of a plan which he believed to be real, a plan to which Orwell may have been privy, or one which he may only have inferred from the political and social events unfolding around him.

We neither know nor care whether the socialist Orwell opposed or supported the plan that he outlines. We are persuaded, however, that he believed it to be a concrete reality, not only because of the many parallels to actual events of the last two centuries, but also because of the convincing human causation which he ascribes to these events, causation obviously based on a deep understanding of the strengths and frailties of our human nature, including that major flaw of being corruptible by power. As we go along, we shall mentally test our hypothesis that his work is the revelation of a Grand Plan, spanning several centuries of time and reaching all the corners of the earth, and aimed at conquering and holding in bondage the entire population of the world.

Orwell refers to the Grand Plan in the past tense, it having been completed and in operation when his novel starts. The plan is spelled out in a fictional writing in *1984* known as *The Book*, which is formally entitled "The Theory and Practice of Oligarchical Collectivism." We would have called it Elitist Socialism, but it's the same thing. The exposition of the theory (in *The Book*) starts by declaring that, from time immemorial, societies have been divided into classes called the High, the Middle, and the Low. The goal of the High is to stay the High, the goal of the Middle is to become the High, and the goal of the Low, to the extent that it has a societal goal, is to abolish all class distinctions and make everyone equal. (In our own society, of course, the High consists of those monied folk we have been calling the banking elites plus, we suppose, the top ranks of their prostituted followers who do their work.  The Middle contains persons in our great middle class, whom Marx labeled the "petty bourgeois."  The Low consists of those in our society who can't bestir themselves beyond football, TV, beer, pizza, and all lesser indulgences.  To Marx, they were the "proletariat"; Orwell called them "proles.")

The Middle are occasionally successful, usually with the help of the Low, in ousting the High and thus becoming the new High.  This arrangement then continues until a new Middle faction arises and is in turn successful in becoming the new High, and the process continues ad infinitum.  When the High falls, it is because it loses either the competence to rule or the will to preserve its status.  Of the three groups, only the Low has never even momentarily achieved its goal (i.e., equality), since each new High, upon attaining its goal, invariably re-suppresses the Low as soon as possible to consolidate its power.

Socialism as a theory (says *The Book*) took root in the early 1800's, but by the end of the century was abandoning the professed aim of liberty and equality for all, and adopting instead, with increasing openness, the goal of dictatorial rule (realized, we might say, by Bolshevism in Russia and Fascism in Germany and Italy).  From the early 1900's, one particular branch of socialism, called Ingsoc for English Socialism, took on the goal of not only ousting and replacing the High, but of doing it with such deliberately thought-out preplanning as to make the new arrangement *permanent*, that is, arresting progress, freezing history at the chosen moment, and stopping forever the ancient Middle/High replacement cycle. Such a goal was deemed both necessary and possible, necessary because machine production had developed so much during the preceding century, and was continuing at such a pace, that economic differences among the classes were in the process of being obliterated, along with the need for any class structure at all. Middle groupings were acquiring so much leisure time that they were enabled to think about, and then work toward, replacing the High rulers. Specifically, "If leisure and security were enjoyed by all alike, the great mass of human beings who are normally stupefied by poverty would become literate and would learn to think for themselves; and when once they had done this, they would sooner or later realize that the privileged minority had no function, and they would sweep it away. In the long run, a hierarchical society was only possible on the basis of poverty and ignorance." The position of power historically maintained by a High class was therefore fundamentally endangered, necessitating corrective attention. (Cf. our Chapter 2 re the Ruskin plan to preserve the English upper class and its values, followed by Cecil Rhodes and his secret society, Milner, the Round Table, etc.)

Fortunately, the technological advances responsible for producing mass affluence also helped make possible strategies for maintaining the hierarchical structure. The development of historical knowledge laid bare (to those who would look) the nature of the prior Middle/High cycles, and therefore the keys to preventing their recurrence. Technical developments in the communication field, including printing, radio, and then television, especially its more lately developed capability of both receiving and transmitting from the same set, made it much easier to both manipulate public opinion and to abolish individual privacy. (Quigley also included, on p. 15 of *Tragedy and Hope*, that by 1930, governments had developed weapons much more powerful than those their citizens could obtain.) During the consolidation of power phase, remaining dangerous opponents were readily liquidated as necessary, and all other sources of public information suppressed, guaranteeing the future uniformity of public opinion on all matters of significance to the new High group.

In this final phase, the Middle and Low were substantially disempowered by stripping all individuals of their physical resources (i.e., homes, land, businesses, etc.), a necessary condition for oligarchical security. The new High, utilizing the nomenclature of socialism, performed this last stage of "collectivization" by having the "Party" (the only existing government) take over whatever remaining property existed in private hands, and then relegating the phrase "private property" to the memory hole. The Low went along willingly, as they were flattered that their goal had thereby been attained of abolishing the hated "capitalists."

*The Book* next examined the ways in which Ingsoc might theoretically be overthrown, and prevention strategies defined to block each way. Four overthrow mechanisms were deemed possible: surrender to an external power, revolt by the Lows, overthrow by a Middle group, or loss of High self-confidence and willingness to rule. The first danger was met by dividing the world into three parts, each being substantially self-sufficient, culturally homogeneous, and of approximately equal strength. Their defensive strengths were made high enough so that each part became essentially unconquerable, even by the other two parts together. Revolt by the Lows (in each part) could easily be avoided by keeping the Lows ignorant of the possibility of any state of life higher than that in which they presently existed. Overthrow efforts from the Middle and loss of faith in the Party within the High were to be avoided by continually enforced individual surveillance and education, backed up by appropriate rewards and punishments, including promotion and perks, or torture and death. The High class was to be kept strong, not by making its membership hereditary, but rather "adoptive," since history has shown family oligarchies to be short-lived compared to organizational oligarchies, such as the Catholic Church, which measured its staying power in millennia. In a word, "A ruling group is a ruling group so long as it can nominate its successors. The Party is not concerned with perpetuating its blood but with perpetuating itself. *Who* wields power is not important, provided that the hierarchical structure remains always the same." (Our banking elites may squabble among themselves, but they remain one in their efforts to wipe out the world's still unconquered middle class.)

The key to keeping the Lows "stupefied by poverty" and therefore ignorant of any better way to live, while simultaneously weakening an entire society to the point that it is unable to become dominant over another society, is, in a word, war – continuous, draining warfare. To that end, the world was divided into three parts, as mentioned above, called Oceania, Eurasia, and Eastasia, an event that was foreseen before the mid 1900's. Following the absorption of the British Empire by the United States, Oceania came to consist of North and South America, the Atlantic islands including the British Isles, Australasia, and southern Africa. Following the Russian absorption of Europe, Eurasia came to consist of Europe and the northern portion of the Asian landmass. After considerable confused warfare, Eastasia came to consist of China, Japan, and the Asian countries south of them, with a fluctuating boundary with Eurasia in the vicinity of Manchuria, Mongolia, and Tibet. North Africa and countries in southern Asia are being constantly fought over by the three major powers for the cheap or slave labor that was available there. (*The Book* doesn't mention a "Trilateral Commission" but we presume that's occurred to you.)

The wars that were to continue among the three world powers were unlike prior wars in human history, in that their purpose was not to conquer an opponent but rather to assure the maintenance of control over one's own subjects in order to keep the structure of the society intact. The wars were therefore shams, impostures, executed by rather small numbers of professional specialists at great distances removed from the population centers, with information concerning them coming to the subject peoples exclusively from the Party-controlled media. Killings and other brutalities were common, however, but secretly controlled and delivered, by rocket bombs and such, by a given ruling government against its own subjects, invariably the proles.

To assure the permanence of such a societal organization, the three powers each had to be substantially self-sufficient, geographically defensible, culturally uniform (to better permit hate to be directed at the other groups), and on a military, economic, and social par with the other powers, all in order to avoid either the incentive or the ability to actually defeat one another in war. The same pyramidal social structure exists in each, and the same dependency on a war economy. No advantage is therefore to be had by one power conquering another, and in fact the existence of each power is now dependent on the continuing existence of the other powers, providing an excuse for the ongoing "warfare." (The words in our Chapter 4 of Rowan Gaither to Norman Dodd concerning promoting convergence with the Soviet Union might be recalled at this point.)

And how does continuous war act to keep the Lows "stupefied by poverty" and thereby assure the maintenance of the social structure? The goal of the wars is to enable the economy to be kept going for the benefit of the High, its military, and its bureaucracy and control personnel (the Thought Police, etc.), but at the same time to assure that any excess production capacity is prevented from producing consumer goods for the lower classes. That excess capacity is instead directed to producing excess military goods which will ultimately rust away or be destroyed in warfare; that is, the excess capacity is deliberately *wasted* in order to turn it away from the production of goods which would result in added leisure or well-being for the lower classes. Those classes are instead continually forced into group activities expressing hatred toward the current enemy (*any* enemy) and dependency upon and love toward their benevolent rulers for protecting them from that enemy. They are thereby led to accept the consumer shortages, the poverty, and the other privations to which they are subjected. Their economic status is kept at the subsistence level, forcing their priorities to be focused on simply acquiring basic food, clothing, and shelter. They are thus denied either the time or the inclination to question the fairness or permanence of their societal condition, or to otherwise evolve into a threat to the established hierarchy. (We have, of course, been subjected in this century to two major world wars, two good-sized no-win wars (Korea and Vietnam), and a host of smaller UN involvements, presently (1996) including an incipient war in Bosnia.)

But why, asks Orwell through the voice of his Party protagonist, does the Party cling to power? "What is our motive? Why should we want power?" He then proceeds to answer his own question: "The Party seeks power entirely for its own sake. We are not interested in the good of others; we are interested solely in power. Not wealth or luxury or long life or happiness; only power, pure power.... Power is not a means; it is an end. One does not establish a dictatorship in order to safeguard a revolution; one makes the revolution in order to establish the dictatorship.... The object of power is power...."

Over what is that power to be exercised, the protagonist then asks. He answers, "The real power, the power we have to fight for night and day, is not power over things, but over men.... [And] how does one man assert his power over another?" He answers his own question: "By making him suffer. Obedience is not enough. Unless he is suffering, how can you be sure that he is obeying your will and not his own? Power is in inflicting pain and humiliation. Power is in tearing human minds to pieces and putting them together again in new shapes of your own choosing.... In our world there will be no emotions except fear, rage, triumph, and self-abasement. Everything else we shall destroy – everything. Already we are breaking down the habits of thought which have survived from before the Revolution. We have cut the links between child and parent, and between man and man, and between man and woman. But in the future there will be no wives and no friends. Children will be taken from their mothers at birth as one takes eggs from a hen.... There will be no art, no literature, no science. There will be no distinction between beauty and ugliness.... All competing pleasures will be destroyed. But always ... there will be the intoxication of power, constantly increasing and constantly growing subtler. Always, at every moment, there will be the thrill of victory, the sensation of trampling on an enemy who is helpless. If you want a picture of the future, imagine a boot stamping on a human face – forever."

This famous picture by Orwell of the ultimate depravity – the worst ultimate result of man's fatal flaw of being corruptible by power – is what we are striving, by writing this book for example, to help future generations to avoid.

Chapter 7

## "REPORT FROM IRON MOUNTAIN
## ON THE POSSIBILITY AND DESIRABILITY
## OF PEACE"

(Foreword by Leonard Lewin. Pub. 1967, Dial Press, NY. Call American Opinion Books, 414-749-3783.)

This remarkable book appeared eighteen years after Orwell's *1984*, and suffers from many of the same speculations as to its origins. It is not a novel, but rather a report written by the members of a 15-man "Special Study Group" commissioned, they believe, by some governmental entity which wished to remain unknown. The report is addressed to that unknown requestor, the work of the group having been completed after about two and a half years of labor. The members of the group knew that they had been carefully screened and selected for the task, that they represented the highest levels of scholarship, experience, and expertise in a wide range of the physical and social sciences, that they possessed years of service in business, government, and academe, and that among them they had access to a vast proportion of the country's resources in the social and physical science fields. The Special Study Group was clearly possessed of outstanding establishmentarian credentials.

The book comes to us because one of the members of the group, identified only as John Doe, approached Mr. Lewin several months after the completed report had been submitted, and sought his help in getting the report commercially published, since he (Doe) felt that the public had a right to be apprised of its existence, even though the group had previously agreed to keep it secret. Mr. Lewin, having agreed to serve in that capacity, wrote a foreword spelling out these circumstances and passing on what little he learned from Doe concerning the study's origin and its participants. He further revealed his personal reaction to the conclusions of the report, conclusions which he said he does not share, but which appear to explain aspects of recent American policies which have otherwise been incomprehensible from a "common sense" viewpoint.

As with *1984*, we shall not indulge in speculation as to the possible motives of persons involved in commissioning, performing, or publicizing the Study's activities, except to suggest the possibility that both *1984* and *The Report From Iron Mountain* may have been created to serve as guides for middle-level workers in the fields of the elites. This would require, of course, a certain skill in reading between the lines, since calling a spade a spade would obviously raise too much public reaction. But let's move right along, starting with a little background on the nature of the Study Group and its operations.

The name Iron Mountain was derived from the name of the location, near Hudson, N.Y., where the first and last meeting of the Study Group took place. The meeting place served to impress and convince the participants of the authenticity of their endeavor. It was a well-equipped underground facility built to survive a nuclear holocaust, and was being used by hundreds of American corporations for the safekeeping of their critical documents. It also even housed substitute corporate headquarters for a number of them, including such major establishment firms as Standard Oil of New Jersey, Shell, and Manufacturers Hanover Trust.

Meetings other than the first and last were held, approximately monthly, at universities, hotels, summer camps, private estates, or business establishments in various parts of the country, but never in the same place twice. Participants were paid travel and per diem expenses by a member identified as the "government contact" who also instructed them not to report those payments on their income tax returns, and to otherwise do whatever was necessary to keep their deliberations secret.

The first meeting was held in August of 1963, though the idea for the study, according to Doe, originated as far back as 1961 with the incoming staff of John Kennedy's administration, mostly, says Doe, "with McNamara, Bundy, and Rusk." Doe further revealed that three of the fifteen Study Group members had been in on the planning which produced the group, but the identities of none of the members (except for Doe) were revealed to Lewin. The last meeting was held in March of 1966, and the report was completed and submitted shortly thereafter. Lewin was ap-proached by Doe during the following winter to arrange for commercial publication. (For reference, recall that John Kennedy was assassinated on November 22, 1963.)

Lewin warned in his foreword that the Report contained presumptions and recommendations which were, on the face of it, outrageous and offensive to ordinary common sense, including such notions that poverty is both necessary and desirable, that the return of slavery as an institution may be desirable, and that budgeting the optimum number of deaths to occur annually in warfare was a proper function of government. With this warning in mind, one cannot help but be mentally probing, as he proceeds through the Report, for the real purposes being served, including the foundation premises upon which the study was based. Doe told Lewin that the purpose stated by the anonymous caller who recruited him was "to determine, accurately and realistically, the nature of the problems that would confront the United States if and when a condition of 'permanent peace' should arrive, and to draft a program for dealing with this contingency." The Report's transmittal letter rephrased these purposes as: "1) to consider the problems involved in the contingency of a transition to a general condition of peace, and 2) to recommend procedures for dealing with this contingency." As the Report's Introduction again rephrased it, the following two questions were to be addressed: "What can be expected if peace comes? What should we be prepared to do about it?"

We are soon led to observe that there is something askew in the logic of the first stated purpose. A

society's "problems" are not nearly as uniquely determined by the presence or absence of "peace" as they
are by other societal characteristics, most particularly
the presence or absence of "individual liberty."  The
question to the Study Group should therefore spell out
as a postulate the status of this elemental characteristic,
since the society's "problems" will be grossly different
depending upon whether its citizenry is or is not "free."

We, as Americans, would naturally assume that
the Study Group would automatically acknowledge,
respect, and seek to preserve the philosophical foundation of our country (the existence of our individual
inalienable rights to life, liberty, and the pursuit of
happiness) along with the mechanics which our forefa-
thers put in place (the U.S. Constitution) to try to
preserve those rights for their posterity, rights which
they had just wrested from Old World monarchs
representative of the entire prior world history of
ongoing despotic rule by whoever managed to acquire
a preponderance of arms.   It soon became clear,
however, that such an assumption was ill-founded, and
that the implicit presumption of the Study Group was
that the condition of individual freedom was to be that
which had historically existed in the Old World,
namely the subservience of the citizenry to an aristo-
cratic elite.

The main question that was to absorb the
group's labor was posed early in the Report's Introduction.  Presuming a world with no war, war preparations, or armaments, were there not certain societal
functions fulfilled in the past by warfare for which

substitute activities would have to be found in a world of peace? Thus, what functions *did* war fulfill? If no viable substitutes could be found to fulfill them, was "peace" even desirable, in terms of "social stability?"

The study member who was the government contact was code-named Able by Doe, who revealed to Lewin that it was Able who challenged the classical definition of war, and suggested that war served other purposes beyond being an extension of diplomacy, or ultimate physical actions in support of a foreign policy, etc. All the other members ultimately came around to his view. It was also Able who, with one other member, drafted the Report, circulated it for review, and then produced the final version. It therefore seems likely that those who conceived the study had pretty well in mind what the study would produce from the beginning.

Of course all of us ordinary folk have a pretty good idea of why peace is desirable. In a few words, war involves lots of us getting killed, usually for the benefit of kings or other elites with whom we have little truck, and even if we physically survive, our savings, i.e., the fruits of our lifelong labors, are expropriated (by inflation or otherwise) and spent on killing others, reducing our ability to lead the good life, and ruining life in its entirety for those who are killed, displaced, enslaved, tortured, etc. All that being so, what is this "social stability" that the Report refers to which may bring into question the desirability of peace?

It took a long time for the Report to get around to defining what it meant by "social stability." But here are a few of the significant steps that we detected on the way. First, in describing the scope of the study, the Report claims that one of the operative criteria was to avoid utilizing any preconceived value assumptions (such as one's right to life or liberty, we assume). But then it proclaims one, since any serious investigation "must be informed by some normative standard.... The stability of society is the one bedrock value that cannot be avoided." The words still remain undefined, however.

The Report next goes directly into the economic effects of disarmament, alleging that such effects would be the same whether disarmament preceded or followed the attainment of peace. The study therefore entirely bypasses the issue of how nations, centered about our own Constitutional Republic, might work to create the desired peace with freedom, for example by jointly defining the conditions, including self-sufficiency and security, which must be satisfied to make nations willing to disarm, and then working jointly to realize those conditions. With a regime of "peace with freedom" established, the institutions then existing could be examined to seek out problems then remaining and recommend programs for dealing with them. The Study, however, avoids looking at what institutional structures might evolve in the production of peace with freedom, though such structures would undoubtedly be very different from those presently existing.

The Report fleetingly describes and then dismisses prior studies leading to mechanistic disarmament procedures. This brief discourse acknowledges that before such scheduled disarmament procedures could begin, genuine agreement of intent would have to be reached among the major powers. We described that above as seeking to define and then realize the conditions which would permit nations to feel secure about disarming. The Report, however, does not mention the attainment of common intent, but rather proclaims that disarmament efforts have been unsuccessful because nations do not *want* peace to reign, and desire instead that the use of war as an institution continue, because war serves certain essential purposes that peace cannot. In point of fact, says the Report, war is not "subordinate to the social systems it is believed to serve." Rather, society's war readiness "supersedes its political and economic structure. War is itself the basic social system, within which other secondary modes of social organization conflict or conspire. It is the system which has governed most human societies of record, as it is today."

We find fault with the above, not respecting its accurate description of how the Old World powers behaved in order to expand their powers at the expense of others (that is, to indulge the fatal flaw of their rulers of being corruptible by power), but most particularly with respect to the purposes and intent of the United States of America, in whose name and for whose benefit the Special Study Group was presumably laboring. George Washington, in his Farewell Address, warned Americans to stay out of Europe's intrigues and wars, which had no legitimate place in our newly constructed country, a country which, for the first time in human history, was put together to be run by the people for the benefit of the people, and not for the benefit of those momentarily powerful persons in governmental office, who would in fact be frequently replaced. The power to make war was carefully put in the hands of the Congress, representing the wide-ranging electorate. The carnage of the Civil War renewed our abhorrence of war, and conspiratorial efforts were required (see Chapter 5) to drag us against our will into World War 1. That produced further revulsion, and further conspiratorial efforts were required to get us into World War 2. That ghastly war fed mass efforts to get us out of the Vietnam War, mass efforts that arose from our increasing conviction that we, the public, were being manipulated, a conviction made possible by our improved historical awareness and our much improved access to current events due to the growth of modern communication media.

We the people do not want war, we know we do not want it, and we are more than willing to support efforts to obtain and maintain peace in the world. To this end we supported the formation of the UN, but were again conned into doing something against our real interests, because the UN is clearly recognized now not as an institution seeking peace with freedom, but rather as the institution charged with acquiring political and military control over the world's peoples for the benefit of today's power elites.

Let's go on with the Report. It next sets about to define what it says are the real functions served by war, and in so doing cannot avoid tipping its hand concerning its previously implicit postulates. It first takes up the economic functions of war. Though war involves waste, it says, such waste has social utility, in that the waste is outside the control of market forces, and is subject instead to "arbitrary central control." That control can be used to "stabilize the advance" of the world's industrial economies, which have "developed the capacity to produce more than is required for their economic survival...." It can also be used as a sort of economic flywheel to balance the economy, and is better for this purpose than wasteful social welfare programs, because the latter, once initiated, become imbedded in the general economy where they are "no longer subject to arbitrary control." In fact, compared to war, "no combination of techniques for controlling employment, production, and consumption has yet been tested that can remotely compare to it in effectiveness...."

One perhaps begins to detect that a major goal, perhaps *the* major implicit postulate, is *control*, and more particularly, arbitrary central control. But, we ask, why do we want to "stabilize the advance" of the industrial economies? Isn't it proper to try to avoid war in order to permit the continuing increase in our own standard of living, as well as the rest of the world's? And isn't war a ludicrous price to pay as a mechanism for smoothing out the ripples in the economy? Aren't better and much less costly mechanisms available? The answers are right around the corner.

The Report has now arrived at its core issue: the hidden *political* functions of war.  And here we run once again into that undefined phrase that we started with: "social stability."  War, we are told, is even more critically needed for maintaining social stability than it is for providing economic stability.  It is fully capable of doing so because a state's war powers constitute "the basic authority of a modern state *over its people*."  In our modern industrial societies, war has served "as the last great safeguard against the elimination of *necessary social classes*."  Our productive economies make it more difficult to "maintain distribution patterns insuring the existence of 'hewers of wood and drawers of water.'"  But fortunately, the arbitrary nature of war expenditures and related military activities "make them ideally suited to *control* these essential class relationships."  Unless a substitute can be found, the institution of war must be continued "to preserve whatever quality and degree of poverty a society requires as an incentive as well as to maintain the stability of its *internal organization of power*."    (Our emphasis added.)

The prime political function of warfare, as understood by the Study Group, is thus seen to be to *preserve poverty* in the society as an aid to maintaining the elite class in control.  The congruence of the Report with Orwell's *1984* is now clear.  What social stability really means is "keeping the Low's in poverty and the High's in power, forever."

The last essential step to completing the Study Group's thesis is to understand why war is so readily accepted by the public, whose members are always the prime losers in any war. The reason, says the Report, is that individual citizens will willingly rise to the defense of their society when they see it being threatened by an external enemy. The enemy, of course, must be formidable and the threat real, or at least perceived to be real. Such a major threat to one's society justifies to the individual the loss of life associated with meeting that threat, including even the loss of one's own life. It may be very difficult, says the Report, to find a substitute for war that produces the desired waste of resources and is at the same time so readily acceptable to the populace. The Report makes no mention of the ease or difficulty of producing wars on demand, perhaps because the means were so obvious that no discussion was felt to be needed.

The final nonmilitary function of war, not necessarily incapable of adequate fulfillment by a substitute, is the loss of life which it produces. This comes under the euphemism of ecological control, aimed at maintaining the world's population at that reduced level at which it may successfully sustain itself within the constraints of the world's agricultural capacity. The Report briefly acknowledges that this Malthusian notion of population control may be approaching obsolescence due to the increasing efficiency with which food and other essentials are being produced, but then quickly dismisses the thought. The chief difficulty with using war for population control, says the Report, is that war regressively kills off a higher proportion of the fittest (our young warriors), instead of our old, weak, and infirm, thereby acting against eugenic improvement. Modern warfare has the promise of improvement in this regard, however, since nuclear warfare will enable millions to be rapidly killed off, and indiscriminately with respect to the weak or the strong. (It really says that!)

The Report further notes, as an incidental matter, that medical science has also exacerbated the problem by removing pestilence as a method of population control, but even worse, it has done so by perpetuating the lives of those who would otherwise have been eliminated by their genetic susceptibilities, thereby eugenically weakening the race. The coming "transition to peace" should probably take these matters into account as well.

The Report then seeks to define substitutes for the essential nonmilitary functions of war which it has allegedly found in the economic, political, sociological, and ecological arenas. In the economic field, there are two important criteria for substitutes: they must be wasteful (involving the destruction of at least 10 percent of the gross national product) and they must be outside the consumer supply and demand system. The first candidates considered are massive social welfare systems, such as cradle-to-grave health care, college education for all, housing for all at the level of the current top 15 percent, environmental purity with respect to air, water, forests, parks, etc., and the elimination of poverty via a guaranteed annual income or other appropriate redistribution scheme. While these schemes may prove useful during the transition to peace, says the Report, they all suffer from the disadvantage that they are too cheap (not as wasteful as war), and would work themselves into a permanent level of expenditure embedded within the general economy, and therefore not subject to arbitrary control.

A second possibility for an economic surrogate is a massive, open-ended space research program having substantially unattainable goals, such as the colonization of Mars, etc. This one might produce sufficient economic waste, and could be extended indefinitely, but lacks the urgency associated with an imminent, credible threat.

In fact, this lack of a credible threat turned out to be the main difficulty with finding *any* viable substitute for the political and sociological functions of war. Any such substitute requires the existence of an "alternate enemy" posing a massive and credible threat, sufficient for one to be willing to give up his life to fight. Of the social welfare programs mentioned above, environmental pollution is perhaps the only one which might be blown up into a big enough threat to convince people that lots of money urgently had to be thrown at the problem. But even this appears to have doubtful viability, even if efforts were made to deliberately poison the environment in various ways in order to enhance the threat. The Report's way around this apparent brick wall was to conclude that, if a viable natural substitute could not be found, *a fake one would have to be invented*. The Study Group didn't wish to pursue that matter any further, at least in print, in order not "to compromise, by premature discussion, any possible option that may eventually lie open to our government."

The Study Group did manage to find an alternate to war for proper population control (an "ecological" function).  The Report declares: "A universal requirement that procreation be limited to the products of artificial insemination would provide a fully adequate substitute for population levels.  Such a reproductive system would have the added advantage of being susceptible of direct eugenic management....  The indicated intermediate step – total control of conception with a variant of the ubiquitous 'pill,' *via water supplies or certain essential foodstuffs* – is already under development." (Emphasis added.)  The only question the Report raised about this matter was whether the imposition of procreation control should or should not await the arrival of peace.  The participants seemed to reluctantly agree that it should, since significant excess manpower would probably be needed in the warfare that was likely to ensue prior to the arrival of the "peace system," and because procreation control would naturally also require the existence of a centrally enforced "peace."

The Report reprises the motivation for the study, now clearly stated, in its summary: "The permanent possibility of war is the foundation for stable government; it supplies the basis for general acceptance of political authority.  It has enabled societies to maintain necessary class distinctions, and it has ensured the subordination of the citizen to the state, by virtue of the residual war powers inherent in the concept of nationhood.... The war system has provided the machinery through which the motivational forces governing human behavior have been translated into binding social allegiance.... The foregoing [political and sociological] functions of war are essential to the survival of the social systems we know today." Except, perhaps, the one created in the late 1700's by Jefferson, Adams, Madison, Hamilton, and their revolutionary compatriots.

After all of this cerebral effort, the Report concludes, "No program or combination of programs yet proposed for a transition to peace has remotely approached meeting the comprehensive functional requirements of a world without war.... The war system cannot responsibly be allowed to disappear until 1) we know exactly what it is we plan to put in its place, and 2) we are certain, beyond reasonable doubt, that these substitute institutions will serve their purposes in terms of the survival and stability of society.... It is uncertain, at this time, whether peace will ever be possible. It is far *more* questionable ... that it would be *desirable*, even if it were demonstrably attainable."

But given the above, the Report goes on to complain how even the "war system" is getting difficult and risky to manage. For example, it is becoming more possible "that one or more sovereign nations may arrive, through ambiguous leadership, at a position in which a ruling administrative class may lose control of basic public opinion or of its ability to rationalize a desired war." Horrors! What if significant leaks were to develop in the media's paper and electronic curtains?

The final recommendation of the study is that a War/Peace Research Agency be created, with unlimited secret funding, and accountable only to the President, to continue research on both how to get to the sought-for permanent peace, and how best to shore up the present war system so that it can continue to be efficiently used until such time as a stable peace is secured. The war studies should include, for example, the "determination of minimum and optimum levels of destruction of life, property, and natural resources prerequisite to the credibility of external threat essential to the political and motivational functions."

One wonders if such a War/Peace Research Agency presently exists.

In our review (Chapter 5) of Griffin's *The Creature From Jekyll Island* we noted that Griffin also had made reference to *The Report From Iron Mountain*. We encourage you to read and absorb his interpretation, which has an emphasis somewhat different from ours. Griffin supplies evidence of the authenticity of the Report by quoting the written assertion to that effect by Harvard's establishmentarian professor John Kenneth Galbraith, who admitted to participating in the study in at least a consultative capacity. We would also like to borrow from Griffin's conclusions concerning the study's importance. He asks why this study differs from any other think tank effort, and then writes (p. 525):

"The answer is that *this* one was commissioned and executed, not by ivory tower dreamers and theoreticians, but by people who are in charge.  It is the brainchild of the CFR.  Furthermore, it should be obvious that the stratagems outlined in the report are already being implemented.  All one has to do is hold the report in one hand and the daily newspaper in the other to realize that every major trend in American life is conforming to the recommendations of the report.  So many things that otherwise are incomprehensible suddenly become perfectly clear:  foreign aid, wasteful spending, the destruction of American industry, a job corps, gun control, a national police force, the apparent demise of Soviet power, a UN army, disarmament, a world bank, a world money, the surrender of national independence through treaties, and the ecology hysteria.  *The Report From Iron Mountain* has already created our present.  It is now shaping our future."

We will have more to say about a major element of that shaping process in our next review.

# Chapter 8

## "THE GREENING"

(By Larry Abraham. Pub. 1993 by Double A Publications, Inc., 2320 W. Peoria #C122, Phoenix, AZ 85029. Tel. (800) 528-0559)

The subtitle of Abraham's book is *The Environmentalists' Drive For Global Power*, and describes how the war-substitute that appeared most feasible to the Iron Mountain study group has been converted into an action program. First, however, let's review the other major possibilities that were considered by that group, and briefly observe what has developed.

A massive social welfare system was proposed, to include health care, college education, modern housing, and poverty elimination for all. We now have myriad programs dealing with these matters, including Medicare, Medicaid, college tuition grants, subsidized housing, and income assistance programs of various kinds, on which we as a nation have spent close to $5 trillion in the 30 or so years since LBJ declared his War on Poverty, without appreciably changing the incidence of "poverty." All this can certainly be considered a world-class effort to produce serious waste, but it has also produced a major backlash among those who are being taxed to pay for it, a backlash which the elites can't control very well. As they predicted, it clearly can't serve their long-term goals.

We also now have a space research program which the public is willing to support at a reasonable level, but "reasonable" is nowhere near enough as a substitute for war.

The environmental issue has clearly been selected as the major policy initiative to be developed. Recall that the Iron Mountain report expressed doubt that this issue would prove to be viable if dealt with only on its inherent merits, since the public would not likely view a sullied environment as a sufficiently severe threat to justify spending massive amounts of money on it, much less give up one's life in such a cause. It might be possible, however, to enhance the environmental threat, or even to *invent a fake issue* if an appropriate real one could not be found, though the conferees thought it better not to further discuss such possibilities in their written report. That, however, is what Abraham discusses at length in his excellent book.

In the first few pages of his book, Abraham plainly states his fundamental thesis. The real goal of the secret elites, he says, "is nothing less than to control natural resources worldwide. The Insiders of Environmentalism realize – even if many innocent bystanders do not – that the wealth of the world consists of the things that men take from the earth, and *they want to control it all....* For what is now being unleashed in the name of 'saving the earth' is nothing less than the most historic grab for power in all of human history."

Abraham then commences to lay out his evidence. In April 1970, just four years after the completion of the Iron Mountain study, President Nixon declared the first Earth Day, and in the same year established the Environmental Protection Agency. Abraham quotes a news article celebrating the 20th anniversary of that first Earth Day: "Government, business, and consumers have spent up to a trillion dollars, by Department of Commerce count, to clean the environment.... The U.S. seems to find three new environmental hazards for each one it conquers." Thus this "war-replacement" project, with its germ of a justifiable excuse for incurring public expenditures, has obviously added mightily to the production of economic waste, but that's hardly its total purpose, as we shall shortly see.

In April 1970 there also appeared an article by insider George F. Kennan in the CFR's journal *Foreign Affairs*, entitled "To Prevent a World Wasteland ... A Proposal." The article, no doubt written for the edification of the worker bees in the fields of the elites, was nothing less than the concrete plan for *implementing* the environmental project suggested by the Iron Mountain Special Study Group. Abraham quotes from the paper extensively, from which one may list the following principal elements of the plan:

- Treat environmental issues as transnational, since water and air contamination are no respecters of national boundaries.

- Create facilities to collect, store, and disseminate worldwide data on all aspects of environmental problems and activities.

- Promote the coordination of present international research and operational environmental activities.

- Establish international environmental standards, and advise and help governments and other organizations on how to meet those standards.

- Most important of all, establish and enforce "suitable rules for all human activities" conducted within the great international media of the high seas, the stratosphere, outer space, and perhaps the polar areas. Since individual governments and their selfish parochial nationals cannot be trusted to make or enforce such regulations, the task must be given to an *international* authority.

- An international body should be created to perform the above functions, including that of enforcing the rules and standards to be created. The body, perhaps called the Environmental Agency, should be empowered to act, not on the basis of agreements between government representatives, but by "collaboration among scholars, scientists, experts, and perhaps also something in the nature of environmental statesmen and diplomats – but true international servants.... The agency would require, of course, financial support from the sponsoring governments ... and one should not underestimate the amount of money that would be required."

Just in case the Establishment workers still don't get it, Kennan specifically spells out that the environmental issue is to replace society's fixation on the then-current Cold War, of which Kennan was a major architect, as Abraham clearly documents. Kennan emotes:

"Not only the international scientific community but the world at large has great need, at this dark hour, of a new and more promising focus of attention. *The great communist and Western powers, particularly, have need to replace the waning fixations for the cold war with interests which they can pursue in common and to everyone's benefit.* For young people the world over, some new opening of hope and creativity is becoming an urgent spiritual necessity. Could there, one wonders, be any undertaking better designed to meet these needs, to relieve the great convulsions of anxiety and ingrained hostility that now rack international society, than a major international effort to restore the hope, the beauty, and the salubriousness of the international environment in which man has his being?" (Abraham's emphasis added.)

*1984* has defined for us the purposes of war as an instrument for controlling a servile citizenry, *The Report From Iron Mountain* has defined the criteria and a suggested replacement for war, and Kennan's article provided a blueprint to install that replacement. It was expected to take about a generation and a half for that replacement to mature, however, and the remainder of *The Greening* describes the forced growth of environmental fervor during that period.

Before going into that, however, Abraham gives us a preview of the elites' most recent assessment of the status of their plan, along with details on how it is to be completed. It appears in a 1991 book by Jim MacNeill called *Beyond Interdependence: The Meshing of the World's Economy and the Earth's Ecology,* published by the Trilateral Commission, and containing a foreword by David Rockefeller himself. The book lays out the major goal to be sought at the 1992 Rio Earth Summit meeting then being planned: "The major purpose of this conference is to launch a global transition to sustainable development." The mechanics laid out for the conference, says Abraham, were to be such as to endow it with "the political capacity to produce the basic changes needed in our national and international economic agendas and in our *institutions of governance* [our emphasis] to ensure a secure and sustainable future for the world community." He quotes *Beyond Interdependence*: "By the year 2012, these changes must be fully integrated into our economic and political life," and then notes that someone up there seems to be setting deadlines for us.

"Sustainable growth" says Abraham is "Insider jargon for Green de-industrialization, global cartelization of natural resources, and international control of the world's economy.... [It] is a new synonym for *Iron*

*Mountain's* 'stability,' i.e., perpetuating Insider control." We have referred to the same term as "social stability," meaning "keeping the Low's in poverty and the High's in power, forever."

MacNeill recommends *environmental taxes* to pay for the real cost of using (replacing?) natural resources. Such costs may be highly speculative, but don't worry, those "environmental statesmen and diplomats" mentioned above can probably handle the job. "Politically," says Abraham, "MacNeill teaches that environmental interdependence means the end of national sovereignty. It will provide the 'external necessity' for a world government with new laws and regulations aplenty." And if some nations don't rush to relinquish their sovereignty, remember that MacNeill says it's OK to accept its piecemeal erosion by the "steady encroachment on their sovereignty by the forces of economic interdependence."

MacNeill's "credible threat," which *The Iron Mountain Report* required, consisted, said Abraham, of "the same old worn-out menu of eco-hoaxes: overpopulation, ozone hole, global warming, deforestation, bio-diversity, acid rain, rising sea levels, soil degradation, *ad nauseam.*" The "alternate enemies" are to consist of those who resist the imposition of international controls over these areas, such as us taxpayers, especially those of us who can still read. To control all of this, MacNeill proposes that a new international environmental super-agency be created.

Listening intently to all the above, the authors of the agenda of the Rio Summit of June 1992 included the following agenda items:

- Adopt an Earth Charter, defining new principles for handling environmental issues into the next century.

- Define an action program to implement the new principles, especially designating the agencies responsible for implementing the first phase of the effort, up to the year 2000.

- Define and sign treaties concerning global warming, deforestation, and bio-diversity.

- Create the necessary long-term international control agencies.

Abraham discusses the outcome of the Summit a little later. For now, he emphasizes just that the elites are deadly serious about their own goals and about the means they have chosen to attain them. "These megalomaniacs," he says, "genuinely *believe* they are the destined elite worthy to rule the world. Environmentalism is merely the ratty, ragged rationalization designed to hoodwink the world into accepting their rule." He digresses briefly to note that these elites have largely managed to identify themselves in their own writings, which few people outside of their own circles ever read. He lists over a dozen such books, including a couple that we have reviewed, and a couple more from which he quotes below. From his review of these and other sources, he says this of their organizational beginnings in the United States:

"The U.S. branch of the Institute [of International Affairs] was called the Council on Foreign Relations (CFR) and was officially founded in 1921. Prior to the formation of the CFR, a tight reciprocity existed between the Round Table group in the U.K. and the Carnegie Endowment for International Peace in the U.S., and once the Council was formed, most if not all of the Carnegie Trustees comprised its original board of directors.

"Dominating the leadership of the U.S. Establishment was the Wall Street lawyer for both Andrew Carnegie and J.P. Morgan, Elihu Root. Root was both chairman of the Carnegie Endowment and the first honorary chairman of the CFR. Orbiting Root were Morgan bank partners John W. Davis (CFR president 1921-33), Dwight Morrow, Thomas Lamont, and Henry Davison, along with other legal powerhouses such as Paul Cravath, Norman Davis, Russell Leffingwell, and Root's special protégé, Col. Henry L. Stimson [FDR's Secretary of War]."

Regarding the political clout which they developed, Abraham quotes from Professor Arthur S. Miller's *The Secret Constitution and the Need for Constitutional Change*: "In other words, those who formally rule take their signals and commands not from the electorate as a body but from a small group of men (plus a few women). This group will be called the establishment. It exists even though that existence is stoutly denied. It is one of the secrets of the American social order. A second secret is the fact that the existence of the establishment, the ruling class, is not supposed to be discussed.... A third secret is implicit in what has been said – that there is really only one political party of any consequence in the United States, one that has been called the 'Property Party.' The Republicans and the Democrats are in fact two branches of the same (secret) party." Abraham notes support of this view from Alvin Toffler's new book, *Power Shift,* which "identifies this consortium as the 'Invisible Party' and agrees with Miller that partisan politics has little or no bearing on the wielding of this all-encompassing power."

Abraham then proceeds to outline how the elites have developed their environmental program over the last 20 years or so. First off, if we're going to replace war with something else, we must start by eliminating the threat of war that has been hanging over us. We do that by eliminating the "credible enemy" which has made us willing to fight the recent Cold War. Lo and behold, the USSR has suddenly become peaceful. Not only that, but it is converting itself into a "Green" image of its former self. Abraham quotes from a New York Times article in August 1991 entitled "Gorbachev Turns Green":

"Soviet diplomacy is preparing a dramatic leap in the concept of 'new world order' that will leave President Bush in the primeval sludge if he doesn't move.... Mikhail Gorbachev gave Mr. Bush a hint to his thinking at their Moscow meeting, proposing that next year's UN conference in Rio de Janeiro on the environment be held *at the summit level* [our emphasis].... Moscow's new idea is not only an astonishing reversal of Soviet attitudes about international relations; it goes beyond accepted notions of the limits of national sovereignty and rules of behavior.... Foreign Ministry officials say they are working on a plan for a global code of environmental conduct. Moscow suggests a convention for all states to sign. It would provide for the World Court to judge states.... This is a breathtaking idea, beyond the current dreams of ecology militants. It is meant to show that the Soviets really take seriously their 'integration' in the world economy. And it is that the environment be [the] topic for what amounts to global policy." National borders must be disregarded, because "Environmental problems ignore borders, and the convention would draw the consequences on the basis of laws applied to all."

We have thus become witnesses to the birth of a "viable replacement for war." Abraham notes, in closing this topic, that the Gorbachev proposal not only "coincided perfectly with what George F. Kennan proposed in his April 1970 article in *Foreign Affairs*," it also presaged precisely what was to be the outcome of the upcoming Rio Summit. But Mr. Abraham doesn't believe that much in coincidences, and treats us instead to a thumbnail history of the art of deception in warfare, an art in which the international con men are highly adept, and in which we, the American public, are the primary "marks."

Abraham next backs up a few years to let us discover how the banking elites will profit even while journeying on their road to world control.  In September 1987, in Denver, Colorado, there occurred a conference called the Fourth World Wilderness Conference.  The 1500 delegates from 60 countries found upon arriving that a conference Declaration had been written for them, stating in part that, because more funding was needed for expanding conservation activities, "a new conservation banking program should be created to integrate international aid for environmental management into coherent common programs for recipient countries based on objective assessments of each country's resources and needs."

These words clearly were not written by the whale lovers and tree huggers in attendance, but more likely by the most major of the several major actors that were found in attendance, who included not only David Rockefeller of the Chase Manhattan Bank, but even the seldom seen (in public) Baron Edmond de Rothschild, representing the interests of his 200-year-old international banking family.  Abraham suggests that we best pay close attention.

Conference papers proposed that up to 30 percent of the world's wilderness land mass, i.e., about 12 billion acres, including whatever natural resources may lie underneath, be set aside for wilderness areas, with title vested in a "World Wilderness Trust."  The new World Conservation Bank (WCB) would participate by financing "directly and through syndicated and co-financing arrangements:

(1) The preparation, development, and implementation of national conservation strategies by developing country governments;

(2) The acquisition/lease of environmentally important land for preservation of biological diversity and watersheds;

(3) The management and conservation of selected areas."

And how are these lands to be acquired? In the Third World, we hark back to the fact of the Third World's unpayable debts, and listen to the conference's plan. It proposes that the WCB "act as intermediary between certain developing countries [e.g., Brazil] and multilateral or private banks [e.g., Chase] to transfer a specific debt [Brazil's debt to Chase] to the World Conservation Bank, thus substituting an existing doubtful debt on the bank's books [Brazil owes Chase] for a new loan to the WCB [WCB owes Chase]. In return for having been relieved of its debt obligation, the debtor country [Brazil] would transfer to the WCB natural resource assets of 'equivalent value'...."

"In other words," says Abraham, "the mega-banks' bad loans [created out of nothing by the 'Mandrake Mechanism'] which are not now collateral-ized would be sold at *full nominal value* to the WCB, instead of their presently discounted value on the open market (as low as 6 to 25 cents on the dollar). The WCB would 'buy' the loan from the existing holder [Chase] and the debtor country [Brazil] would have to collateralize the loan with wilderness areas. If [i.e., when] the debtor failed to pay, the WCB, or whoever its stockholders happen to be [Rockefellers, Rothschilds, etc.], would end up with vast tracts of land and everything below it.

"Now you see why I've been warning for years that the mega-banks were just not going to fail. The fix is in. What was proposed in Denver was the 'Proposal' of Kennan over 20 years ago.... The name of the game is the creation of world banks, regional currencies, multinational trusts, giant foundations, land expropriations, and massive transfers of natural re-sources – the cartelization of the world's natural resources – which will ultimately evolve into transfers of national sovereignty...."

We might recall at this point our discussion toward the end of Chapter 1 of Henry Kissinger's National Security Council Study Memorandum 200 recommending that a program of population reduction be aimed at a list of 13 Third World countries that produced raw materials that the U.S. needed. As reported by William Engdahl (p. 164), Kissinger noted in the Memorandum "how much more efficient ex-penditures for population control might be than [expenditures for] raising production through direct investments in additional irrigation and power projects and factories," such as would be required if the coun-try's population and standard of living were permitted to rise. We wondered aloud in Chapter 1 what the hidden rationale for such a policy might be. Now it's getting much clearer. The elites wish to reduce the targeted Third World populations to a bare subsistence level in order to reduce to a minimum the costs of producing the raw materials on the lands which the elites are presently trying to wrest from those target countries in the name of world environmentalism.

In the United States, the methods are different. They depend upon the poor brainwashed citizen being willing to be taxed (or to use "government" money, no matter how it is created) in order for the government (ultimately to be synonymous with "elites") to "buy" vast additional tracts of U.S. real estate.  In order for this to work, the media must keep up its bombardment of environmental horrors on the psyches of us ordinary folks.  Abraham quotes from an arbitrary sampling of such material to remind us just how deeply we are swimming in such intellectual sewage.

We are constantly reminded that the costs of the overall environmental cleanup program will be immense, no doubt to reinforce the claim that the danger is critical and imminent, and to get us used to thinking in terms of throwing hundreds of billions of dollars a year at the problem.  For instance, the New York Times article of August 1991, which was quoted above, projects environmental cleanup after the military production of the last 30 years or so to take 30 years and cost $400 billion.  Vice President Al Gore's book *Earth in the Balance* suggests that needed environmental activities would cost on the order of $100 billion per year, or about 2 percent of the GNP, though this is quite a bit lower than the *Iron Mountain* assertion that the economic waste of the war substitute must reach at least 10 percent of the GNP.   That probably means we'll have to keep activated for a little while longer the annual drug losses of around $400 billion, the welfare waste of another $200-$300 billion, plus a little war now and then, such as in Bosnia, to keep more excess billions flowing into the Pentagon as well.

Abraham then launches into an outline of the personnel and programs constituting the environmental onslaught in the United States. He notes that we should not be surprised to find that the figures at the helm of each and every one of the major environmental foundations (such as the World Wildlife Fund, the Heritage Trust, the Nature Conservancy, the National Wildlife Federation, The Sierra Club, the World Wilderness Congress, Conservation International, and the Center for Earth Resource Analysis) are key members of the elite political organizations previously and repetitiously identified (i.e., the Royal Institute of International Affairs, the Council on Foreign Relations, the Bilderberger Group, the Club of Rome, and the Trilateral Commission). Abraham spends a whole chapter on mini-biographies of 20 of these "Eco-Prophets," as he calls them, namely David Brower, McGeorge Bundy, Helen Caldicott, Barry Commoner, Paul Ehrlich, Dave Foreman, Jay Hair, Denis Hayes, Amory Lovins, J. Michael McCloskey, Ralph Nader, William Reilly, Jeremy Rifkin, John D. Rockefeller III, Laurence Rockefeller, William Ruckelshaus, John Sawhill, J. Gustave Speth, Maurice Strong, and Russell Train. We'll pick out just one of these gentlemen to say a few words about, namely Maurice Strong.

Mr. Strong is a multimillionaire Canadian with Establishment credentials starting with President, World Federation of United Nations Associations; co-chairman, World Economic Forum; member, Club of Rome; trustee, Aspen Institute; trustee, Rockefeller Foundation; and on and on for a dozen more lines of type, including heading up the Rio Earth Summit in June 1992. Abraham reports: "To buttress the Earth Summit, Strong formed the *Business Council for Sustainable Development*, 'a blue-ribbon group of 50 eminent business leaders from all regions of the world ... to promote a clear understanding of and commitments to environmentally *sustainable development* within the private sector at the highest corporate level.'" Strong appointed members to the council, many of whose names are not familiar, but whose company affiliations certainly are, including Asea Brown Boveri, Chevron, Volkswagen, Alcoa, Dow Chemical, Royal Dutch Shell, and du Pont. Holding this little sketch of Mr. Strong in mind, Abraham continues:

"In May 1990 Daniel Wood interviewed Strong for *West* magazine. Strong presented the idea that the only way to save the planet from destruction is to see to it that the industrialized civilizations collapse... Wood recounts the conversation:

[Strong] has a novel he'd like to do.... [In] the novel's plot, the World Economic Forum convenes in Davos, Switzerland. Over a thousand CEOs, prime ministers, finance ministers, and leading academics gather ... to attend meetings and set

economic agendas for the year ahead.... "What if"
[says Strong] "a small group of these world leaders
were to conclude that the principal risk to the earth
comes from the actions of the rich countries? And
if the world is to survive, those rich countries
would have to sign an agreement reducing their
impact on the environment. Will they do it?"....

Strong resumes his story. "The group's conclusion is 'no.' The rich countries won't do it. They
won't change. So, in order to save the planet, the
group decides: isn't the *only* hope for the planet
that the industrialized civilizations collapse? Isn't
it our responsibility to bring that about?

"This group of world leaders," he continues,
"form a secret society to bring about an economic
collapse... These aren't terrorists. They're *world
leaders*. They have positioned themselves in the
world's commodity and stock markets ... and have
engineered, using their access to stock exchanges
and computers and gold supplies, a panic. Then,
they prevent the world's stock markets from closing. They jam the gears. They hire mercenaries
who hold the rest of the world leaders at Davos as
hostages. The markets *can't close*. The rich
countries ..." And Strong makes a slight motion
with his fingers as if he were flicking a cigarette
butt out the window.

I sit there spellbound. This is not *any* story-
teller talking. This is Maurice Strong. He knows
these world leaders. He is, in fact, co-chairman of
the Council of the World Economic Forum. He
sits at the fulcrum of power. He is in a position to
*do* it...."

Abraham concludes that Strong's megalomania-
cal daydream speaks for itself, that he has surrounded
himself with a group of people who believe in the
coming of an apocalypse, and that a *cult of personality*
is appearing around him. "Strong," says Abraham, "is
part of a terrifically dangerous group of elitists who
actually believe they are Plato's 'philosopher kings.'
They alone are fit to rule the world. After all, without
their guiding light, nothing 'can save humankind from
itself.'"

Recalling that *Iron Mountain* noted that only
the *perception* of impending catastrophe was necessary, Abraham includes a couple of chapters on how
the elites are doing at creating this perception. The
first has to do with the one-sided media barrages on the
various environmental issues, the second on environmental brainwashing of kids in the public schools. On
the elites' side in the media effort is the ownership and
expert use of the mass media; on our side is scientific
truth. Though the printed and spoken words on the
one side vastly outnumber those on the other, truth and
skepticism are still winning out among the public, as
indicated by polls which ask people to define what
they believe to be the most important problem facing
the country. Results: 34 percent - economic problems;
27 percent - the drug crisis; 10 percent - poverty and
homelessness; and 4 percent - environmental problems.
Abraham presents a reading list of literature refuting
the various environmental calamities which are
claimed to beset us. The mass media drumbeat continues, however.

Abraham then outlines with what ease and effectiveness the "green" message is cleansing the brains of our next generation in the public schools. He quotes a New York Times article of November 1989: "Educators and environmentalists say that schools across the country are reporting an increase in class-room demand for environmental education.... Government officials and other spokesmen ... go to schools with [various environmental] messages. Several teachers describe the campaign as brainwashing for a good cause.... By and large the environmental groups are active and moving into education." Abraham notes that these "environmental groups" involve not only private organizations, such as the National Audubon Society, but large corporate entities as well, including Dow Chemical, AT&T, Exxon, and 3M. "Is it only an accident," asks Abraham, "that all [of these corporate entities] are also members of the National Wildlife Federation's Corporate Conservation Council as well as Maurice Strong's Business Council for Sustainable Development?" He winds up his discussion of the green indoctrination of our children with a look at *Captain Planet* and similar programs on children's TV.

The next couple of chapters are devoted to debunking a few of the specific ways that we are being told that the sky is falling. This is the fun part, because whenever the claims are racked up against measurable facts, the claims and their claimants suddenly lose their credibility. Abraham takes on briefly the issues of the population explosion, global warming, the ozone hole, and acid rain.  This is fun reading, and I won't steal it from him.  You should read it yourself.

He does introduce a final issue, however, which we must discuss.  It involves a legal ploy long ago developed by the elites, but now being increasingly used in the name of environmentalism, to bring our citizenry under the much more direct control of government bureaucrats who are enabled to define and enforce their own arbitrary "law."  The legal starting point is with the Congress, which, against the long-term best interests of the country, "delegates authority to an independent agency with no specific powers, only a general 'mandate' for enforcement.  The EPA is only the latest example of a legacy most exemplified by the fearsome power of the IRS.  In varying measure, these agencies are cop, judge, and jury.  They all possess legislative powers, executive powers, and judicial enforcement powers – which means they can define law [and] impose fines, civil penalties, injunctions, and in some cases even criminal sanctions.  Legal proceedings have been removed from a 'judicial' to an 'administrative' setting.  We are no longer protected by a presumption of innocence.  These entities operate on a *presumption of guilt.*  Administrative law replaces constitutional and common law rights...."

Abraham continues: "Objective law affords prior notice so that people can *avoid* criminal acts.  But when the law becomes subjective, when legislatures refuse to define offenses but issue only generalized mandates to bureaucracies ('clean up the air,' 'protect the environment' ...) then the very definition of the law becomes unknowable, [and] liable to change with the bureaucrats' subjective perceptions."

Given the above, Abraham concludes that the purpose of this "law" is not to save the environment, but to change the law itself into an institution better suited to controlling our once-independent citizenry. Of course, congressional delegation of such bureaucratic authority is unconstitutional on at least two counts: that the Constitution does not grant to Congress the power to delegate its legislative authority to other agencies, and that it does not grant Congress the power to legislate concerning the "environment." Such action appears to be an obvious violation of the Tenth Amendment to the Constitution, and, so long as it stands, is a major threat to our God-given natural rights of life, liberty, and the pursuit of happiness, and a major tool in the hands of the elites who wish to dominate us.

Abraham includes as an appendix an article written recently by scholar Brooks Alexander entitled *The View From Iron Mountain,* reprinted by permission. It seeks to answer the question of the authenticity of *The Report From Iron Mountain,* and evaluates the available evidence. It's a highly interesting interpretation from yet another party of one of the most significant publications of this last century, a publication which created a significant stir immediately after its appearance, and which continues to resist efforts by the elites to relegate it, once and for all, to the memory hole.

Chapter 9

# "THE POLITICS OF HEROIN"

(By Alfred W. McCoy. Pub. 1991 by Lawrence Hill
Books, Brooklyn, NY.)

This book is subtitled *CIA Complicity in the
Global Drug Trade.* It is the product of about 20 years
of research and travel by Professor McCoy, primarily
in Southeast Asia, tracking down the mechanics of the
international drug trade. The first edition of the book
was published in 1972 under the title *The Politics of
Heroin in Southeast Asia.* McCoy is presently
professor of Southeast Asian History at the University
of Wisconsin-Madison.

We take up this and the two following books
because they deal with entities utilized by the elites
which concern themselves not with foundation grants,
or monetary manipulation, or media propaganda, or
secret diplomacy, but rather with highly physical, very
illegal, and therefore always covert, means to attain
various ends which the elites deem important enough
to justify such means. We won't presume to assign a
motivation to the elites' apparent effort to perpetuate
the "drug war," though we can't refrain from pointing
out its $400 billion annual cost to the American public
which we estimated in the previous chapter, certainly
an attractive source of "waste" which the Iron Moun-

tain Study Group may actually have considered but left unrecorded.

McCoy starts by sketching the history of the drug trade.  Opium was first mentioned in Greek texts in the fifth century BC and in Chinese texts in the eighth century AD.  Its use remained local until western traders discovered its commercial potential, starting with the Portuguese in the sixteenth century, followed by the Dutch and then on a much larger scale by the British in the eighteenth and nineteenth centuries.  Starting in 1773, the British East India Company established a monopoly on the production of Indian opium, transported it to China and bartered it for Chinese tea, silk, and porcelains, and shipped and sold those goods back in Britain and other European countries for vast profits.  This triangular trade depended first upon political control in India and second upon military force in China, the latter necessitated by Chinese efforts to ban opium, efforts which were defeated by the two opium wars which the British successfully waged against the Chinese in 1839 and 1856.  By 1900 the Chinese had become the world's greatest opium consumer, having about 13.5 million addicts in its population of 400 million.  Its annual production had grown to over 35,000 tons, over 85 percent of the world's total, making China also the world's greatest producer.

The poppy produces the opium from which morphine and heroin are chemically derived.  Germany's E. Merck and Co. discovered in 1805 how to extract morphine from the opium sap, and began commercial morphine manufacture in 1827. An English chemist first synthesized heroin (diacetyl-morphine) in 1874, and in 1898 Germany's Bayer Company commenced commercial production of heroin as a pain reliever. (One year later they discovered aspirin and began marketing it as well.) Bayer advertised heroin as non-addictive, and it was included in countless patent medicines in America, Europe, and Australia. The AMA in 1906 approved its use as a substitute for morphine, which was finally recognized as being addictive.

Cocaine likewise became known to the western world in the nineteenth century. Noting the Andean Indian practice of chewing coca leaves, European firms began efforts in the 1850's to extract the active element. Merck was successful, and began commercial manufacture of cocaine. Sigmund Freud experimented with it and gave it a ringing endorsement, including "its ability to cure morphine and alcohol addiction." For a few-score years it enjoyed legal manufacture, by Parke-Davis Company for example, and widespread use in medicines, tonics, and even foods of various kinds. Coca-Cola contained a dose of cocaine until 1903, around which time the medical community started becoming aware of its addictive nature.

It took 10 more years for Congress to get stirred to action, but in 1914 it passed a law requiring a doctor's prescription to purchase heroin or cocaine. The law was widely circumvented, but by 1923 was strengthened into an effective federal ban on sales of essentially all narcotics, accompanied by the creation of the first drug enforcement agency, the Treasury Department's Narcotics Division.

The termination of legal distribution of narcotics did not end addiction, however, and criminal syndicates grew up to supply the demand for both alcohol and narcotics. But whereas alcohol prohibition was terminated in 1933, ending its criminal involvement, the narcotics ban has remained permanent, says McCoy, "making the illicit heroin traffic the most constant source of income for organized crime in America."

The Treasury's Narcotics Division came a cropper in 1929 when a grand jury found it protecting New York City drug dealers, including the notorious Arnold Rothstein, the leading organizer of the city's criminal syndicates in the 20's. Congress then created in its place the Federal Bureau of Narcotics (FBN), and President Hoover named Harry Anslinger, a young Prohibition officer, as its director. Anslinger ran it with enthusiasm through the 30's, confining his efforts to domestic suppression.

But after World War 2, when the U.S. sought to extend its drug suppression activities overseas, Anslinger faltered. According to McCoy, "In retrospect, it seems that Anslinger's intelligence connections compromised his bureau's anti-narcotics mission. As a strong anti-Communist and a specialist in counterintelligence, Anslinger maintained close ties to the U.S. intelligence community. During World War 2, he had lent his bureau's key personnel to form the Office of

Strategic Services (OSS), forerunner of the CIA [Central Intelligence Agency], thereby setting a postwar pattern of cross-fertilization between the two agencies." Anslinger thereafter denied the primacy of Southeast Asia's Golden Triangle as the prime source of postwar opium, claiming erroneously that the Chinese Communists controlled that trade, and otherwise steering his agency around any position or activity in opposition to the interests or positions taken by the CIA.

We noted in our own Chapter 1 on Engdahl's *A Century of War* that the British helped us form our international intelligence agencies, housing our OSS in the London offices of the British intelligence services. Staffed in part by Anslinger's drug fighters, the OSS metamorphosed into the CIA, which was formally created by President Truman in 1947 to prosecute espionage and covert action projects against the USSR in the Cold War which was then just starting. Whatever else may be said about the CIA, its genes may be seen to have come from persons involved for two centuries in the British Far Eastern drug trade, persons with extensive knowledge and involvement with the organized criminal syndicates handling illegal narcotics in the United States, and persons with anti-Communist mind-sets.

As a prelude to his main theme, McCoy goes into some detail concerning the organizational familiarity between the wartime intelligence agencies and the criminal syndicates. Very briefly, in 1942 the Office of Naval Intelligence (ONI) approached the Sicilian-

American Mafia who were "in charge" of the New York waterfront to seek their help in preventing German espionage and sabotage on the docks. The ONI was shortly referred to Lucky Luciano, then in a New York prison for prostitution racketeering, and to his good friend Meyer Lansky, patriot, who assured the Navy that Luciano would be trustworthy. Luciano and Lansky represented the "new generation" (following the death of Arnold Rothstein in 1928) of the Italian and Jewish Mafia respectively, with their friendship and pact of assistance going back to their youthful boyhoods on the streets of New York. A deal was struck: the ONI would define its problems to Luciano, who would advise Lansky of what was to be done, and Lansky would relay the orders to "whomever he thought appropriate" to get the job done. Among other services, the ONI learned, via Luciano and Lansky, what it needed concerning coastal waters around Sicily, where Italian army files could be found on Sicily, and who (among the Sicilian Mafia) would be helpful to Patton in defeating the Italian garrison on Sicily. When the war was over, the Mafia in Sicily was stronger than ever, having earlier been reduced to near impotence by Mussolini. In addition, Lucky Luciano's prison sentence was commuted by New York Governor Thomas E. Dewey, upon the request of American military intelligence officers, and Luciano was deported back to Italy.

McCoy then lays out the theme of his book. The number of U.S. addicts had dropped from around 200,000 in 1924 to perhaps 20,000 by the end of World War 2, largely due to the wartime disruption of the heroin supply and transport organizations. McCoy observes:

"With American consumer demand reduced to its lowest point in fifty years and the international syndicates in disarray, the U.S. government had a unique opportunity to eliminate heroin addiction as a major American social problem. Instead, the government – through the CIA and its wartime predecessor, the OSS – created a situation that made it possible for the Sicilian-American Mafia and the Corsican underworld to revive the international narcotics traffic. These operations were the first signs of the CIA's willingness to form tactical, anti-Communist alliances with major narcotics dealers, whether in the cities of Europe or the jungles of the Third World. During the forty years of the Cold War, several of the CIA's covert action allies were to play a significant role in sustaining a global narcotics industry that supplied the United States."

McCoy then goes to the CIA's first involvement. Back in Sicily, Lucky Luciano proceeded to construct one of the most successful narcotic syndicates in the history of the trade. He started by diverting heroin legally manufactured by Schiaparelli, a respected Italian pharmaceutical firm, and smuggling it to destinations in North America where it was received and distributed by his long-time associate, Meyer Lansky. Luciano had himself visited Cuba in 1947, met with the American syndicate leaders, and distributed lavish bribes to appropriate Cuban officials. Cuba was to be the focal point of North American distribution. Lansky was placed in charge, not only of organizing the remaining American heroin distribution network, but also of managing Luciano's entire financial empire in America. In this role he was responsible for collecting the enormous flood of North American drug cash and seeing that it got properly distributed, i.e., to the workers within the cartel, to bribed authorities, and of course back to Luciano who saw to the monetary distribution within Europe and Asia, no doubt including his own Swiss bank accounts. It was reportedly planned that the heroin transshipments within Cuba were to be managed by Santo Trafficante, Jr., a Lansky lieutenant and son of a Sicilian-born Tampa gangster. (His name will crop up again in this and in our next chapter.)

In 1950, Italian pharmaceutical regulations underwent a tightening, and Luciano turned to an alternate source of supply which he had under development. He began receiving morphine base from a major Lebanese wholesaler who received opium grown in Turkey and processed it in Lebanon into the much more compact morphine base. The Lebanese operation was secured politically by extensive bribing of Lebanese airport directors, customs officials, narcotics police, etc., arrangements which Luciano had considerable experience with, and no doubt inquired carefully about when making his arrangement with his new supplier.

He was now in need of the sophisticated chemical labs which could produce heroin from the morphine base. He established and operated a number of such secret labs in Sicily under the watchful direction of local Mafiosi, but they only operated successfully for five years or so (up to 1954) when the Italian police and press became aware of what was going on. Luciano saw that it might be wise to shut down the chemical operations so close to his command center, and utilize instead the services of an alternate processing center being run by the Corsican criminal syndicates in Marseille, on the southern shore of France. Anticipating this usage, Meyer Lansky, on a trip he had made to Europe in 1949-1950 to help arrange the financial labyrinth for handling and hiding drug proceeds from tax authorities, had also toured through France and held lengthy discussions with Corsican syndicate leaders on matters of mutual concern. A year or so later, the first heroin labs began appearing in Marseille. The highly successful route from Turkey to Lebanon to Marseille to the United States was to dominate the international heroin trade for the next twenty years.

McCoy outlines the political history in and around Marseille in great detail. In brief, Marseille had for many years been a rough laboring town, strongly populated by Corsican gangster elements, but also a stronghold of the French Communist Party and powerful Communist labor unions. The Corsican syndicates struck bargains with local French fascists during the 30's, and with Nazis during the occupation years, to support those political regimes in return for relatively free rein in running their "businesses."

Upon the beginning of the Cold War, the European Recovery Plan (the Marshall Plan) was instituted, and in early 1947 Congress appropriated $400 million to "fight communism."  According to McCoy's sources, President Truman "used it overtly in Greece and Turkey and covertly in France and Italy, through the CIA, to support ... democratic political parties." The CIA, established in September 1947, was going to be the operative agency to do this covert fighting.

Marseille was to be the primary port of entry of Marshall Plan goods.  The dock workers and other Marseille working people, feeling economically put upon, commenced wildcat strikes and demonstrations, supported by the Communist Party.  The strike spread throughout the country.  Truman, fearing a Communist coup, ordered the CIA to help break up the strike.  It did so, by providing millions of dollars to the French Socialist Party to procure their help in fighting the Communists.  Thereupon the Socialist Minister of the Interior called up military reserves to fight the strikers, and the lead Communist union shortly backed out.  In Marseille, the Socialist mayor purged Communist supporters from the police units.  The CIA joined the physical fray by supplying arms and money to Corsican gangs so that they could help the Communist-purged police forces assault the Communist picket lines and harass their union officials.  The CIA then mounted a media assault on the people, promising to withhold recently shipped foods unless the dock workers unloaded them immediately.  All this pressure proved sufficient, and the strike was, for the moment, broken.

These events established the Corsican Guerini brothers as the new leaders of the Corsican underworld, with the CIA and the French Socialists beholden to them. A substantial repeat of the strike occurred 3 years later, with the CIA again supplying money, and the Corsicans the brawn. This time, the Communist unionists were ousted from the docks, and the Corsicans won control of the waterfront. The stage was now set for the "unforeseen consequence" which Lansky was just at that time discussing with the Corsican leadership. Marseille's first heroin laboratories were opened in 1951, just a year or so after the Marseille waterfront was secured, courtesy of the anti-Communist efforts of the American CIA.

The clinching political safeguard which guaranteed success appeared to be located at the apex of the French government. McCoy points out, "Under the terms of their informal alliance with France's Gaullist government, the Marseille syndicates manufactured their heroin exclusively for export. Marseille may have become the world's largest heroin producer, but France remained drug-free – an essential element in the political equation that allowed this illicit industry to operate. Protected and connected, the Corsicans, according to the Federal Bureau of Narcotics, produced an estimated 80 percent of America's heroin supply." McCoy further points out that, toward the end of the Guerini reign, around 1970, they could no longer enforce their prohibition on domestic drug trafficking, and France started developing its own heroin addiction problem.

It is thus apparent that during the 50's and most of the 60's, French national administrations were aware of the heroin traffic and secretly permitted it to operate. One French agency which was itself involved was the Service d'Action Civique (SAC). It was a force of some 5000 men, many of them French and Corsican gangsters, created by General de Gaulle for the purpose of providing street protection at pro-Gaullist rallies, breaking up opposition demonstrations, providing bodyguards for government officials, and performing "dirty" (i.e., illegal) missions for French police and intelligence agencies. In return for their services they were granted broad immunities, which many abused to the point of being arrested for heroin smuggling.

A second, and much more important, French agency that was involved with the traffic was the French intelligence agency called the SDECE, the equivalent of our CIA. McCoy relates: "Moreover, informed observers were convinced that some of SDECE's top intelligence officers had been organizing narcotics shipments to the United States to finance SAC operations." McCoy describes an instance of an American undercover drug sting operation being exposed to the targeted French smugglers by a high-ranking SDECE officer. He continues, "The extent of SDECE's involvement in the heroin trade was finally exposed in November 1971 when a New Jersey prosecutor indicted Colonel Paul Fournier, one of SDECE's top supervisory agents, for conspiring to smuggle 45 kilos of heroin into the United States.  On April 5 a U.S. customs inspector ... had discovered the heroin concealed in a Volkswagen camper and arrested its owner, a retired SDECE agent named Roger de Louette.  After confessing his role in the affair, de Louette claimed that he was only working as a courier for Colonel Fournier.  Fournier's indictment rated banner headlines in the French press and prompted former high-ranking SDECE officials to come forward with some startling allegations about SDECE's involvement in the heroin traffic."

In point of fact, France's official protection of their domestic heroin operations goes back to the early Corsican takeover of Marseille.  McCoy reports: "After the CIA withdrew in the early 1950's, Marseille's Corsicans won political protection from France's intelligence service, the SDECE, which allowed their heroin laboratories to operate undisturbed for nearly 20 years."  This will not be the only cooperative tie that we will discuss between the CIA and the SDECE, clearly two birds of a feather.

In the early 70's, the European drug traffic started into a steep decline, owing primarily to the start of serious French suppression efforts (because of the revelations noted above and of the growing French addiction problem) and also because of American pressure which resulted in Turkey's plan, announced in 1967, to reduce and eventually abolish opium production, a plan which was completed in 1972.  Thus, in the late 60's, the Corsican and Mafia traffickers saw that they were going to have to rely upon an alternate source of supply. With Luciano having died in 1962, and Lansky retired at age 66 to Israel, the organization of the new source of supply fell to Lansky's heir apparent, Santo Trafficante, Jr.   He observed that Southeast Asia seemed to be the Mafia's most promising source, since (1) it presently grew over 70 percent of the world's illicit opium, (2) Corsican syndicates were already there supplying morphine to the international markets, and (3) Chinese-operated laboratories in Hong Kong were producing some of the best high-grade heroin in the world.   So in 1968, Trafficante boarded a plane for Southeast Asia.

McCoy then backs up in time to relate something of the history of the peoples and culture of Southeast Asia, with emphasis on opium production, and most particularly the central economic position accorded it by the French colonial administration. Colonial control was acquired over the bulk of the region by the late 1800's.  The French managed their own opium distribution monopoly for the 40 years prior to World War 2, first utilizing opium grown and shipped from India, and later from Iran and Turkey. Its use was "taxed" and produced about 15 percent of French Indochina's tax revenues.

During the war, the opium flow was cut off and the French decided to raise it locally, to keep the taxes coming in from the addict populations. They granted power and influence to local leaders of the Hmong hill tribes in return for the efforts of those leaders to encourage the hill farmers to cultivate poppies.  The system was very successful, except the French violated one of their own rules in northwestern Vietnam by recruiting Tai leaders of lowland rice-growing country to be the controlling brokers of the Hmong farmers in the surrounding hill country. This produced the animosity of the Vietnamese Hmong which resulted in the Dien Bien Phu catastrophe for the French when they attempted to re-establish postwar control over their former colonial regions in the first Indochina War in 1954, losing both the war and their Southeast Asian empire. McCoy's account provides a highly interesting view of Southeast Asian history from a uniquely different perspective. The official, deliberate French policy of using opium as a revenue producer is duly noted, and may help to explain how the French could rationalize their actions previously noted in Marseille.

Immediately after World War 2, Southeast Asia's home-grown opium was supplemented by some legal opium from Iran and a much greater illegal supply smuggled from China. In 1949 the Chinese supply was cut off by the Communist victory in China, its ban on opium production, and the massive detoxification program forced on the Chinese population. Iranian production was then banned, making that source illegal, and thus more uncertain. Domestic Southeast Asian production was therefore indicated, which would involve the United States this time, and would make the Southeast Asian Golden Triangle the largest single opium-producing area in the world. McCoy notes that these changes in the patterns of the international narcotic drug traffic came about primarily as a result of decisions made by governments (i.e.,

France, China, Iran, and the United States), and not due to unilateral decisions made by criminal syndicates, who could only be charged with taking advantage of the illegal cash flow that was made available to them.

The French were involved with raising opium in Laos and northern Vietnam and selling it to the opium dens of Saigon. The U.S. was involved with opium raised in Burma and Thailand, supplying the dens of Bangkok, Thailand's capitol city. McCoy details the history of each development at great length.

In French Indochina, the French army found that standard battle tactics didn't work, and that the guerrilla assistance of the Hmong hill dwellers was a necessity. The French bought that assistance covertly by purchasing the Hmong farmers' opium, transporting it to Saigon, and selling it to the large addict market there, with any surplus going to the Corsican underworld running the illicit export market. This secret operation, called Operation X, was run as a joint endeavor of the French military and the French Intelligence Service, the SDECE, all under the ultimate authority of the French Ministry of War. The American CIA in Vietnam, in the person of Col. Edward G. Lansdale, found out about Operation X in July 1953, "complained to Washington that the French military was involved in the narcotics traffic, and suggested that an investigation was in order." He was told by Washington to drop any investigation, since it would only serve to embarrass a good ally. "Washington" clearly knew what was going on.

The French defeat at Dien Bien Phu in May 1954 and the peace agreement negotiated in Geneva by Vietnamese, French, Russian, Chinese, British, and American delegates and signed on July 20 did not deter the French military from continuing the war covertly. They were supported by a criminal organization of river pirates known as the Binh Xuyen, who had been installed by the French as the legal administrators of Saigon, France's "Pearl of the Orient," the richest and most important city in French Indochina. The Binh Xuyen ran the opium dens in Saigon, along with the city's gambling, prostitution, and other criminal enterprises, and were sufficiently ruthless and locally knowledgeable to keep the Communist Viet Minh terrorists out of the city.

France's last gasp as a colonial power in Southeast Asia was in a war over the control of Saigon, and therefore over the source of funds (i.e., from heroin addicts) for any future military or other activities. Opposing the French military and the Binh Xuyen, in the spring of 1955, were the Vietnamese Army (the ARVN) and the American CIA, led locally by Edward Lansdale. The war was actually a fight between the United States and France over who was to control Saigon and South Vietnam. It was a battle by proxy, actually fought by the Binh Xuyen criminals against the ARVN. It was a savage house-to-house battle in which whole blocks of Saigon were leveled. In the end, Lansdale and the ARVN won, and immediately thereafter, in a May 8-11 meeting between French Premier Edgar Foure and the American Secretary of

State John Foster Dulles, France agreed to leave Indochina and let the U.S try its hand at managing it.

Thus ended France's colonial empire in Southeast Asia. But why did the United States wish to get involved? Why did it *fight* France for the privilege? Part of the answer may be perceived in the fact that the U.S. in the early 50's had paid about 78 percent of the costs of the French Expeditionary Corps, and "hundreds of American advisors had served with the French units." It was only after Dien Bien Phu that cooperation between the French and the Americans began to unravel. A larger part of the answer may be seen by rolling the clock back to the end of World War 2 and looking at American activities in Southeast Asia, particularly in Burma and Thailand.

In January 1949, the Chinese Communists rolled into Yunnan province, and remnants of the Kuomintang's Nationalist army (KMT) straggled into neighboring Burma and Indochina. In the latter, the French disarmed, interned, and later repatriated the stragglers to Taiwan. The Burmese tried the same, but were initially unsuccessful due to their own military weakness. More importantly, in November 1950, upon the entry of massive Chinese forces into Korea, President Truman approved a plan put forward by the Office of Policy Coordination (OPC) and the CIA to covertly train and equip the KMT remnants in Burma for an invasion of southern China, presumably to relieve the pressure on Korea. Doubters were put aside by the CIA's insistence that, though the tiny force would start out as a pinprick, it would ultimately be successful because of the millions of patriotic Chinese who would join the counterrevolution once it was started.

With their authority in hand, the CIA set up covert channels for getting military equipment to the KMT, including a shipping front and a "commercial" airline actually purchased by the CIA, and it helped the KMT recruit and organize a viable army, which actually mounted three separate invasions of China – in June 1951, July 1951, and, after heavy-duty reinforcement by the CIA, again in August 1952. Each invasion force consisted of about 2000 men plus CIA advisors, several of whom were killed. Each invasion failed to attract any millions of supportive Chinese, and each was easily defeated by huge Communist forces and driven back into Burma. At that point, support from the existing CIA channels dried up, and the thrust of future KMT activities, coinciding in time with the incoming administration of Dwight Eisenhower, was entirely redirected.

Instead of training, arming, and organizing for exerting pressure on China, the KMT spread out into the great bulk of northeastern Burma, substantially conquering it. They then took over the opium production in that region, vastly increasing production by coercively imposing taxes on the farmers, to be paid in opium, just as the French were doing in Laos and northern Vietnam. The vastly expanded opium yields were shipped out to Thailand, mostly by a system of mule caravans which the KMT had organized soon after their arrival in Burma. Even before the failed

Chinese invasions, the caravans had carried opium on the way out and arms on the way back into Burma, supplementing the arms and drug flows that were also carried in and out by unmarked CIA airplanes.

The Burmese government complained to the UN in March 1953. Publicly embarrassed, the U.S. called a conference in May with Burma, Taiwan, and Thailand at which KMT withdrawal from Burma was agreed to. (It was at about this time that Lansdale was "discovering" French drug operations in Vietnam.) The KMT didn't go along, however, and various foot dragging was engaged in, involving, among others, the newly appointed U.S. ambassador to Thailand, William Donovan, who will be remembered as the founder of the OSS. When all the flak had died away, and some KMT had been removed to Taiwan, so many remained that the Burmese were finally led to mount a major military offensive against them in March 1954. The KMT were momentarily routed, and its general announced the dissolution of the KMT army. Nevertheless, some 6000 troops remained in Burma, and would remain in full control of opium production for another seven years. Only by 1961 were they finally defeated by the Burmese and driven into Laos. Upon this victory, the Burmese were enraged to find American arms and ammunition of recent manufacture left behind by the KMT. They also found three refineries for morphine base that had been operated by the KMT. Opium production in Burma had by then expanded from the 1946 level of 80 tons per year to between 300 and 400 tons per year.

The clincher concerning the CIA involvement with Burmese opium took McCoy to Thailand. Very briefly, the official who received the Burmese opium in northern Thailand was, for about 10 years starting in 1948, General Phao Siyanan, the notoriously corrupt director of Thailand's national police, and the secret kingpin of Thailand's drug trade. General Phao, who had murdered his way into power, had about 40,000 national police at his disposal. His last obstacle to power was a rival who had about 45,000 army personnel at *his* disposal. Phao's final victory came upon the CIA's selection of Phao to receive *its* support, including, says McCoy, "naval vessels, arms, armored vehicles, and aircraft [delivered] to Phao's police force. The CIA denied similar aid to his rival, and by 1952 General Phao had consolidated his political power. "By 1953," says McCoy, "the CIA had at least 275 overt and covert agents working with Phao's police and had delivered [via the CIA shipping front] $35 million worth of assistance."

Phao took control of the Bangkok vice rackets, including the delivery of opium to Bangkok's addict population. His police protected the CIA's delivery of arms to the KMT in Burma, and obtained also the control of the opium delivered by the KMT into Thailand. He was shortly able to build "a virtual monopoly on Burmese opium exports." This man, says McCoy, "whom a respected Thai diplomat hailed as the 'worst man in the whole history of modern Thailand'" was nevertheless praised by U.S. Ambassador William Donovan, the founder of the OSS, saying that Phao's police constituted "a tough and well-trained police force."     Accordingly, General Phao was awarded the Legion of Merit in 1954 for "exceptionally meritorious service" by the U.S. Secretary of the Army.

Phao's reign lasted only three more years, when he was finally overthrown by an army coup, and he flew off to Switzerland, no doubt to be closer to his ill-gotten gains.  The factions assuming power in Thailand threw the CIA agents in Phao's police out of the country, closed the existing opium dens, and in 1959 prohibited opium use or distribution.  The addicts remained, however, and the trade simply went underground, to be run by Bangkok's Chinese syndicates rather than the army, but protected as usual by secret payoffs to the reigning politicians and the Thai military.

McCoy notes that by the beginning of the 60's, Thailand's opium production had grown from 7 tons per year to over 100 tons per year.  The total production in the Burma-Thailand-Laos area had grown to perhaps 700 tons per year, making the Golden Triangle the largest single opium growing region in the world, courtesy of the French SDECE, the American CIA, and various purchased political and military officials in Southeast Asia.  The region was fully capable at this time of supplying essentially the whole world should the need or opportunity arise.

McCoy's story then goes back to the 15 years or so following the French defeat in Saigon in 1955 by the American CIA.  It's a fascinating account, including the naive years in support of Ngo Dinh Diem, in which the Americans attempted to create and run South Vietnam with a more or less honest officialdom, followed by their support of the overthrow (and murder) of Diem on November 1, 1963, and their acceptance in 1966 of the return of a corrupt and opium drenched administration, that of Premier Nguyen Cao Ky, which was capable of freeing Saigon of Communist terrorists.  Ky in turn ultimately lost substantial power to General Nguyen Van Thieu in 1968, changing the names of the high-level officials dealing in drugs, but not the fact of drug-dealing and other corruption.  Throughout the Ky/Thieu period, the CIA and the U.S. embassy in Saigon supported the regimes, denying charges raised in the U.S. Congress and elsewhere that the regimes were corrupt, or were supporting themselves by drug trafficking, though the evidence presented by McCoy to the contrary is overwhelming.  He shows, for example, that Lansdale and his CIA subordinate and former OSS officer, Lucien Conein, were well aware in 1966 that then-Premier Ky had agreed to let the Corsican underworld "start making large drug shipments to Europe in exchange for a fixed percentage of the profits."

McCoy continues his narrative with the developments in the Golden Triangle in the period from 1960 to 1975.  In Burma, the KMT were driven out and into Thailand, where they were protected and granted secret bases next to Burma from which to operate.  They continued to run their heavily armed donkey caravans into Burma to pick up opium from the farmers and return most of it to Thailand, paying "duties" to the Thai officialdom, and selling the opium to Chinese syndicates for domestic distribution and export to Hong Kong. In Thailand, the KMT, being skilled in mountain warfare among the Hmong tribesmen, and with American financial support, helped the Thai military keep down Communist insurgency. In return, the KMT was given a free hand to manage their caravans into Burma and were also permitted to operate modern heroin labs in their secret bases.

But the main thrust of the American involvement in the Golden Triangle during these years was in Laos. This unfortunate country was bordered on the east by northern Vietnam, on the west by Burma, on the north by China, and on the south by Thailand. After the fall of Dien Bien Phu, it was subject to infiltrative attack by the Communist Pathet Lao. McCoy reports: "For 15 years, 1960-1974, the CIA maintained a secret army of 30,000 Hmong tribesmen in the mountains of northern Laos – participants in a covert war that remains the largest single operation in the agency's forty-year history [as of 1991]."

The strategy followed that of the French before them, except that the CIA was not directly involved with buying and selling opium, as the French had been. The CIA merely *facilitated* the trade. The CIA's purpose was to recruit an army of local tribesmen who were familiar with the terrain, who could be convinced that they had something to lose if the Communists were to take over, and who would fight in the stead of American combat contingents that would otherwise be necessary. The Hmong army would be mobilized via a

Hmong commander chosen by the CIA, Major Vang Pao. He approached local tribesmen, offering to supply rice to them and buy opium from them if they would raise it instead of rice, provided they would supply young men to join the Laotian mercenary army. The later sale of the opium to Chinese or Corsican syndicates supplied funds for rice purchases and arms and other supplies for the secret army, thus reducing the CIA's direct costs. "In effect," says McCoy, "the CIA's support for the Hmong opium crop insured the economic survival of the tribal villages, thereby allowing the agency to make its annual harvest of Hmong children. More important, control over the opium crop reinforced the authority of the CIA's Hmong commander, General Vang Pao, transforming him from a minor officer into a tribal warrior who could extract adolescent recruits from villages no longer willing to accept the war's high casualties."

The strategy was successful, at least for a while, largely because of the CIA's Air America network of agile aircraft which tied the Hmong villages into an integrated whole, transporting rice to the villages, recruits to battle, and opium to market. However, in the larger picture, the strategy was substantially defensive, and the offense undertaken by the Communist forces eventually overran northern Laos. The CIA then turned to a scorched earth policy, forcing the Hmong to leave their villages and retreat away from the advancing Pathet Lao, denying the Hmong manpower to the conquerors. But by 1973, Vang Pao's army had been reduced from a peak of 40,000 to a remnant of 10,000, with the Pathet Lao threatening the

Laotian capitol of Vientiane. The Royal Lao government then signed a cease-fire with the Pathet Lao, effectively ending the secret war. The CIA's Air America gave up all its Laotian facilities in June 1974. Vang Pao attempted to fight on for some time, but in May 1975 was evacuated by a CIA plane just prior to his capture, and shortly thereafter spent a half a million dollars on a cattle ranch and other real estate in Montana. By the end of 1975, some 30,000 Hmong refugees had fled Laos into Thailand.

By 1970, opium production in the Golden Triangle had reached nearly 1000 tons per year, and had by then become highly interesting to the Corsican, the Chinese, and the Mafia syndicates. The Corsicans had been there for years, having followed the French military into Indochina after World War 2, and having been engaged in narcotics smuggling with their compatriots in Marseille ever since. The Chinese had for some years received opium and morphine smuggled into Hong Kong, converted it into high-grade heroin, and shipped it to various world markets. They also sent master chemists skilled in that conversion into the Golden Triangle area to help the various local powers there set up heroin labs which came into production by early 1970. The Mafia showed interest starting in about 1965 with the arrival of John Pullman, Meyer Lansky's "courier and financial expert," for a visit with certain Chinese entrepreneurs in Hong Kong with whom he probably wished to make certain financial and other strategic arrangements. At about the same time, a "young Mafioso from Tampa, Florida" named Frank Furci arrived in Vietnam, engaged in various joint enterprises with the local Corsican gangsters there for about three years, was ejected and went to Hong Kong, where he introduced himself to the Chinese drug lords.  While there, he was visited by Santo Trafficante, Jr. and one of his lieutenants, Dominick Furci, who also happened to be Frank Furci's father.  Santo, of course, was probably there to discuss how the business empires of Meyer Lansky and of the Chinese drug kingpins might synergistically prosper.

The first visible upshot of these several events was that a plague of heroin addiction started among American GIs in 1970.  Army medical officers estimated in 1971 that 10 to 15 percent of the GIs were users, and a White House task force in 1973 found that 34 percent of GIs in Vietnam had "commonly used" heroin.  The heroin was smuggled from the Golden Triangle laboratories to every conceivable location in Vietnam close to American soldiers, where it was pressed upon them by an army of pushers, including street peddlers, roadside stands, pimps, prostitutes, and even officers in the Vietnamese army.  The distribution network was set up by the Ky/Thieu political regimes, run for their financial benefit, and protected by their officialdom, including elements of their army, navy, customs, police, and anyone else they needed.  Whenever questioned by U.S. newspapers or congressmen, the CIA and U.S. Embassy officials in Saigon denied the involvement of Vietnamese officials.

But why would the Vietnamese willingly bring this scourge on American soldiers who were trying to save Vietnam from the Communists?  The answer, says McCoy, was money, about $88 million per year, coming from about 20,000 GI addicts each spending about $12 per day for heroin. That cash was used in the same way as the French found it useful – to hold together the politically corrupt infrastructure that seemed to be necessary in the post-colonial Vietnamese culture.

Following the American evacuation from Vietnam in 1975, the Golden Triangle heroin labs did not go out of business, but continued shipping their product out via Bangkok. The Hong Kong labs also continued in operation. Heroin destined for the U.S. was sent from Bangkok and Hong Kong to Chile and then to Paraguay. Morphine from Bangkok was also sent to Marseille, converted to heroin, sent to Argentina, and then sometimes to Paraguay. Santo Trafficante would then deal with the problem of getting it from Paraguay and Argentina into the Mafia distribution system in the U.S. This system was available to serve the American addicts coming home from Vietnam, and helped mightily to fuel the heroin plague with which our country is still struggling. Heroin made this sorry chapter of American history even worse than most of us realized at the time.

McCoy details what he knows of the Hong Kong Chinese syndicates. They originated in Shanghai, but moved out of there to Hong Kong just before the Chinese Communists arrived. They possessed the world's best expertise in the chemical process of creating high-grade heroin from morphine base. They organized the smuggling of opium and morphine by sea from Bangkok to Hong Kong. They created the heroin labs in the Golden Triangle. In the late 60's they had started significant heroin production and were heavy into it in the early 70's. They organized the heroin smuggling from Hong Kong to South America and elsewhere, for delivery to Mafia types who would get it to the American market.

During these same years, poppy cultivation in Turkey had been abolished, and the French were busily suppressing heroin production in Marseille, to protect the French population. Notwithstanding the growing evidence that the great bulk of the heroin arriving stateside originated in the Golden Triangle under the management of the Chinese criminal syndicates in Hong Kong, the U.S. State Department, says McCoy, "clung to its belief in Turkey's importance. Convinced that the root of the problem still lay in the Mediterranean and unwilling to confront the political consequences of thinking otherwise, America's diplomats were reluctant to apply the same political leverage in Southeast Asia as they had in France and Turkey."

What "political consequences?" We presume that McCoy is referring to the secret knowledge held by our political elites that the United States had just fought a war which had produced, with our complicity, the greatest illicit heroin production and delivery network that the world has ever seen, and that the population of the United States was the primary targeted market. We can't help but wonder how those Iron Mountain scholars would have graded this activity on its potential for promoting "economic waste."

McCoy isn't through.  The United States was involved in a second anti-Communist war run covertly by the CIA which resulted in the development of a second major heroin production area, rivaling the Golden Triangle.  The war lasted from 1979 to 1989. The battleground was Afghanistan.  The Communist threat was supplied by Russia.  The CIA client was the neighboring country of Pakistan, specifically in the persons of General Zia ul-Haq, who was newly running the country following a military coup, and his chosen Afghan guerrilla client, Gulbuddin Hekmatyar. Hekmatyar ended up being the enforcer for opium production in the neighboring Afghan highlands, plus its collection and delivery to heroin labs in Pakistan, all under the protection of General Zia, and using arms supplied by the CIA and American "military aid."

The origins of the above conflict are interesting. In April 1978, Communist elements in the Afghan army had thrown out the previous dictator and established a pro-Soviet regime.  Then in April 1979 Zbigniew Brzezinski, President Carter's National Security Advisor and conduit to our elites, convinced the National Security Council to be "more sympathetic" to the fledgling anti-Communist resistance.  A month later, a CIA special envoy arrived in Pakistan to interview Afghan resistance leaders, and selected Hekmatyar, the man recommended by Pakistan's Inter-Service Intelligence agency, through which General Zia intended to prosecute the upcoming conflict.  A half-year later, Russia invaded Afghanistan, President Carter made a public display on TV denouncing Leonid

Brezhnev, and sent Brzezinski out again to twist some arms and rustle up some arms for the resistance. He got them, from China, Egypt, and Saudi Arabia, plus of course some from the CIA itself. President Reagan later followed up with a $3 billion program of military aid to Pakistan.

President Carter had a White House advisor on drugs, Dr. David Musto, who warned Carter and his Council on Drug Abuse about militarily supporting the opium-growing guerrilla resistance. "I told the council," he recalled, "that we were going into Afghanistan to support the opium growers in their rebellion against the Soviets. Shouldn't we try to avoid what we had done in Laos? Shouldn't we try to pay the growers if they will eradicate their opium production? There was silence." By the end of the 10-year war, the Afghanistan-Pakistan border area had emerged into a major heroin production region, complete with political protection. World opium production was then up to 4200 tons, with 73 percent of it coming from the Golden Triangle and most of the rest coming from the CIA's Afghan guerrilla clients. The American public barely knew that anything was going on in Afghanistan, and certainly not anything that was going to exacerbate the American drug problem.

Finally, McCoy looks briefly at the CIA's covert war against the Nicaraguan Sandinista government, waged at the same time that the U.S. was being deluged in a sea of cocaine. Though much remains to be uncovered, some outlines have emerged. President Reagan in 1981 ordered the CIA to commence a covert action in support of the Contras' fight against the Sandinistas, following their overthrow in 1979 of the anti-Communist Somoza government. The U.S. Congress refused in 1984 to continue supporting the Contras, following which a "civilian" support effort was mounted, led by Lieutenant Colonel Oliver North. He recruited retired General Richard Secord, who in turn recruited Thomas Clines, an ex-CIA compatriot from their days together commanding the CIA's secret war in Laos. Clines and Secord raised money, bought airplanes, and hired veterans of former clandestine operations as pilots, mechanics, etc., as required to procure and ship arms to the Contras.

The planes flew arms and supplies from the U.S. to supply points in Costa Rica and Honduras on the borders of Nicaragua, and frequently returned to the U.S. loaded with cocaine. The cocaine had started in the high valleys of Peru and Bolivia, was accumulated in the town of Medellin, Columbia, and was thence sent by air and other means toward the United States, with at least some of it going to way-stations in Central America. The Medellin Cartel presumably paid the Contras to help deliver the cocaine to the United States, thus providing the Contras with money to pay for arms to fight their war. The CIA then acted as at least one of the smuggling agencies which brought the cocaine back into the U.S. Presuming all this to be accurate, the parallels to the CIA operations in Afghanistan, Laos, Burma, and Marseille can easily be drawn, which McCoy proceeds to do, quite adequately.

For a little more background on Somoza's overthrow during the Carter presidency, in Somoza's own words, see *Nicaragua Betrayed* (by A. Somoza, Western Islands, 1980). Roughly speaking, his book details how he was militarily overthrown because of various actions and inactions of the United States, creating the excuse for the later patriotic efforts of the CIA to save Nicaragua from the Communists. By 1982 Americans were spending annually about $29 billion on cocaine, more than on any other single illicit drug. Its use continued to rise through the rest of the 80's, particularly upon the advent of crack cocaine, a form which could be sold for as little as $10 a dose, and thus much more salable to juvenile users.

McCoy finishes up by summarizing America's 70-year history of trying to suppress or interdict narcotic drugs aimed at the United States, and then briefly discusses alternative ways of dealing with the drug plague. He toys with regulation, or partial legalization, but we believe that solutions which we ourselves have offered, and will discuss in the last chapter, better hit the mark. McCoy's only suggestion with which we wholly agree is contained in his final sentence, i.e., rescind the CIA's covert action authority and close down its covert action apparatus.

Chapter 10

## "FINAL JUDGMENT"

(By Michael Collins Piper. Pub. 1995 by The Wolfe Press, Washington, DC. Tel. 1-800-522-6292.)

Piper has subtitled his book *The Missing Link in the JFK Assassination Conspiracy.* We take up this book not simply to lay out the evidence which many investigators have accumulated concerning the Kennedy assassination conspiracy, but also to further pursue our reason for reviewing McCoy's book, *The Politics of Heroin.* Where McCoy introduces us to the illegal strong-arm activities of our own CIA, acting in concert with organized crime in its world-wide drug trafficking, Piper, in investigating the Kennedy assassination, draws a picture of cooperative illegal activities in a number of additional arenas by the secret intelligence agencies of the United States, France, and Israel, i.e., the CIA, the SDECE, and the Mossad, all of which have histories of utilizing the services of organized crime elements in pursuing their various goals. Our approach will be to review the ties Piper has unearthed among the three intelligence agencies, and then the ties existing between each one of them and organized crime. The picture which emerges is one of vast *criminal* power available to those secretly manipulating the affairs of the world, in addition to the monetary, social, and political power we have discussed in our earlier chapters.

McCoy discusses perhaps the first cooperative venture involving the CIA and the SDECE: the securing of Marseille for the use of Corsican gangsters for heroin manufacture and drug transit. During these same years, the late 40's and early 50's, the CIA was helping establish the KMT "army" in Burma, financed by opium the CIA helped the KMT to transport out of Burma and through Thailand. At the same time, the U.S. was funding the French in their war against the North Vietnamese, which also utilized the services of Hmong hill tribes in raising opium to help finance the war. The SDECE and the French military ran that show, which was eventually lost at Dien Bien Phu in 1954. The CIA won the right to continue the Vietnamese War, and mounted a major effort in Laos from 1960 to 1974, copying the strategy of the French military and the SDECE of financing the war by the cultivation and sale of drugs, selling even to American military personnel who were fighting that hated "anti-Communist" war in Southeast Asia.

Piper discusses another CIA-SDECE tie, connected with General Charles DeGaulle's fight with the French Secret Army Organization (OAS) over granting independence to Algeria. (DeGaulle became French President in 1958. Algeria attained independence in 1962.) Piper indicates that the OAS, like the CIA, was highly compartmented, with projects kept secret from all except those who were directly involved and had a "need to know." The Algerian question had created a split within the body politic of the French nation, and most particularly among French politicians and bureaucrats, specifically including the French secret service, the SDECE. Piper references sources which indicate the heavy involvement of SDECE officers in support of the OAS and its goals, goals which included multiple attempts on DeGaulle's life.

Likewise, in the United States the CIA was similarly compartmented. Piper's narrative repeatedly involves James J. Angleton, the CIA's Chief of Counterintelligence under Allen Dulles and then Richard Helms. Angleton, says Piper, served as American intelligence liaison with the SDECE after World War 2 and "maintained close friendships with a number of French intelligence officials throughout his career." During this period of DeGaulle's struggles with the OAS, the CIA "was actively engaged in an effort to topple ... DeGaulle, lending aid and support to the French Secret Army Organization that was fighting DeGaulle's decision to grant independence to Algeria." John F. Kennedy was *supporting* DeGaulle and his Algerian position at this very same time, indicating the degree of autonomy which the CIA was secretly enjoying.

Another connection involved a Frenchman named Jean Souetre, an OAS mercenary who had approached the CIA a few months before the JFK assassination allegedly with information concerning Communists in the SDECE. A CIA document dated about four months after the assassination was uncovered in 1977, which reported that the SDECE wanted help in locating Souetre, and asking why American authorities had expelled him from the U.S. immediately after he had been picked up in Dallas "within 48 hours after Kennedy's death." Souetre, the document said, sometimes went under the name Michel Mertz. Mertz was in turn identified, says Piper, by former CIA insider Robert Morrow, as a member of one of the assassination teams that killed Kennedy. Further, says Morrow, "Mertz was on the Angleton-supervised CIA ZR/Rifle Team of foreign mercenaries where he was known by his code name, QJ/WIN." If you are left wondering about these specific matters, so are we, and so is Piper.

The final tie to be noted involves the CIA's James Angleton and the then deputy chief of the SDECE, Col. Georges deLannurien. Piper says (p. 241): "In a private communication to this author after he read the first draft of *Final Judgment,* a former high-ranking retired French diplomat and intelligence officer stated (based on his own inside knowledge) that a French team – professional assassins – were the actual shooters in Dealey Plaza...." [More about this in a moment.] The unidentified diplomat wrote to Piper indicating that the assassination team had been hired "through the good offices of ... Col. Georges deLannurien. 'It was no coincidence,' he wrote, 'that on the very day of the execution of the President by the French team that [deLannurien] was in Langley meeting with James Jesus Angleton....'

"According to the diplomat, 'There are no coincidences in the suspicion business – just cover-ups. The case of Communist infiltration of the French secret service was an appropriate cover-up to justify the presence of the French deLannurien at Langley, Virginia.'

"Obviously, Angleton and deLannurien were together for a very specific purpose: damage control – making sure that the assassination cover-up fell into place after the crime itself had been committed.

"Angleton himself told the House Assassination Committee that deLannurien had come to his office for just that purpose: seeking assistance in routing out Communist moles in the SDECE."

We go next to the ties which Piper discusses between the SDECE/OAS and the Mossad, the Israeli intelligence agency. The prime issue here revolves around the antipathy felt by the Israelis toward General DeGaulle for granting independence to Algeria. Algeria was a predominantly Muslim state, though it contained a substantial Jewish minority. Piper quotes the Washington Post of March 20, 1982: "Diplomatically, France, shorn of Algeria, returned under President Charles DeGaulle to its traditional policy of friendship with the Arabs – much to the chagrin of Israel and the 200,000 Algerian Jews who had lived peacefully alongside their Arab neighbors until emigrating to France." Piper points out elsewhere (p. 31): "Israel, of course, saw the emergence of another independent Arab republic as a threat to its security, and anyone favoring Algerian independence [e.g., Charles DeGaulle, or John Kennedy] was, thus, advocating a policy deemed threatening to Israel's survival."

The OAS, including its supportive elements within the SDECE, were therefore found to be enjoying covert financial and other support from the Israeli Mossad and other entities supportive of Israel. Piper quotes Israeli historian Benjamin Beit-Hallahmi: "During 1961 and 1962, there were numerous reports of Israeli support for the French OAS movement in Algeria." Historian Stewart Steven is also quoted: "When in 1961 the OAS was created, it was a natural development that Israel, as keen on [French retention of Algeria as a colony] as the OAS themselves, should lock themselves into the [OAS]." An SDECE report supportive of DeGaulle charged that funds from the Israeli Bank Hapoalim were routed to the OAS in Paris via Guy Banister in New Orleans, about whom more will be said shortly.

We now go back to the retired French diplomat and intelligence agent who corresponded with Piper. He told Piper that it was at the behest of the Israeli Mossad that Col. Georges deLannurien arranged for the physical execution of John Kennedy. Specifically, Piper writes: "According to the French intelligence officer, then-Mossad assassination chief Yitzhak Shamir (later Israeli prime minister) arranged the hiring of the assassination team through the good offices of the deputy chief of the SDECE, Col. Georges deLannurien."

We'll get to Piper's discussion of the Israeli motivation for the crime in a few minutes, but in explanation of the Mossad's contracting of the physical assassination with the SDECE, Piper quotes the French officer: "Never the Prime Minister of Israel would have involved Mossad people, American Jews, or CIA personnel in the execution part of the conspiracy. Even the CIA contracts the services of other members of the intelligence community (they like the French style) to wash dirty linens. The right hand does not know what the left did. The cover-up team doesn't know who executes. And the executioners are not interested in the aftermath of their mission. They don't care less."

DeGaulle continued to have trouble with the Mossad after JFK was killed, though he managed to survive assassination efforts directed at himself. After an incident in 1965 involving the Mossad and various elements in his own SDECE, he furiously set about to clean house within the SDECE, and simultaneously expelled the Mossad from France and ordered the termination of all intelligence cooperation between France and Israel. Historian Stewart Steven described the expulsion as "a severe blow, perhaps the most severe the Israeli secret service has ever suffered.... DeGaulle was never to forgive Israel."

We go next to the ties between the Mossad and the CIA. We'll discuss here just three of the many ties which Piper discusses. They are embodied in the names Angleton, Shaw, and Rafizadeh.

Piper devotes a whole chapter to discussing the relationship of the CIA's James Angleton with the Mossad and other of Israel's support entities in the United States and elsewhere. He was recruited into the OSS directly out of Yale University, entered the CIA after it was formed in 1947 following the abolition of the OSS, and by 1954 assumed the position of chief of CIA counterintelligence, under the patronage of Richard Helms, who became CIA director under Lyndon Johnson. Angleton was given his own secret slush fund to operate with essentially as he wished. According to one researcher quoted by Piper, Angleton was the "official CIA liaison for all Allied foreign intelligence agencies" – most particularly including the Mossad. A friend is further quoted: "That's the job that was so sensitive and that's the one that you don't read about. While he was liaising with everyone, he was getting them to do favors for either the CIA ... or for his own agenda.... He could use his contacts with Israeli intelligence, which he kept to himself, as authority for whatever line he was trying to push at the CIA.... No one was going to contradict him, since no one else was allowed to talk to Israeli intelligence."

Piper then quotes Angleton's biographer, Tom Mangold: "I would like to place on the record, however, that Angleton's closest professional friends overseas ... came from the Mossad, and that he was held in immense esteem by his Israeli colleagues and by the state of Israel, which was to award him profound honors after his death." In fact, says Piper, "Following his death in 1987, a monument was unveiled in Israel by its government in his honor."

Piper goes into detail about a number of the joint ventures undertaken by Angleton and the Mossad. These included a plot to kill the Egyptian President Nasser, a similar plot against Israel's enemies in Syria, and, very importantly, an effort to assist Israel in their development of nuclear weapons and to cover up that secret development. This latter effort went to the heart of the disagreement between John Kennedy and the Israeli prime minister David Ben-Gurion, and also between JFK and the CIA.

There is much more, but let us hurry on to Clay Shaw. Shaw's name came to the attention of the public when he was tried in New Orleans by District Attorney Jim Garrison as being a conspirator in the JFK assassination. Though Garrison could not himself prove it, Piper indicates that assassination researchers are substantially unanimous concerning Shaw's CIA affiliation. Garrison suspected it because of the ties which he found between Shaw and Guy Banister and David Ferrie, both having histories of CIA involvements and both tied to pre-assassination contacts with Lee Harvey Oswald, presumably as his CIA "handlers." Piper repeats the claim of one researcher that Shaw was, in fact, "Banister's immediate superior in coordinating CIA operations out of New Orleans."

Further, Shaw had been assigned to the OSS while a young army officer in Britain during World War 2, and had at that time become a good friend of Winston Churchill. This was the same entrée into the intelligence world that we noted above for James

Angleton, and yet also for a third gentleman of great interest, Louis M. Bloomfield. Bloomfield was later hired by J. Edgar Hoover, says Piper, "to serve as a recruiting agent for the FBI's counterespionage division, Division Five. Through this position, Bloomfield became a working partner of Division Five chief William Sullivan, a close friend of James J. Angleton, the Mossad's CIA ally. Sullivan was Angleton's 'man inside' the FBI."

Both Shaw and Bloomfield were directors of a company called Permindex, which was in turn a subsidiary of an organization based in Rome called Centro Mondiale Commerciale (CMC), which translates to World Trade Center. "Permindex" is an acronym for PERmanent INDustrial EXpositions, in accordance with the stated function of CMC which was to establish a worldwide network of trade expositions. Piper lists a few of the other board members, remarkably including a couple with significant ties to Meyer Lansky's organized crime network. The CMC founder, he says, was one Georges Mandel, an Eastern European Jew who Italianized his name to Giorgio Mantello. One of the chief shareholders of CMC, says Piper, "was the Banque De Credit International of Geneva (BCI), established by Tibor Rosenbaum, the longtime Director for Finance and Supply of Israel's Mossad.... BCI also served as a depository for the Permindex account." Piper identifies several of the BCI directors, including "Ernest Israel Japhet, also chairman and president of the Bank Leumi, the largest bank in Israel," plus two men, Ed Levinson and John

Pullman, connected with Meyer Lansky's crime network.

Piper quotes author Paris Flammonde: "Actually it was soon to become evident that the seemingly vast, mighty structure [the CMC] was not a rock of solidarity, but a shell of superficiality; not constructed with mass, supporting promise, but composed of channels through which money flowed back and forth, with no one knowing the source or the destination of these liquid assets."  In short, says Piper, it was a money laundry, a joint venture between the CIA and the Mossad, with ties to organized crime, which we will discuss presently.

Public controversy arose in Europe in 1962 over Permindex involvement with assassination plots against President DeGaulle, involving funds from the Israeli Bank Hapoalim routed to the OAS via Guy Banister in New Orleans.  Permindex was thereupon expelled from Switzerland and Italy, and was subsequently relocated in Johannesburg, South Africa, the move being managed by Dr. David Biegun, the national secretary of a New York organization called the National Committee for Labor Israel, Inc., whose parent organization in Israel controlled the Israeli Bank Hapoalim, referred to above.

As with the case of Angleton, there's much more detail about Shaw that Piper goes into, but you really must get the book yourself.  Let's go on to our last name suggestive of CIA/Mossad ties – Mansur Rafizadeh.

Rafizadeh was the former chief of the SAVAK, which was the secret police of the Shah of Iran, with whom Rafizadeh later broke. The SAVAK was created in 1957, said Rafizadeh in his memoirs, at the joint urging of Israel, the United States, and Britain. Only 4 years earlier, CIA director Allen Dulles and his deputy director Richard Helms had organized a coup in Iran, ousting the elected Prime Minister Mossadegh and installing the Shah, as we outlined in our Chapter 1. Helms and the Shah, says Piper, had been schoolmates as children in Switzerland, a relationship that was capped by Helms finally becoming U.S. Ambassador to Iran.

The CIA and the Mossad cooperated in training SAVAK recruits. To this end the CIA maintained an operation called the International Police Academy in Washington, which trained recruits for both the SAVAK and the Mossad. It was run by one Joseph Shimon, friend of Chicago Mafia boss Sam Giancana among others of questionable character. Shimon once testified before the Senate Intelligence Committee concerning his participation with Giancana and CIA operatives in Miami in assassination plots against Fidel Castro.

Piper's proximate reason for bringing up the SAVAK has to do with the assassination of JFK's brother, Robert F. Kennedy. He describes the thesis put forward by former CIA contract agent Robert Morrow. In Piper's words: "Simply put, Morrow's thesis is this: that the murder of Robert F. Kennedy was a CIA contract hit, carried out through the CIA's long-standing ally in international intrigue, the SAVAK, the secret police of the Shah of Iran – an intelligence agency created in part by Israel's Mossad itself, and tied closely to the Mossad." Piper outlines the available evidence in support of this thesis.

Before going into the ties of the CIA, the SDECE, and the Mossad to organized crime, let's spend a few moments examining the common origins of these agencies. We noted in Chapter 1 that Engdahl noted in his *A Century of War* that the CIA got its start as the OSS, which was created as an adjunct to and in the London offices of the British intelligence agency which Engdahl calls the Special Operations Executive (SOE). Piper adds a few more specifics. Louis Bloomfield, who, with Clay Shaw and James Angleton, had joined the OSS during the war, had in 1938 been recruited into Britain's counterintelligence agency, the same SOE, reporting to another Canadian, Sir William Stephenson. British intelligence, in the person of Sir William Stephenson, appears to be the common key we are seeking.

Stephenson's job in 1938 was to set up British intelligence activities in the United States. Stephenson, the reputed role model for the fictional James Bond, with Louis Bloomfield as his top aide, worked in Operation Underworld, the anti-Nazi activities undertaken during World War 2 by the FBI and the Office of Naval Intelligence utilizing the services of Lucky Luciano and Meyer Lansky. After the war, Stephenson and Bloomfield, says Piper, "were integral to gun-running operations on behalf of the Jewish terrorist underground that later emerged as the government of the new Jewish State in 1948." (Recall that Engdahl had noted that the British purpose for establishing Israel – a small country dependent on Britain and surrounded by squabbling Arabs – was to project British control into the oil-laden Middle-East.) Stephenson in addition worked after the war with a U.S. army counterintelligence officer named General Julius Klein on the task of setting up the Mossad, the secret service of the new Jewish State, and training its officers. Stephenson, said Piper, "became a critical player in the establishment of Israel's Mossad." The British were even involved in the creation of the Iranian SAVAK, according to Mr. Rafizadeh. This omnipresence of British Intelligence is strongly suggestive of control by British political elites, and therefore also by the dynastic banking families listed by Carroll Quigley to whom those politicians are subservient.

We go now to the organized crime ties. The SDECE's cooperative arrangement with the Corsican Mafia in Marseille, in which the SDECE protected the Marseille labs that were producing heroin for American consumption, was discussed at some length in our Chapter 9. Also discussed was the secret SDECE Operation X, involving the French collection of Hmong opium and its delivery to Saigon's controlling criminal gang (the Binh Xuyen) for sale in Saigon's opium dens, utilized as a means of financing the French Indochinese War against the Communist Pathet Lao.

The CIA ties are much more extensive, and seem invariably to involve "The Chairman of the Board" of American organized crime, Meyer Lansky, or one of his subordinates. It was Lansky with whom the Office of Naval Intelligence (ONI) directly dealt in Operation Underworld, described briefly by Piper and much more extensively by McCoy.

But to understand Lansky, a couple of preliminaries are mandatory. First, there was for many years not one, but two branches of "organized crime": the "Sicilian Mafia" and the "Jewish Mafia." The former contained mostly Italian names, such as Lucky Luciano, Frank Costello, Joe Adonis, and Sam Giancana; the latter contained Jewish names, including Meyer Lansky, Micky Cohen, and Bugsy Siegel. The two organizations were for many years in a state of "cooperative competition" which was finally resolved in favor of Lansky upon the retirement, death, or deportation of all those capable of leadership challenges from among the Sicilians. Lansky was not at all bashful about helping along such retirements, deaths, and/or deportations, as Luciano ruefully came to realize.

Second, Lansky for years remained immune from federal prosecution, the only top crime figure (except for his heir Santo Trafficante) to remain untouched. The Justice Department twice refused IRS requests to prosecute him. How come? It went beyond just the "help" that Lansky gave the ONI during the war against the Nazis. Piper tops off his list of evidences on the matter by identifying the carrot and the stick Lansky used against FBI Director J. Edgar Hoover. Piper relates from the biography of the Chicago Mafia chieftain Sam Giancana: "The Giancanas say that Hoover had worked out a deal with Lansky's boyhood friend and criminal associate Frank Costello. The New York mobster would pass horse race betting tips to columnist Walter Winchell, a Hoover intimate. Winchell, in turn, would pass the information on fixed races to Hoover. Hoover would arrange his real bets through his associates, while making minimal bets on his own ticket at the horse races. According to the Giancanas, 'Hoover won every time.'"

The stick, as reported by 1993 author Anthony Summers in his Hoover biography *Official and Confidential*, was that Lansky was blackmailing Hoover with pictures of Hoover engaged in homosexual activity. Summers reports that the pictures were also held by James J. Angleton and his former OSS chief William Donovan. This, of course, would explain Hoover's hands-off policy toward Lansky, and would also explain FBI reticence concerning any investigation of various CIA peccadilloes, up to and including the assassination of John F. Kennedy.

Third and last, in Piper's words: "It was the Meyer Lansky Organized Crime Syndicate that played a pivotal role in the establishment of Israel. Lansky, you see, was Israel's modern-day 'Godfather.' Lansky was with Israel from the beginning." To be more specific, the intellectual outlooks of Lansky and the

Mossad with respect to the fortunes of the new Israeli state were identical.

CIA (and OSS) ties to the Corsican Mafia in Marseille, to Lansky in Operation Underworld, and to various parties dealing with opium cultivation and transport in Indochina and Afghanistan (including Meyer Lansky and Santo Trafficante) have been thoroughly covered in our review of Alfred McCoy's book in Chapter 9. Piper notes that Angleton, working for the OSS in Britain and Italy during the war, had contact with the Lansky-linked Operation Underworld. By 1951, Angleton was stationed in Rome doing OSS counterintelligence work, where he was supporting "the underground Jewish network that ran down from Eastern Europe through Italy to the ports where shiploads of immigrants were loaded for Palestine." One of his contacts was Teddy Kollek, who was later to be the mayor of Jerusalem. Kollek, says Piper, was engaged in arms smuggling to Palestine in conjunction with Meyer Lansky and Major Louis M. Bloomfield, the aforementioned deputy to Sir William Stephenson. Angleton was obviously aware, even as he worked for the American OSS, of the illegal activities of Meyer Lansky in acquiring and smuggling arms into Palestine.

The Giancana biography referred to above also claimed that Mafia figure Carlos Marcello, the New Orleans "boss" (at the sufferance of Meyer Lansky, the real boss), "was a co-conspirator with the CIA in gunrunning operations and a fervent supporter of the anti-Castro exiles. It was an arrangement ... aimed at returning Cuba to its pre-Castro glory – meaning its lucrative casinos and vice rackets [which Lansky had previously run]." The biography elsewhere had Sam Giancana showing his brother an ancient Roman coin and declaring: "Look, this is one of the Roman gods. This one has two faces ... two sides. That's what we are, the Outfit and the CIA ... two sides of the same coin." Piper quotes a great deal of additional detail concerning the personnel and activities of the joint CIA / Organized Crime activities to assassinate Fidel Castro, which the CIA labeled Operation Mongoose. Included were General Edward Lansdale directing the operation, assisted by Ted Shackley and Thomas Clines, all also much involved in the CIA war and drug operation in Indochina. Included also was CIA operative E. Howard Hunt, who was later personally implicated in the JFK assassination conspiracy. Piper concludes, "So it was that the CIA and Organized Crime entered into a complex – and controversial – liaison for a mutual aim: the elimination of Cuban dictator Fidel Castro. There is no question that Trafficante, [Johnny] Rosselli and Giancana did indeed help coordinate assassination plots against Castro with representatives of the CIA.... However, as one author succinctly put it: 'Lansky was the top man in the CIA-Mafia plot against Castro.' All of [his subordinates'] operations in league with the CIA were being conducted with Lansky's approval and under Lansky's watchful eye."

Rosselli and Giancana were later murdered, effectively shutting them up, but the 1992 Giancana biography alleged that "The Outfit" and the CIA were also jointly planning JFK's assassination, though Piper suggests that that operation was probably only one of several "false flags" set up by whoever the master assassination planners were to direct suspicion away from the true culprits. Nevertheless, the Giancana biography had Sam explaining: "The politicians and the CIA made it real simple. We'd each provide men for the hit. I'd oversee the Outfit side of things and throw in Jack Ruby and some extra backup, and the CIA would put their own guys on to take care of the rest." Piper notes that Santo Trafficante, being Meyer Lansky's chosen heir, remained untouched, dying of kidney failure in 1987. Anything that Trafficante contributed to the Kennedy assassination, however, Meyer Lansky surely knew about and approved.

The Giancana biography also detailed the cut that Sam Giancana said the CIA was getting from the drug traffic being managed by Santo Trafficante: "The CIA looked the other way – allowing over $100 million a year in illicit drugs to flow through Havana into the United States. It was an arrangement similar to all the rest they'd made, he said. The CIA received 10 percent of the take on the sale of narcotics, which they utilized 'for their undercover slush fund.' Such illegally earned moneys were stashed away by the CIA in Swiss, Italian, Bahamian, and Panamanian accounts."

One last tie which Piper outlines between the CIA and Organized Crime involves Jack Ruby. Piper quotes sources detailing Ruby's gunrunning activities under the guidance of the CIA both to Castro before his takeover of Cuba and to Castro's opponents afterwards. Ruby was clearly well-known to both the CIA and the FBI before the JFK assassination. Piper relates: "[Reporter John] Henshaw also wrote that Texas Attorney General Waggoner Carr was being kept under surveillance by the FBI because he had undisclosed evidence: 'The evidence includes a copy of the missing film taken moments before Jack Ruby shot and killed Lee Harvey Oswald. The film covers Ruby's progress through the FBI and police screens guarding the entrance of the Dallas Police headquarters. Two cameramen had been assigned by a Dallas TV station to cover the entrance, but were ordered by federal agents to knock off film footage which showed a high official of the Justice Department escorting [Ruby] through the two security screens.'" A suspicious person might smell the hands of CIA and/or FBI persons here as well, acting in concert with The Outfit.

We finally get to ties between the Mossad (plus its organizational appurtenances) and Meyer Lansky's organized crime apparatus. We'll start with the primary tie and flesh it out a little from there. That primary tie is in the person of Rabbi Tibor Rosenbaum. As we mentioned above in our discussion of Clay Shaw, Rosenbaum was the long-time Director for Finance and Supply of Israel's Mossad. To serve Israel's purposes, Rosenbaum created the Banque de Credit International in Geneva, Switzerland. Rosenbaum, having earlier served as international vice president of the World Jewish Congress, and as a co-founder of the World Zionist Congress, and as a director of the Jewish Agency in Geneva, attracted deposits from such agencies into his BCI. The bank, says Piper, "was very much an Israeli government /

Mossad operation, critical to the survival of the Jewish State."

But the tie to Organized Crime? Piper continues: "BCI was to become Meyer Lansky's primary overseas money laundering bank – sharing those money laundering services that the bank provided to Israel's Mossad. In fact, during its heyday, BCI included among its board of directors two longtime Lansky associates, Edward Levinson and John Pullman.... Levinson was one of the operators of the Fremont Casino in Las Vegas, a front man for Lansky's close friend, Joseph 'Doc' Stacher, and a frequent business partner of Bobby Baker, reputed 'bagman' for Lyndon Johnson. John Pullman ... was Lansky's key international money handler." Recall that we encountered Pullman in our previous chapter, who was then traveling to Hong Kong for Lansky to cement deals with the Hong Kong heroin merchants.

One of the real keys to the Lansky / Israeli tie, says Piper, was money. Lansky needed a network to launder his criminal proceeds. Israel needed money to survive. It was a natural marriage of interests. The importance to Israel of those early money-raising efforts is described by reporter Jim Hougan: "During the Second World War [Rosenbaum had become] a hero of the resistance through his underground activities on behalf of the Jews. After the War he became a delegate to the World Zionist Congress in Basel, where plans were made for the creation of Israel.... This was at the height of Zionist terrorist attacks in Palestine. A superb clandestine operator, Rosenbaum is said to have been instrumental in providing weapons to the Haganah and Stern Gang. That would tend to explain why the [BCI], 'Rosenbaum's Baby,' became gambling czar Meyer Lansky's Number One conduit abroad.

"Rosenbaum was more than a friend to the Jews, however.... The newspaper *Ha'aretz* solemnly declared, 'Tibor Rosenbaum is Israel.' And the paper wasn't far from wrong.... Rosenbaum's bank ... served as a source of secret funds for the Mossad, Israel's intelligence service, and as one of the country's primary weapons brokers. At one point 'as much as ninety percent of the Israeli Defense Ministry's external budget flowed through [the BCI].'

"In economic matters he was equally important, founding the Israel Corporation with the help of Baron Edmond de Rothschild, a French aristocrat committed to the Zionist cause. The raison d'être of the Israel Corporation was to raise money among the world's Jews, money to be invested in a variety of public and semi-public Israeli enterprises. By finding money abroad to fund development projects in 'the homeland,' Rosenbaum and Rothschild freed Israeli tax moneys to be spent on the country's critical military needs....

"The mix of Mob, Mossad, ... and Rothschild moneys was an intoxicating one in which the common denominator appears to have been a love of Israel. Certainly Rosenbaum ... shared that affection with Lansky and the French baron."

Let's flesh out the structure a little more. Says Piper: "It was in 1947 that Rudolph Sonneborn (husband of New York publisher Dorothy Schiff) set up an entity known as the Sonneborn Institute. It was this institute that provided the Jewish Haganah, and later the Irgun, in Palestine with arms and money. The Institute's coordinator for arms smuggling to the Jewish underground was Louis Bloomfield. Working with Bloomfield were liquor baron Samuel Bronfman ... and Lansky himself." Bloomfield, you will recall, was aide to Sir William Stephenson in Operation Underworld during World War 2, was later a director and board chairman of Permindex, and was also the attorney and front man for the Bronfman bootlegging family of Canada, which built its fortune working with the Lansky Organized Crime Syndicate in the illegal liquor trade, and which now owns a controlling interest in Time Warner, the giant American media conglomerate. Sam Bronfman's family and members of Meyer Lansky's "Jewish Mafia" provide major financial support to the Anti-Defamation League of B'nai B'rith (ADL), whose origins go back to 1913, when it was incorporated by one Sigmund Livingston as a public relations entity whose prime purpose was to defend Jewish mobsters in New York City. It was thereafter used for that purpose by Arnold Rothstein in the 20's and by Meyer Lansky up through the 60's. J. Edgar Hoover, who protected Lansky from prosecution, had a foundation named in his honor which was established by the ADL. The first president of the foundation was Rabbi Paul Richman, the Washington director of the ADL.

The difference between Piper's book and the many other books that have been written about the JFK assassination is that Piper decided to follow the leads that were associated with motivation as opposed to the mechanics of the deed, such as how many shots were fired, from where, and how they might have bounced around, etc.  He asked instead such questions as Who gained by JFK's death? and Who was capable of mounting such a masterfully orchestrated cover-up?  This led him to examine the motivations of the major covert action agencies which we have discussed above.  So let's turn finally to the relationships which Piper has uncovered between John Kennedy and each of the SDECE, the CIA, the Mossad, and Organized Crime.

Taking the SDECE first, John Kennedy had announced his support for DeGaulle's policy of granting independence to Algeria.  In so doing he earned the enmity of the French Secret Army Organization (OAS), and also those elements within the SDECE supportive of the OAS.  As Piper describes it, "The debate over Algerian independence had sparked a major crisis within France, and the French OAS, which fought Algerian freedom, considered John F. Kennedy an enemy second only to Charles DeGaulle."  These facts make it understandable how a "French" team might plausibly have been recruited to perform the JFK assassination, as Piper says was reported to him by a French ex-diplomat and intelligence officer.

JFK and the CIA parted company on at least three major policy issues: Algeria, the Bay of Pigs, and Vietnam.  Over Algeria, we noted near the beginning of this chapter that the CIA was secretly engaged in supporting the effort by the OAS to overthrow French President Charles DeGaulle. Piper does not say whether or not Kennedy was aware of such CIA help. The CIA, however, was fully aware of Kennedy's support of DeGaulle, producing what amounted to at least a one-sided disagreement, if not a direct confrontation.

The second issue was the Bay of Pigs. Kennedy and the CIA each blamed the other for the operation's failure. Piper quotes from Mark Lane's *Plausible Denial:* "John F. Kennedy made it clear that he planned to destroy the CIA. The *New York Times* reported on April 25, 1966 ... that 'as the enormity of the Bay of Pigs disaster came home to him, [Kennedy] said to one of the highest officials of his Administration that he wanted 'to splinter the CIA in a thousand pieces and scatter it to the winds.' He clearly was not suggesting a modest legislative proposal or executive order to modify or reform the organization. The total destruction of the Agency was his apparent objective." Piper further quotes from *Plausible Denial* describing the preliminary steps Kennedy actually took in trying to bring the Agency to heel.

The third issue was Vietnam. Piper again quotes Mark Lane: "[In October 1963, New York Times columnist Arthur] Krock pointed out that John F. Kennedy had gone to war against the CIA.... The columnist stated that President Kennedy sent Henry Cabot Lodge, his Ambassador to Vietnam, with orders to the CIA on two separate occasions, and in both cases the CIA ignored those orders, saying that it was different from what the agency thought should be done. In other words the CIA had decided that it – not the President – would make the decisions as to how American foreign policy should be conducted."

Kennedy sent Defense Secretary McNamara and General Maxwell Taylor on a fact-finding trip to Vietnam. They returned and reported that they believed that the U.S. could withdraw all personnel from Vietnam by the end of 1965. Col. Fletcher Prouty thereupon commented in his book *The Secret Team*: "Now we can see why they chose that date. This was the date that the President had used in his own discussions with his closest advisors. They all knew that he planned to announce a pullout once he had been re-elected." The CIA, of course, heavy into its "anti-Communist" war in Indochina which was as a side effect developing the Golden Triangle opium trade, wanted no part of JFK's withdrawal plans.

Piper, in investigating these policy differences between Kennedy and the CIA was also aware that many Kennedy assassination researchers were now convinced that the CIA had at least some partial role in the assassination. He devotes an entire chapter to the assassination facts developed by attorney Mark Lane, who reported in his own book, *Plausible Denial*, his experiences in a related trial. The trial actually involved a libel case, but the jury was asked to find for the defendant based on the jury becoming convinced that the CIA was in fact implicated in the assassination. The jury forewoman issued a statement upon the release of Lane's written account of the trial, saying: "Mr. Lane was asking us [the jury] to do something very difficult.   He was asking us to believe John Kennedy had been killed by our own government.  Yet when we examined the evidence closely, we were compelled to conclude that the CIA had indeed killed President Kennedy."  Piper, of course, only holds in his book that the CIA was a major conspirator, but did not necessarily employ the man who held the gun that shot the bullet that killed the President.   The trial outcome suffered a mysterious media blackout, explaining why you probably never heard about it.

Next we look at John Kennedy's policy differences with Israel and its Mossad.  There were perhaps three significant issues: Algeria, nuclear weapon development, and Palestinian resettlement.   We discussed earlier how Israeli leaders felt that a new Arab state of Algeria would represent an added threat to the security of Israel, and since both Kennedy and France's DeGaulle were supportive of Algerian independence, those two men were to be regarded as enemies of the Israeli state.   The feeling toward Kennedy, however, went much deeper.   The Israelis felt that Kennedy had betrayed them.   JFK's father, Joseph P. Kennedy, Sr., as Ambassador to Great Britain in the late 30's, had been supportive of Neville Chamberlain and of his policy of appeasing Hitler. Later in his life, he renounced his former views and pledged his support for the Jewish community.   That community remained suspicious of him, however, and was even more so following John Kennedy's Senate speech proclaiming his support for an independent Algeria.

Kennedy, however, recognizing in 1960 that he needed both money and votes from the Jewish community, made moves to appease the pro-Israel lobby, very successfully, it turned out. His contact with the lobby was Abraham Feinberg, president of the Israel Bond Organization, who later acknowledged, "My path to power was cooperation in terms of what they needed – campaign money." Kennedy met with Feinberg "and a host of other wealthy Jewish Americans" in Feinberg's New York apartment. The group agreed to support Kennedy to the tune of $500,000. Kennedy, said Feinberg, "got emotional" with gratitude. To his own intimates, however, Kennedy was outraged. He said that he was told, "We're willing to pay your bills if you'll let us have control of your Middle East policy," and he vowed that if he did get to be President, he was going to do something about eliminating the influence of special interest lobbies – especially foreign pressure groups – in American election campaigns. After his election, he *did* introduce such campaign reform legislation, and he *did* proclaim an even-handed Middle Eastern policy – that the United States "will act promptly and decisively against any nation in the Middle East which attacks its neighbor," a policy clearly directed at both the Israelis and the Arabs. Israel, says Piper, "was not happy."

Of much greater import, however, was Kennedy's stance on nuclear weaponry. Upon becoming President, he was informed by the Eisenhower administration that Israel was secretly developing nuclear weapons at a desert site known as Dimona. Kennedy was determined to support a non-proliferation policy, however, and set about, as one of his primary concerns, to derail the Dimona development. Therefore, says Piper, "from the very beginning of his presidency, John F. Kennedy found himself at severe odds with the government of Israel."

Israeli Prime Minister David Ben-Gurion publicly announced that the Dimona project was for the purpose of studying "desert flora and fauna." Charles DeGaulle, who had helped Israel design the Dimona nuclear reactor as a power plant, was not amused. Nor was John Kennedy. According to Israeli historians Raviv and Melman, writing in 1990, Kennedy met with Ben-Gurion, stated his position, and demanded periodic international inspection of the site. Ben-Gurion resisted, and there thus began what amounted to a "secret war" between Kennedy and Israel, which was not resolved until Kennedy was killed and replaced by Lyndon Johnson. Author Seymour Hersh, writing in 1991, said: "Israel's bomb, and what to do about it, became a White House fixation, part of the secret presidential agenda that would remain hidden for the next thirty years." Hersh, further noting that this secret war had never been noted by any of Kennedy's biographers, evoked the following comment from Piper: "If indeed it had been, ... the mystery behind the JFK assassination might have been unraveled long, long ago."

For here, found in 1990, was the missing motivation. The relations between Ben-Gurion and Kennedy deteriorated down to the level of personal hatred. Ben-Gurion, who, according to Abraham Feinberg, hated old Joe Kennedy as an "anti-Semite," harbored a contempt for the younger Kennedy, says Piper, that "was growing by leaps and bounds – almost pathologically." Hersh writes that on Kennedy's part, he was getting fed up with the fact that the Israeli "sons of bitches lie to me constantly about their nuclear capability." Hersh then wrote, "Kennedy's relationship with Ben-Gurion remained at an impasse over Dimona, and the correspondence between the two became increasingly sour. None of those letters has been made public." Given the fact of Piper's present book, those letters today would be of very great interest.

Kennedy further proposed, said Piper, that Palestinian refugees "either be permitted to return to their homes in Israel or be compensated by Israel and resettled in the Arab countries or elsewhere. Former Undersecretary of State George Ball, writing in 1992, quoted as follows from a Ben-Gurion letter commenting on the Kennedy proposal, sent to the Israeli Ambassador in Washington for him to convey to Jewish leaders in America: "Israel will regard this plan as a more serious danger to her existence than all the threats of the Arab dictators and kings, than all the Arab armies, than all of Nasser's missiles and his Soviet MIGs.... Israel will fight against this implementation down to the last man."

Author Seymour Hersh reported that in one of Ben-Gurion's last communications with Kennedy he wrote: "Mr. President, my people have a right to exist ... and this existence is in danger." He then demanded that Kennedy sign a security treaty with Israel. Kennedy refused, whereupon David Ben-Gurion, on June 16, 1963, resigned from office. Piper suggests that it was at this time, just before his resignation, that Ben-Gurion gave the order to the Mossad's assassinations chief, Yitzhak Shamir, to proceed with plans for Kennedy's assassination.

In summary, JFK would not countenance a nuclear Israel, and Israel perceived Kennedy's Palestinian resolution and nuclear non-proliferation policies as threats to Israel's very existence. From Piper's perspective, with this strong motivational information newly in hand, the rest of the known elements of the assassination conspiracy fell easily into place, with only a few final pieces of the puzzle to be inserted in the future. Let's put several of these last pieces in right now by examining the relationship between John Kennedy and the Organized Crime empire of Meyer Lansky.

The story is simple in its outline. Back in 1927, Joe Kennedy Sr. had a shipment of his bootleg whiskey from Ireland hijacked by a Luciano-Lansky mob in southern New England, with considerable loss of life, and significant financial loss to Kennedy. Things were smoothed over, but Lansky biographers said that Kennedy held a grudge against Lansky from that time on, and, in fact, "passed the hostility on to his sons."

When Lansky later found out that Kennedy was sympathetic to the Nazi movement, Lansky was furious, and "swore a blood revenge on the whole [Kennedy] family."

Papa Joe Kennedy also transgressed the territory of the "Jewish Mafia" in Detroit during Prohibition days, and a Detroit contract was taken out on him. He went to the Chicago Mafia boss Sam Giancana to beg for his life, and Sam intervened on his behalf, putting Kennedy ever after in Chicago's debt. Years later, Joe Kennedy again went to Sam Giancana, this time to ask for his help in getting his son John elected President. Giancana, said his biographers, asked what the quid pro quo would be, and Kennedy responded, "You help me now, Sam, and I'll see to it that Chicago – that you – can sit in the goddamned Oval Office if you want…. He'll be your man. I swear to that. My son – the President of the United States – will owe you his father's life. He won't refuse you, ever. You have my word."

Mafia money thereafter poured into JFK's campaign, and following some questionable vote-counting in Illinois, he was elected. The aftermath, however, was not what Giancana and his boss Lansky expected. Says Piper, "Soon after JFK assumed the presidency, an unexpected war on organized crime began. Robert Kennedy, who had cut his teeth prosecuting mobsters as a counsel for the Senate's 'racket's committee' was named attorney general, and it was apparent that he was taking his new job seriously." Sam Giancana, says his biographers, responded: "It's a brilliant move on Joe [Kennedy]'s part. He'll have Bobby wipe us out to cover their own dirty tracks, and it'll all be done in the name of the Kennedy 'war on organized crime.' Brilliant. Just fuckin' brilliant."

Seth Kantor, Jack Ruby's biographer, summarized the fallout of the double-cross: "As Attorney General, [Robert F. Kennedy] got more indictments on members of America's criminal industry than had any previous prosecutor, pursuing them relentlessly. Meyer Lansky, for instance, no longer was safe behind the bolted doors of that industry's executive suite." Bobby Kennedy had bypassed Hoover's FBI and put together a Justice Department group called the Organized Crime Division, and "was stalking Lansky's secret operations in the Bahamas and Las Vegas."

If *you* were running Organized Crime, wouldn't you feel a little peeved at the Kennedy family?

We can't resist at least touching on one additional "detail" that Piper covers involving The Mob. That has to do with the death of Marilyn Monroe. The Mob, in the person of Micky Cohen, Lansky's man in Los Angeles, arranged for Marilyn, "America's sweetheart," to meet President Kennedy at a Hollywood party. Kennedy, as was his wont, took the bait, and a continuing affair commenced. This "arranged liaison" had a serious ulterior purpose, however, which was for Marilyn to find out what Kennedy planned for U.S. policy toward Israel. Marilyn resisted these demands, insisting that she had neither any knowledge of or interest in politics, but pressure on her to find out nevertheless continued. She was found dead on August 5, 1962. Piper relates a great deal more about the circumstances, and suggests that, in the light of all the other matters he has discovered and integrated with respect to the JFK assassination, it seems highly plausible that Marilyn was killed because Israel / Lansky / Cohen could not risk having Marilyn ever talk about what had been demanded of her. You will find Piper's account of these matters highly interesting.

Following JFK's death, what happened with respect to all the issues that JFK's enemies were concerned about?

1. The Dimona nuclear reactor went critical in early 1964. That event elicited no reaction from President Johnson, who raised no objection to Israel's continuing nuclear weapons development.

2. Major military aid to Israel was started in LBJ's fiscal 1965, and turned into a flood in fiscal 1966. Writing in 1984, author Stephen Green said: "America has given Israel over $17 billion in military aid since 1946, virtually all of which – over 99 percent – has been provided since 1965."

3. Kennedy's plan to withdraw from Vietnam was reversed by Johnson just a few days after the assassination. In the following months the American commitment was increased "from under 20,000 troops to approximately a quarter of a million."

4. The autonomy of the CIA, including its covert action branch, was preserved.

5. The Kennedy war against Organized Crime came to an immediate and sudden halt, protecting, among

others, J. Edgar Hoover's FBI empire. The Golden Triangle heroin development continued, and drug smuggling, money laundering, and the addiction of American youth continued apace.

In short, the international intelligence agencies, acting in concert with the international organized crime rings, displayed in the JFK assassination affair their immense capabilities for controlling the course of history. The cover-up, of course, required the services of additional agencies in the service of our elites, particularly the mass media, as Piper discusses at some length.

But we take particular interest in the revelations concerning the British antecedents of Permindex, the CIA, the Mossad, and Israel itself, since they suggest even higher-level ties back to the banking families identified by Carroll Quigley and others whose books we have reviewed in our previous chapters. In our next chapter we will undertake to trace the circle of influence back to that starting point.

Chapter 11

## "DOPE, INC."

(By the Editors of *Executive Intelligence Review* (EIR). Commissioned by Lyndon H. LaRouche, Jr. Pub. 1st ed. in 1978, 2nd ed. in 1986, 3rd ed. in 1992 by EIR, PO Box 17390, Washington, DC 20041-0390.)

McCoy's *The Politics of Heroin* describes how the cultivation and distribution of drugs have in recent times been secretly promoted by American and French governments via the activities of their covert intelligence agencies. Piper's *Final Judgment* enlarges the picture by including the British and Israeli governments and agencies, and uncovering a scope of criminal enterprises larger than just the drug trade which has been undertaken by these agencies in cooperation with the world's organized crime rings. The EIR's *Dope, Inc.* seeks to identify the kingpins at the top of the drug trade by examining the origins of the trade, by studying the paths via which drug profits are laundered, and by tracing the ownership of the controlling corporate entities.

The first few chapters of *Dope, Inc.* serve to update the 1986 edition to 1992, and are also useful in further fleshing out the subject matter of McCoy's and Piper's books. McCoy discusses the cocaine trafficking attendant to the Nicaraguan Contra affair, but the

EIR is less bashful about naming names: "Colonel [Oliver] North was the day-to-day operations officer for the Contra resupply program.  But it was Vice President George Bush, the former CIA director, who was formally in charge of the entire Reagan administration Central America covert operations program." Reagan created and placed Bush in charge of the secret "Crisis Pre-Planning Group" with North as its secretary.  In that capacity, North "ran the Central America spook show – under George Bush."  The EIR quotes memos from North's personal notebooks which indicate that North was fully aware of the cocaine traffic to the United States which was generating funds from American addicts to pay for Contra arms.

According to the EIR, North and other administration officials were also involved in the arms-for-hostages swap with the Lebanese terrorists who were holding American hostages.  Negotiations were conducted with a Syrian drug and arms smuggler named Mansur Al-Kassar, who was a supplier of arms to the PLO, a black market partner of Syria's Vice President Rifaat al-Assad, and a known business associate of Medellin Cartel boss Pablo Escobar Gaviria.  North did not manage to get any hostages freed, though Al-Kassar's drug-running activities were protected, and though he received, in one transaction that was uncovered, $1.5 million from North for Soviet-bloc arms which went to the Contras.  Al-Kassar's drug-runners were suspected of being involved in the bombing of Pan Am Flight 103 over Lockerbie, Scotland, on December 21, 1988, as was publicly suggested by U.S. Rep. James Traficant among others.  Syria's role in the flourishing Middle-Eastern heroin and hashish trade into Europe, along with Al-Kassar's possible role in the Flight 103 bombing, have both been deliberately covered up, says the EIR, by British and American intelligence agencies.

Columbian and Middle Eastern dope trafficking seems to the EIR to have a recurring common denominator of Israeli involvement. In April 1989, the EIR says, "a DEA and U.S. Customs Service report was covered in the media alleging that New York's Republic National Bank was serving as a money-laundering facility for Middle East and Ibero-American narcotics-trafficking organizations. Republic National Bank is owned by Edmond Safra, a prominent Jewish banker of Lebanese descent" having world-wide banking operations. The report said that Safra and his bank were part of a money-laundering network run out of the Zurich-based Shakarchi Trading Co., which "operates as a currency exchange company and is utilized by some of the world's largest drug-trafficking organizations to launder the proceeds of their drug-trafficking activities.... Shakarchi Trading Company maintains accounts at the Republic National Bank of New York...." Mr. Safra, the EIR notes, in 1989 donated "a reported $1 million to his favorite charity – the Anti-Defamation League."

(The EIR goes way beyond the brief description of the ADL which appears in Piper's book, which simply painted the ADL as a public relations support arm of the "Jewish Mafia" going back to 1913, with Arnold Rothstein and Meyer Lansky its primary early beneficiaries. The EIR devotes a 49-page appendix to the ADL, which we will briefly review in a few moments.)

On December 15, 1989, a Columbian army shoot-out with Medellin Cartel boss Rodriguez Gacha occurred. Gacha was killed, and shortly thereafter large stockpiles of cartel arms were seized, the majority of which were found to have been made in Israel. After months of investigation, it was determined that "Israeli intelligence ... had been providing weapons and terrorist training to the Medellin Cartel's assassination squads in collaboration with British mercenaries.... The funds to purchase the weapons ... had been provided by the U.S. State Department through a program personally run by Assistant Secretary of State Elliott Abrams," who later pled guilty to Iran-Contra crimes."

EIR continues: "The trainer of Rodriguez Gacha's killer squads was a reserve Israeli army colonel named Yair Klein.... In a parallel operation, a group a British mercenaries also engaged in training the cartel hit squads.... The involvement of British intelligence in the CIA-Mossad Columbia deal was further confirmed when Louis Blom-Cooper and Geoffrey Robertson, both officials of Amnesty International, which is funded by British intelligence, were deployed to cover up the official U.S., British, and Israeli government sponsorship of the Klein operation...."

A shipload of Israeli arms was transferred on April 24, 1989 in the British Crown Colony of Antigua, to a Panamanian-registered ship, *Sea Point*, and "shuttled off to Rodriguez Gacha in Columbia…. The escrow deposit to ensure that the hundreds of guns left Israel on time had come through the Miami branch of the Israeli Bank Hapoalim" into which Elliott Abrams had deposited the funds to purchase the arms. On December 20, 1989, just a few days after the start of the Gacha shoot-out, the U.S. under President Bush invaded Panama, overthrew General Noriega, and installed in his place "a local Panamanian lawyer, Guillermo "Porky" Endara. A review of court records shows that President Endara and several of his law partners were the owners of record of the ship *Sea Point* in April 1989 when the ship had delivered the Israeli weapons to Rodriguez Gacha…. [Furthermore,] in Panama City, Endara was the co-owner, along with Rodriguez Gacha, of the drug money-laundering Banco Interoceánico." The British-Mossad-CIA intelligence combine thus lost or disposed of a former drug ally (Gacha) in Columbia, but almost simultaneously picked up a new one (Endara) in Panama.

A little more light is shed on this matter by the EIR: "In 1986, in Panama, Gen. Manuel Noriega closed down First Interamericas Bank after it was proven that the bank was owned by the Cali Cartel. In December 1989, U.S. occupation forces invaded Panama … and proceeded to place four members of the board of that same First Interamericas Bank in power – as President, attorney general, president of the Supreme Court, and minister of the Treasury. The result: Drug running in Panama has *grown* since Noriega's ouster." Bush's strategy? "Specifically, a working alliance has been created between the U.S. government and the Cali Cartel, against the Medellin Cartel of Pablo Escobar and Rodriguez Gacha. The result has been ... that the Cali Cartel has become dominant among the different Columbian groups ... all with behind-the-scenes American approval." It seems clear that Washington wants the drug trade to continue, but that it also wants to be able to hire and fire those who it chooses to participate in the trade.

The EIR published a report in November 1990 detailing the growth of narcotic revenues over the immediately preceding years. The totals were astonishing, and contradicted the Bush administration's optimistic reports on the same subject. Growth was phenomenal in cultivation and street sales of all the major drugs – heroine, cocaine, and marijuana. Street sales of all drugs throughout the world had increased from $175 billion back in 1977 to $558 billion in 1989. Cumulative sales from 1977 to 1989 of drugs raised only in Ibero-America (Mexico and South and Central America) is nearly $2 trillion, dwarfing even Ibero-America's gigantic foreign debt of $430 billion. Worldwide addiction continues to grow. Some 70 million Americans are estimated to have used drugs at some point, with many of these remaining as addicts. Consumption has jumped throughout South America, including such places as Brazil, Peru, and Columbia. More millions of people are users in India, Iran, Pakistan, Egypt, and other Asian countries. Europe is another very large market, with an unknown number of consumers.

Very little of the money raised from street sales is returned and kept by the countries raising the drugs. Some of the money is laundered by businesses having high cash turnover, such as restaurants and casinos. A great deal of it is sent out of the country in suitcases and deposited in off-shore banks which don't have the laws which U.S. banks do requiring cash deposits over $10,000 to be reported to the IRS. The great bulk of the $558 billion annual revenue (in 1989) is deposited in banks elsewhere. "Although no precise figures are available," says the EIR, "a leading anti-drug prosecutor in Switzerland, Paolo Bernasconi, told Italy's *La Stampa* newspaper in January 1990 that the leading money-laundering centers include the United States (Miami and Wall Street), Canada, Great Britain, and, of course, Switzerland."

Further, far from fighting the trade, the banks are fighting to get their share: "As the London *Economist* wrote proudly in June 1989: 'It is obvious that drug dealers use banks.... The business ... has become part of the financial system.... If you had morals or ethics in this business, you would not be in it.'" The EIR further writes, "As one banker stated in an off-the-record discussion in London in 1986: Dope 'is the biggest source of new financial business in the world today.... I know banks which will literally kill to secure a chunk of this action.' The banker worked for one of Wall Street's biggest investment houses, Merrill Lynch."

The EIR insists that any strategy of fighting the drug trade must aim at the drug proceeds. "A competent war on drugs must begin with a war against the banking institutions and bankers who 'launder' Dope, Inc.'s ill-gotten gains." And: "Shut down the drug money-laundering by the major Anglo-American banks, and the dope cartel would choke to death on its own profits!" And: "Dope, Inc.'s vulnerable flank is the international network of banks and other financial institutions that 'launder' the cartel's $558 billion per year in gross revenue.... Action by governments against the drug bankers could rapidly shut down Dope, Inc." And yet, says the EIR, "no government has ever touched the *system* which allowed [the drug trade to develop]. At best, a few accounts here and there have been seized. To this day, money-laundering is not even a criminal offense in 8 out of the 15 industrial nations. In the United States, the center of the problem, government action is a joke: No top management has *ever* been charged or prosecuted for criminal money-laundering activity."

There is negligible opium or cocaine presently being grown in the U.S., says the EIR, but the same can't be said for marijuana. In fact, the 1987 U.S. pot harvest was valued by the EIR at $33.1 billion, barely less than the receipts tabulated by the USDA of the largest single farm commodity in 1987, which was cattle and calves yielding $33.8 billion. Marijuana receipts were greater than any grain crop, or in fact any other commodity excepting cattle. The major pot-growing states were Hawaii, Washington, Oregon,

California, and a set of relatively impoverished states running from Arkansas and Missouri through Georgia and North Carolina. A great deal of the financial stress on farmers which helped produce this situation was the high-interest policies of the Fed imposed during the 80's, which devastated *all* businesses which had become dependent upon low-cost credit. The EIR relates instances in which banks actually suggested to financially stressed farmers and ranchers that they try their hand at the profitable marijuana business to help get their bank loans paid off.

We made reference near the beginning of our review to the appendix which the EIR has included on the Anti-Defamation League (ADL). It's an amazing compendium of information which utterly frees one of the misapprehension that the ADL is simply an honorable, upright, civic-minded institution supporting Judaism. The appendix goes into detail concerning the following matters related to the ADL and its operations:

- **What Is It?** Basically, a public relations front for the Rothstein-Lansky branch of American Organized Crime, though it operates formally as a tax-exempt public interest organization under Section 501(c)3 of the Internal Revenue Service Codes.
- **Structure and Key Personnel:** It is an organization having a National Commission of about 150 members, a National Executive Committee, officers, and a number of standing committees. Membership is by nomination or invitation only. The standing committees and their chairmen are listed.

Nine operatives in the "active core" of the ADL are listed, some of whom are mentioned below.

- **Ties to Organized Crime:**  This gets interesting.  First mention is of former ADL national chairman Kenneth Bialkin, who, says the EIR, masterminded the $60 million looting of Investors Overseas Service (IOS) by financier Robert Vesco, an indicted fugitive living in Havana and charged with complicity in Medellin Cartel cocaine smuggling from 1974 to 1989.  In January 1980, a jury ordered Bialkin's law firm to pay $35 million to the victims of the IOS looting, and found Bialkin to be instrumental in that fraud.  The IOS was believed by law enforcement officials to have been used by Meyer Lansky as a conduit for laundering his illicit drug profits.

  A second mention is of the Sterling National Bank of New York City.  It was charged by Italian authorities in January 1982 of looting $27 million from the Banca Privata Italiana.  The chairman of Sterling, says the EIR, "both at the time of the alleged theft and today, is Theodore H. Silbert, another honorary vice-chairman of the ADL and the former head of the ADL Appeal, its major fundraising arm.  Law enforcement sources have identified Sterling National as a mob front since its founding in 1929 by Meyer Lansky associate Frank Erickson."

  The EIR alleges: "A listing of ADL financial contributors and award recipients over the recent decades reads like a 'Who's Who' of the Meyer Lansky international crime syndicate.  Longtime Lansky cronies such as Victor Posner, Hollywood attorney Sidney Korshak, and Moe Dalitz all appear as ADL patrons. The same pattern holds true at the regional levels of the ADL." Lots more detail is given.

The final major mention is the Canadian Edgar Bronfman, an honorary vice chairman of the ADL. His family's criminal dynasty started with his father Sam, who, with Arnold Rothstein, was dispatched to Hong Kong in 1920 to arrange for supplies of opium, and who further organized the smuggling and retail distribution of the illegal drugs. A nephew of Edgar Bronfman "was named in a 1972 Montreal Crime Commission report as an intimate of local crime boss Willy Obront." Further detail is quoted from *The Bronfman Dynasty* by Peter C. Newman. The Bronfmans' present holdings include Seagrams Corp., including its majority share in E. I. du Pont de Nemours Co. The EIR says that, upon the appearance of the 1978 edition of *Dope, Inc.*, which prominently mentioned the Bronfman clan, Quebec police sources said that Bronfman ordered his attorneys to sue EIR for libel, but that, "after careful deliberation, the attorneys strongly argued against such an action." Bronfman instead poured money into the ADL, which then commenced a campaign of shrill attacks against Lyndon LaRouche and the EIR.

- **Ties to the Soviet Union:** The extensive relationships are detailed between major ADL figures, including Edgar Bronfman and Dwayne Andreas, the president of the Archer Daniels Midland grain giant, and communist bloc leaders, including the East German communist dictator Erich

Honecker, and Mikhail Gorbachev, who ascended to power in Moscow in 1985. Some of the purposes were "to improve ADL coordination with the KGB in running pro-Gorbachev propaganda inside the United States" and "to move in on the 'lucrative new markets' in the liberated nations of Central Europe – on behalf of organized crime." Ties between the Soviets and the ADL are described going back as far as the mid-30's, involving also the Soviet spy rings operating during World War 2.

- **Ties to the Nicaraguan Contra Program:** The ADL's ties to this covert program for developing the South American drug trade are extensively described by reference to the participation of several eminent ADL figures, including Carl Gershman, the director of the National Endowment for Democracy (NED), the administration's agency for secretly funding the Contras; Rabbi Morten M. Rosenthal, who, with NED funding, produced a study pronouncing that the Sandinistas were "anti-Semitic," aimed at marshaling Jewish support for the Contra effort; Kenneth Bialkin, the attorney for Saudi billionaire Adnan Khashoggi, whose money purchased arms for Iran via the good offices of Col. Oliver North, as part of the arms-for-hostages negotiations; Willard Zucker, who ran the Lake Resources front company in Geneva, Switzerland, which laundered the Iranian arms profits to the Contras; Edmond Safra, who, with Willard Zucker, owned the corporate jets used by Oliver North and National Security Advisor Robert MacFarland in traveling to secret conferences in Iran.

- **Domestic Terrorism:** The ADL's activities as agent-provocateur within groups involving the civil rights movement, the Ku Klux Klan, the Nazis, the anti-war movement, and the paramilitary Right are described, with the ADL frequently cooperating with the FBI's Division Five in these matters. This collusive work is shown to have extended to bombings, assaults, jury-tampering, and other illegal activities.

- **International Terrorism:** The EIR focuses on the ADL efforts concerning the preparation for and/or the cover-up after the murders of Indian Prime Minister Indira Gandhi and Swedish Prime Minister Olof Palme. Prime Minister Gandhi was murdered in October 1984, perhaps because she was moving toward American and away from Soviet military assistance. During the immediately preceding months, a Sikh "extremist" group had threatened and predicted her death, and had formed the World Sikh Organization. That organization has had assistance and ongoing communication with the ADL, with its leader Surjit Singh being "a close personal friend of ADL Honorary National Chairman Kenneth Bialkin."

Prime Minister Palme's murder in February 1986 was apparently to cover up the massive arms and drug trafficking by American, British, Israeli, and Soviet agencies that became known to him from documents obtained following a police raid which he ordered on a trafficker in his own country. He thereupon undertook to halt the flow of arms from Sweden to the Persian Gulf, and his murder shortly followed. The ADL's involvement in the cover-up is described, as is the proof uncovered by the Swedish police of the KGB's prior knowledge of the assassination.

- **Penetration of Law Enforcement:** Despite its ties to organized crime and other less-than-legal activities outlined above, the ADL has, with the help of the FBI, "managed to conduct a highly successful campaign to insinuate itself into the day-to-day workings of virtually every major police department and sheriff's department in the United States." The methods and some of the results of this activity are described.

Other matters discussed, which we will not go into here, include involvement with Israeli / Palestinian politics, ties to Mossad operations, support of efforts by the major Midwest grain cartels to liquidate the independent family farmer, and even the support of cultism, followed by the creation of "deprogramming" entities to which parents of cultists would pay big bucks to recover their children, both physically and mentally, from the clutches of those same cults. Study of these matters, and in fact the entire appendix on the ADL, is highly recommended, since the nature of the ADL is so grossly misunderstood in our country, and since its works are so pernicious.

Our strategy at this point will be to delve into the core of the first edition of *Dope, Inc.*, plainly exposing the tie we presumed would appear between the dynastic banking families and the conspiratorial combination of intelligence agencies and organized crime rings described by Piper. We will then end by updating the organizational structure of that combine as was seen by the EIR in their 1986 edition of *Dope, Inc.*

As McCoy related, the Portuguese and then the Dutch preceded the British in running the drugs from India, where the opium was raised, to China and elsewhere in Southeast Asia, where it was consumed. "By 1659," says the EIR, "the opium trade had become second only to the trade in spices, for which opium was a medium of exchange. By 1750, the Dutch were shipping more than 100 tons of opium a year to Indonesia," where, according to one historian, they took good advantage of one of opium's side effects: its use broke down the moral resistance of its users.

The British East India Company (BEIC) started getting involved in 1715, when they opened an office in Canton, on the Chinese coast. They nibbled around the edges of the trade until 1757, when, by military victory, they turned the prime opium-growing area of Bengal (now Bangladesh) into a Crown Colony. Profits went into the pockets of local BEIC officials, however, and did not accrue to England or even the BEIC itself until the effective coup in 1783, when, in the EIR's words, "the dope trade took over Britain."

The coup was organized by Lord Shelburne, who proposed to take two bankrupt entities, the BEIC and Britain, which was hugely in debt at the end of the Revolutionary War, and combine them into a single going concern. Drug profits would henceforth go to the BEIC *and* to Britain, and Britain's political establishment would protect and enhance the operations of the BEIC, particularly its profitable drug trade. Shelburne struck an alliance with the BEIC's Lawrence Sullivan, "whose son had subcontracted for the private opium monopoly in Bengal," and Anglo-Dutch banker Francis Baring. Then with money from the opium trade and with the support of the monarchical patronage machine, "Shelburne bought the Parliament in 1783, lock, stock, and barrel," and consolidated an unbeatable financial and political power.

Shelburne's proposed program for returning Britain to greatness was, says the EIR, to "expand the opium traffic and subvert the United States – both under the banner of free trade. The first achieved crowning success with the Chinese Opium War; the second not until the twentieth century."

As early as 1787, the British Secretary of State proposed that Britain force the opium market into China. Jardine Matheson was one of the trading companies entrusted to covertly manage the opium exportation from India to China, hiding the BEIC's involvement. The drug trade soared, and by 1830, "opium was the largest commodity in world trade." In China, local criminal gangs called Triads (analogous to American "Mafia") were selected by the British trading companies to distribute their opium into the hinterlands. The Chinese Emperor finally resisted by seeking to expropriate the opium in the warehouses of the trading companies, and the British declared war. It was over very quickly, since "The Chinese forces, decimated by ten years of rampant opium addiction within the Imperial Army, proved no match for the British." The peace treaty, signed in 1842, delivered, besides monetary reparations, British extraterritorial control over the 'free port' of Hong Kong, "to this day [in 1978] the capital of Britain's global drug-running."

Britain's official policy of using mind-destroying drugs to enhance British commerce was laid out in an 1841 memo from British Prime Minister Lord Palmerston to the British governor-general of India: "... we must unremittingly endeavor to find, in other parts of the world [than Europe], new vents for our industry [opium].... If we succeed in our China expedition [i.e., the Opium War], Abyssinia, Arabia, the countries of the Indus, and the new markets of China will at no distant period give us a most important extension to the range of our foreign commerce."

The process was repeated in the Second Opium War, ending with the joint British-French siege of Beijing in October 1860. Out of this war, "the British merchant banks and trading companies established the Hongkong and Shanghai Corporation, which to this day serves as the central clearinghouse for all Far Eastern financial transactions relating to the black market in opium and its heroin derivative." The British had thus completed the process of opening up all of China, as Lord Palmerston had sought in 1841, and now controlled about seven-eighths of the Chinese drug trade, which doubled again by 1880. Its modus operandi had been:

- Addict the target population, "to sap the vitality of the nation."
- Utilize the military as needed to install and protect the drug trade.
- Use profits to fund a criminal infrastructure to carry out the trade.

The EIR then outlines ties created by the British merchant bankers to American bankers and traders, and something of how certain of them were drawn into the drug trafficking business. Some of the familiar names which come up are John Jacob Astor and his descendent Waldorf Astor, who was chairman of the Council of the Royal Institute of International Affairs (RIIA) during World War 2. John Murray Forbes of Boston was U.S. agent for Baring Brothers, the "premier merchant bank of the opium traffic from 1783 to the present day." Several other Boston families were involved in the trade, including the Hathaway and Perkins families. The leading banker for this group of families became the House of Morgan. Thomas Nelson Perkins became the chief Boston agent of the Morgan Bank. Morgan partner Willard Straight spent 1901-1912 in China as assistant to Sir Robert Hart, the head of the Chinese Customs Service, and thus the leading Britisher conducting the opium traffic. Straight then became head of the Morgan Bank's Far Eastern operations. Today (i.e., 1978), the chairman of Morgan Grenfell, which is 40 percent owned by Morgan Guaranty Trust, is Lord Catto of Cairncatto, who sits on the "London Committee" of the Hongkong and Shanghai Bank.

The bulk introduction of drugs into the United States came about by the introduction of coolies onto the West Coast. They were transported there by the same British trading companies who were running the slave trade to the South. Some 117,000 coolies entered in 1846 alone, a great many of them being opium addicts. The opium followed them, laying the foundation for the later drug trade out of the Chinatowns of the major West Coast cities. Lincoln outlawed the coolie traffic in 1862, but it continued without significant pause up to the turn of the century. By 1875, officials estimated that 120,000 Americans in addition to the Chinese coolies were addicted to opium.

As Americans and others around the world began to perceive addiction problems in their own back yards, efforts were made to shut down the traffic, efforts which the British sternly opposed. A Hague Convention was passed in 1905 (which the British signed and then evaded), and a proposal was brought to the League of Nations Opium Committee in 1923 aimed at worldwide reduction of both production and consumption to 10 percent of current values, a proposal which the British publicly and vehemently opposed. By 1927, British statistics showed that about 26 percent of British Far Eastern colonial revenues were derived from opium, providing a believable rationalization for their adamant support of the drug trade.

The next major step, taken in 1920, was Prohibition. Basic opium supply was now available, and its transport into the country was simple enough. What was needed was a criminal infrastructure to deliver it on American streets. The effort started by mounting a campaign in both Canada and the U.S. to outlaw liquor. The agitation for Prohibition was not spontaneous. Rather, it was deliberately funded by American families who had been drawn into the British web. The Women's Christian Temperance Union (WCTU) and its offshoots "enjoyed the financial backing of the Astors, the Vanderbilts, the Warburgs, and the Rockefellers." Tax-exempt foundations were also brought in, "especially the Russell Sage Foundation and the Rockefeller Foundation."

Prohibition commenced first in Canada, running from 1915 to 1919. During this period, the Canadian criminal infrastructure for the delivery of British (and Scotch) booze was developed, centered largely on Canada's Bronfman family, who "established the local mob contacts in the United States [which would soon be needed], and consolidated contractual agreements with the Royal Liquor Commission in London." In the United States, the Prohibition Amendment was ratified in 1917, but only went into effect via the Volstead Act in January of 1920. Canadian Prohibition terminated just one month earlier, giving the Bronfman's free rein in their own country to import and manufacture distilled spirits, and to move that liquor into the hands of the American organized crime rings under development.

The scheme worked like a charm. The needed street gangs were spawned, and those capable of managing their internal organization rose to the top, with Meyer Lansky being the final emergent kingpin. Even though Prohibition was repealed in 1933, narcotic drugs remained illegal, and the criminal gangs were enabled to continue honing their skills by branching out in other directions, including casino gambling, prostitution, extortion, loan-sharking, etc. Narcotics, however, was not to become their really big business until the supply was further developed after World War 2, the monetary pathways developed for handling the anticipated flood of illicit cash, and a cultural climate created "conducive to fostering drug addiction."

The British stayed demurely above all this illegal fray. The heroin they sold to Arnold Rothstein and Meyer Lansky in the 20's was sold legally. What the buyers did with it was their own business. Likewise the booze the British sold to Joe Kennedy and the Bronfman family was legally sold, and what those buyers did with it was likewise their own business, simply a matter of "free enterprise" at work.

The EIR next plunges into how the monetary end of the drug system works. It looks first at the size of the trade. Annual street sales in the U.S. of the three major drugs (heroin, cocaine, and marijuana) amount to about $233 billion, according to House Select Committee on Narcotics in 1986. The worldwide trade is accordingly estimated at about $500 billion. The first question, says the EIR, is "How is it possible that $500 billion in dirty money ... can remain outside the control of the law?" It is obvious that no one bank is large enough to handle this volume of money. The EIR answers its own question: "A huge chunk of international banking and related financial operations has been created solely to manage dirty money." And who is capable of creating such a network? "British banking operations [comprise] the only possible banking network that could handle the requisite volume of illegal traffic." That network has become qualified to do so, says the EIR, by virtue of having handled the trade for about a century and a half, by controlling the political jurisdiction over the major off-shore banking outlets (whose records are invisible to target governments), by controlling the world trade in gold and diamonds (used to hide the routes of illicit cash flows), and by possession of the needed connections to organized crime, law enforcement, and intelligence agencies around the world.

Off-shore banking occurs largely in Britain's old island colonies around the Caribbean, as in the Bahamas and Cayman Islands, and "with very few exceptions ... is under the thumb of the British oligarchy." The bulk of the net drug proceeds in the U.S., i.e., after paying off the crime rings engaged in street distribution, are then "laundered" by including such cash in bank deposits made by companies normally handling large volumes of cash, such as casinos, race tracks, sports stadiums, commodity or other brokerages, restaurant chains, and even department stores. Once such a deposit is made, the illicit money is wired to an off-shore bank, following which it is lost in an electronic maze of transfers substantially impossible to trace, even if investigative agencies had access to off-shore banking records, which they do not.

The trick is making that first laundering deposit and then transferring the money out of the depositing bank in such a way as to make the transaction disappear or appear normal to the bank's computers and to later auditors. The EIR devotes a chapter of *Dope, Inc.* describing some of the illegal ways in which this can and has been done, usually involving an inside conspirator in the bank accepting the deposit, in addition to the needed conspirator(s) in the business establishment making the deposit. However, says the EIR, "If the reader is beginning to suspect that thousands of bankers and IRS officials are all in on the game, we emphasize that no such thing is, or could possibly be the case. Dope, Inc. is a tightly run little network. What makes it effective is that there is nothing 'abnormal' about it; it is built into the business structure of the United States and a number of other countries." The "good news" part of this is that the group of conspirators is small enough to be successfully attacked. As the EIR put it, "We know their names and addresses, and how to mop them up."

The EIR relates an instructive example at this point which involves a small American airline suspected of delivering dope to various urban crime centers, while simultaneously contracting with the Federal Reserve to deliver cleared checks. The airline was partially owned by Airborne Freight of Seattle, controlled by a New York bank called Allen and Co., the Allen being Meyer Lansky's investment banker Charles Allen. On the board of Airborne Freight was one James H. Carey, an executive Vice President of

Chase Manhattan Bank. Carey had previously worked at Hambro's, the leading British merchant bank, for its then president Richard Hambro, immediately following which he became CEO of First Empire Bank, a joint venture between Hambro's and Macy's. First Empire did banking for the Jacobs brothers, who ran a major money-laundering branch of Lansky's empire. Carey's sponsors at Hambro's, says the EIR, "were among the best-connected of Britain's elite: Richard Hambro's uncle, the late Sir Charles Hambro, was chief of Britain's Special Operations Executive during World War 2, the superior of Sir William 'Intrepid' Stephenson" who we have met a number of times before.

But the "choke point" of dirty money was in Hong Kong, where the huge money volume dwarfed legitimate economic activity. The drug money estimated by the EIR to have flowed through Hong Kong in 1978 was $10 billion, about twice Hong Kong's total money supply. The EIR therefore focused its attention upon Hong Kong and set about to trace that money flow back to its origins in the British-controlled syndicates in America.

The core of control is at the Hongkong and Shanghai Bank (the "HongShang"), created by the British after the Second Chinese Opium War. The bank, says the EIR, "is the semi-official central bank for the Crown Colony, regulating general market conditions, holding excess deposits of the myriad smaller banks, providing rediscount facilities, and so forth. The HongShang is also the financial hydra unifying the production, transportation, and distribution of Asia's opium." The colonial government and the bank "often work closely together," as the London *Financial Times* is quoted, though neither entity makes any banking statistics public. Sitting adjacent to the HongShang in the Crown Colony are "213 deposit-taking finance companies, as well as 34 local banks and 104 bank representative offices" via which the HongShang receives deposits from and tenders payments to the external world.

One of the bank's chores is to finance the cultivation and acquisition of each year's new crop. This goes a little beyond legitimate agriculture, since the financing must cover not only the equivalent of seed, fertilizer, and equipment, but also transportation on pack mule trains, chemicals for heroin laboratories, smuggling to ports of embarkation, private armed security forces, and official bribery as required at each step along the way. Opium from the farm costs about $100 per pound, grows to $200 at the Thai border, becomes $2000 per pound for heroin out of the laboratory, and ultimately grows to about $2 *million* per pound on the streets of San Francisco, Los Angeles, or Chicago. The HongShang must see that the finances are in place to pay for each new year's heroin supply, at $2000 per pound, before any of the heroin ever reaches the final markets. Some portion of that seed money is probably available from retained earnings by the several participants in the production, transportation, and marketing processes. However, any and all credit which the HongShang may have to extend within Southeast Asia, which the EIR says might amount annually to around $150 million, can readily be handled, particularly when it is realized that a much larger stream of money is coming into the area than is going out.

The larger stream is labeled "reflow" by the EIR, and consists of the cut that the Far Eastern end of the dope trade is receiving out of the overall profits realized by the trade, the great bulk of which comes about from the huge price markups at the street level. "In other words," says the EIR, "the Hong Kong networks are directly represented in the Western 'organized crime' segment of Dope, Inc., and take their cut in the form of a reflow of the retailing profits. Scattered bits of evidence ... indicate that this is, in fact, how these syndicates operate."

The business structure managing the drug trade in Southeast Asia consists of "the old British banks and trading companies, including the HongShang, Jardine Matheson, Charterhouse Japhet, Swire's, and the Peninsular and Orient Lines" plus a second satellite group of "overseas Chinese networks, under the control of London and Beijing." This latter group is indispensable to the HongShang: "The essence of the bank's drug control is its intimate relationship to scores of expatriate Chinese banking families scattered throughout the Far East. The British and Dutch connection to these families dates back to the first East India Company penetration of the region. The central banking role of the HongShang expresses an agreement that grew out of a century of official opium trade and continues through to the present." The Bangkok Metropolitan Bank is cited as an example. The bank developed the Golden Triangle's major source of acetic anhydride, an essential component of heroin production. It has reported links to the Triads, the expatriate Chinese secret society involved in much of the legwork of the drug trade. Yet the Chairman of the Bangkok Bank, Chin Sophonpanich, "is actually nothing more than a subcontractor of the Hongkong and Shanghai Bank."

The Chinese expatriate community handles a large percentage of the legitimate commerce of the Southeast Asian region, much of it in partnership with the HongShang. The corrupt segments of that community which handle the drug trade "have provoked a long series of clashes with national authorities.... The one exception is the British possession of Hong Kong, the center of illegal operations in the area, where smugglers are members of Hong Kong's high society...."

A critical element in managing the finances of the drug trade is the use of gold and diamonds to hide the route of money transfers from point A to point B. As the EIR puts it, "One bar of gold looks like any other; changing a bank balance into gold or diamonds, and then changing it back into a bank balance, is like crossing a river to avoid bloodhounds." The trade simply could not be run without these commodities. These facts led the EIR to examine where the gold and diamonds that were readily available in Hong Kong came from.

First, the Hong Kong gold market was found to be run by a company called Sharps Pixley Ward, 51 percent owned by the HongShang. The Hong Kong diamond market was found to be monopolized by the Union Bank of Israel, which was wholly owned by Israel's largest finance house, Bank Leumi. Following each of these commodities back to their source brought the EIR to Harry Oppenheimer in South Africa.

Taking gold first, the market in Hong Kong involved a daily trading volume in the hundreds of millions of dollars, on a par with the other major gold markets in London and Zurich. The EIR quotes from an address by British expert Timothy Green of Consolidated Gold Fields, Ltd. at the Gold Conference of the London *Financial Times* in October 1972: "It is a fact that both in 1970 and 1971 at least 500 tons of gold – that is to say half of all South Africa's production, or 40% of total gold production in the non-Communist world – passed through unofficial [i.e., illegal] channels on the way to its ultimate destination. These unofficial channels usually start in gold markets such as Beirut [since defunct], Dubai, Vientiane, Hong Kong, and Singapore.... Their chief role – their raison d'être – is as distribution centers for smuggling.... Dubai has become the largest gold market in the world, except for London and Zurich." In 1970 and 1971 the Dubai market transmitted about 200 tons of gold, about one-fourth of South Africa's production, into a golden pipeline toward India and the East. The EIR notes, "The dominant commercial and gold market force in Dubai is the British Bank of the Middle East, a 100% subsidiary of the Hongkong and Shanghai Bank."

Many more details about the mechanics of illegal use are discussed, but we'll try to keep focused on the bigger picture. Hong Kong, says the EIR, "depends entirely on the London gold pool for its supplies [of gold]. The London gold pool is the same operation as the Hongkong and Shanghai Bank, controlled by the same London families whose drug-running activities go back 150 years." The EIR then offers up its details, including:

There are two major South African gold companies: Anglo-American and Consolidated Gold Fields. The Anglo-American chairman is Harry Oppenheimer. In 1980 Oppenheimer also took 28% control of Consolidated Gold Fields. The gold pool consists of five firms which meet daily to "fix" the day's gold price. "Examining these firms individually," says the EIR, "we discover such a manifold of connections that it is meaningless to speak of the London and Hong Kong gold markets as anything but branch offices of the same operation."

The first London pool member, Sharps Pixley, has a subsidiary Sharps Pixley Ward, which is 51% owned by the HongShang. Other cited ties: Sharps Pixley is itself fully owned by the London merchant bank Kleinwort Benson, whose employee George Young "was the number-two man of British intelligence throughout the 1960s." Kleinwort Benson's deputy chairman is Sir Mark Turner, the chairman of Rio Tinto Zinc, which was founded a century ago by a member of the Matheson family with the opium-trading profits of Jardine Matheson. Members of the Matheson family are still large shareholders in the HongShang.

The second pool member is Mocatta Metals, a majority share of which is owned by Hong Kong's second largest bank, the Standard and Chartered Bank, whose predecessor, the Standard Bank, was created a century ago by Cecil Rhodes. Standard and Chartered has for years been closely interlocked with the Hong-Shang. Mocatta Metals' current chairman is Dr. Henry Jarecki, who has of late been investigated for illegal activities. The EIR says that European intelligence sources have alleged that Jarecki's money laundering activities in the New York City area have helped fund the activities of the Mossad. Other details are discussed.

The third pool member is Samuel Montagu, which is wholly owned by the Midland Bank. Midland also owns 20% of Standard and Chartered, thus standing behind Mocatta Metals as well. Sir Mark Turner, mentioned above, "is a director of both Midland Bank and Samuel Montagu. The Montagu family is heavily intermarried with the Rothschilds, Montefiores, and Samuels. One of the family's protégés is HongShang board member Philip de Zulueta."

The fourth pool member is N.M. Rothschild and Sons, which commenced Hong Kong operations in 1975. The Rothschild name appeared in our earliest reviews, and will frequently appear again.

The fifth and last member of the London gold pool is Johnson Matthey. Both it and N.M. Rothschild and Sons are "interlocked several times over with both the HongShang and the major South African gold producers, Consolidated Gold Fields and Anglo-American, who control between them 90% of South Africa's gold output."

Going briefly to diamonds, the second commodity facilitating the opium trade, we noted above that the Hong Kong market was under the financial control of Israel's largest finance house, Bank Leumi. That bank in turn is under the control of Barclays Bank, "on whose board sat Harry Oppenheimer and the Oppenheimer family itself." Harry Oppenheimer, who is first of all the manager of the largest South African gold producer, Anglo-American, is also the presiding manager of the De Beers Corporation, which runs the worldwide diamond cartel. De Beers was created in 1888 by Cecil Rhodes (again!). Today the diamond cartel sells raw diamonds to 300 secret, select customers, following which the purchased diamonds are sent to either Antwerp or Ashqelon, Israel for cutting. The Israeli processing is financed by Bank Leumi, the Antwerp processing by the Banque Bruxelles-Lambert. The latter bank is "controlled by the Lambert family, the Belgian cousins of the Rothschilds." I think that we could fairly say at this point that a pattern has emerged.

Whereas the "reflow" of drug profits to the HongShang and other destinations in the Far East is no doubt desired to be entirely in laundered, readily negotiable form, some portion of it apparently trickles in in small U.S. bills which still require laundering, since Hmong peasants and other legmen in the trade much prefer goods, gold, or their own local currency. One such laundering attempt by the HongShang and five other Hong Kong banks illustrated this need when an American bank receiving large cash deposits from them was caught by the U.S. Treasury department, and fined $2.25 million, for not reporting deposits greater than $10,000 from 1980 to 1984 aggregating some $3.43 *billion.* The bank in question was the Crocker National Bank of San Francisco, which is closely tied to the HongShang. "Indeed," says the EIR, "the Hong-Shang is the parent company of the Crocker Bank," with both of them being owned wholly or in part by the London-based Midland Bank. Note that the fine amounted to about 60 cents per $1000 of illegal deposits, a truly negligible laundering "cost."

The true nature of the drug and supportive financial operations in Hong Kong are well-known to U.S. officialdom. The EIR notes, "In testimony before the House Select Committee on Narcotics Abuse and Control in 1984, Assistant Secretary of State Dominick Di Carlo pointed to Hong Kong as 'the major financial center for Southeast Asia's drug-trafficking. Hong Kong-based trafficking organizations operate through-out the world.'" The EIR further quotes a 1984 Presidential Commission on Organized Crime which noted that the currency being repatriated from Hong Kong in small bills "exceeds the total volume of all currency transactions with any European country," including France and West Germany. The commission discounted any notion that the flood of small bills could be anything other than dope money.

There is one aspect of the drug trade which is *not* well known, however, or which is at least officially denied. That is the matter of the involvement of the People's Republic of China (PRC). On this issue, the EIR takes explicit exception to the allegations of Alfred McCoy in his *The Politics of Heroin*. The issue is important enough for us to clearly identify.

With respect to PRC involvement, McCoy claims in his book: 1) that Harry Anslinger, the first director of the Federal Bureau of Narcotics, was wrong in claiming PRC involvement; 2) that the Golden Triangle opium cultivation and collection area excluded any portion of the PRC, specifically Yunnan province; 3) that all opium production within mainland China was terminated upon the Communist conquest; 4) that Vietnamese officials were primarily responsible for pushing drugs onto American soldiers, in order to raise money to support their corrupt political infrastructure; and 5) that the Hong Kong drug business was run by the heads of Chinese criminal syndicates who had fled from Shanghai just before the Communists arrived.

The EIR takes issue with each of these claims, even to the point of alleging that McCoy was led to make them because of his own sympathy with the anti-Vietnam War movement, and his desire to help stop the war by exposing the U.S. government's complicity in promoting the drug trade. The EIR's footnote on

Part III, Chapter 7 says in part (p. 278): "Experts on the Southeast Asian theater at the time McCoy wrote simply doubt the author's integrity. McCoy had available to him a mass of documentary evidence showing that roughly half the Golden Triangle growing area lay within the confines of Communist China's Yunnan province.... McCoy simply chose to ignore this evidence, or, more accurately, to attempt to refute it with unsubstantiated assertions.... *McCoy's book cannot be taken seriously as far as the PRC issue is concerned.*" [EIR's emphasis]

With respect to the PRC, the EIR updates to 1992 what it first wrote back in 1978, and also adds an entirely new appendix covering the PRC's involvement. The EIR's evidence is extensive. They start by quoting comments made by Chinese Prime Minister Chou En-lai in a 1965 conversation with Egyptian President Nasser: "Some of [the U.S. troops in Vietnam] are trying opium, and we are helping them. We are planting the best kinds of poppies especially for the American soldiers in Vietnam.... Do you remember when the West imposed opium on us? They fought us with opium, and we are going to fight them with their own weapons.... The effect this demoralization is going to have on the United States will be far greater than anyone realizes."

It is through the triad of the PRC and the British and expatriate Chinese in Hong Kong that the PRC will realize its share of the drug trade profits, says the EIR. It quotes from a Reuters report of Sept. 25, 1982 in which British Prime Minister Margaret Thatcher flew to Beijing to consult with PRC elder statesman Deng Xiaoping on the future of Hong Kong. From there she flew to Shanghai to have lunch with Sir Y. K. Pao, an expatriate Chinese and British knight who is a board member of both the HongShang and the Chase Manhattan Bank, and who runs Hong Kong's World-wide Shipping, which manages the world's largest merchant fleet. From there she went to a shipyard in Shanghai and performed the naming ceremony for one of Pao's new ships, called *World Goodwill*. She told the Shanghai mayor, "The ship is the symbol of the close relation between China, Britain, and Hong Kong."

The EIR continues, "Since the late 1950s, Beijing has deliberately integrated its external financial affairs with the top British drug-running firms in Hong Kong and Macao and the overseas Chinese drug wholesaling and dirty money networks throughout the Orient.... Beijing's financial dependence on Hong Kong is a matter of public record. On Oct. 2, 1978, Chase Manhattan's newsletter *East-West Markets* estimated that the financial flow into mainland China in 1978 (excluding [payments for] exports) through Hong Kong would total $2.5 billion.... Beijing does all its banking through Hong Kong, largely through the Hongkong and Shanghai Bank, and secondarily through the Standard and Chartered Bank. The aston-ishing $2.5 billion financial reflow back to Communist China represents the fruits of Beijing's twenty-year program of moving into the higher echelons of the drug traffic, by agreement with the British.... Beijing's current policy represents a direct line of continuity between the current regime and Britain's nineteenth-century corrupt collaborators in China. Correspondingly, the fortunes of the Beijing Communists are linked to the opium trade and the British oligarchy. They have staked China's economy – its capacity to import urgently needed foreign goods – on the opium trade."

Much more detail and lines of evidence are offered by the EIR in the update of their old material, including the complicity of the PRC intelligence service, the PRC's participation in the Hong Kong gold market, Hong Kong's act of self-protection by moving its heroin labs out of Hong Kong, another joint venture between Sir Pao and the PRC in 1980, born out of an earlier discussion with Margaret Thatcher in London, and more.

Then in their new appendix, the EIR seeks to summarize the then-present (1992) state of the PRC involvement. The cover-up of the PRC's drug war against us far exceeds in effectiveness the Warren Commission attempted cover-up of the Kennedy assassination. The PRC cover-up was orchestrated by Henry Kissinger following his trip to China in 1972. Nixon fought it, but was outmaneuvered and eventually driven from office. The PRC never did stop growing and distributing opium, though they outlawed its domestic consumption, ruthlessly enforced that proscription, and brought production under state monopoly control. "Corroborated reports indicate that today [1992] the PRC is the world's largest opium producer, [at] 800 metric tons of opium per year....

The Hong Kong-based *Liberation Monthly* reported in December 1989 that the PRC provides 80% of the high-quality heroin selling on the international market.... A *San Jose Mercury* article, published May 16, 1975, explained why [such details were seldom seen]: 'A secret federal report, the *Mercury* has learned, pinpoints the PRC as the producer of quantities of heroin that have been detected in the Bay area. The report ... supposedly is being kept under wraps ... for fear its release could affect détente between the U.S. and China." This makes it clear enough that official Washington is well aware that the PRC is growing and distributing drugs to the U.S. It's only the public that doesn't know.

The EIR appendix discusses the drug routes out of the Golden Triangle, including the Yunnan province, and something about the local controlling entities. It quotes the Thai police chief who predicted that the 1989 opium harvest would increase to 2000 tons, over triple the 600 ton yield in 1981. The new figure includes PRC opium raised in Yunnan and smuggled into Burma for delivery through Thailand. Eyewitnesses are quoted concerning the Yunnan operations. Several PRC leaders of the drug operations are identified. Also discussed is Beijing's relatively new attempt to bring distribution under their own in-house control in place of that of the expatriate Chinese, since the latter are too prone to invest their profits in legitimate businesses outside of the PRC instead of sending it all back to mainland China. Gang warfare has broken out in such places as Amsterdam over this issue.

The EIR then backs up a few years to further examine the recent origins of the current PRC-British drug venture. The EIR's sources are recently released documents of both the U.S. State Department and Britain's Royal Institute of International Affairs (RIIA) covering the years of the Communist conquest of China. The EIR recalls first that the RIIA was created in 1919 by Lord Milner, in furtherance of the tasks he undertook as administrator of the Rhodes Trust to fulfill the wishes of Cecil Rhodes. Those wishes were expressed in Rhodes' will (somewhat abridged) as follows:

"To establish a trust, to and for the establishment and promotion and development of a secret society, the true aim and object whereof shall be the extension of British rule throughout the world ... and especially the occupation by British settlers of the entire continent of Africa, the Holy Land, the valley of the Euphrates, the islands of Cyprus and Candia [Crete], the whole of South America, the islands of the Pacific not heretofore possessed by Great Britain, the whole of the Malay Archipelago, the seaboard of China and Japan, the ultimate recovery of the United States of America as an integral part of the British Empire, the consolidation of the whole Empire ... and finally, the foundation of so great a power as to hereafter render wars impossible and promote the best interests of humanity."

In support of this strategic policy, the events respecting China and Britain during the World War 2 period went something as follows. Britain became convinced during 1942 that they would lose the support of the American public if they disavowed the Atlantic Charter's declaration in favor of self-determination for all, and instead insisted upon retaining autonomy over their enclaves in the Far East. In particular this included the portion of Shanghai which they administered, Shanghai coincidentally being the world's center for refining opium into heroin. The RIIA and its offspring, the Institute of Pacific Relations (IPR), therefore proposed and pushed an alternative policy of fostering Maoism.

Why? One clue appears in a 1976 book by Peter Vladimirov, the Soviet liaison to Mao Zedong's wartime headquarters in the north-central Chinese city of Yenan, in which Vladimirov alleged that Mao supported the continued cultivation around Yenan of opium as a major cash crop, a practice begun before Mao's arrival. He also questioned Mao's "close contact with American visitors connected to the IPR." A second clue appeared in a 1978 issue of the RIIA's journal *International Affairs.* Victor Farmer, of the RIIA's Far Eastern Committee, is reported to have stated following a 1944 visit to the Far East: "I have met some [Chinese] Communists and their ideas are very open-minded. If you could get rid of this ultra-nationalist clique in the saddle at present in Chungking ... I think that the way would be open for a compromise with the Communists; and an effective compromise."

An "effective compromise" was in fact obtained, primarily through the efforts of Sir John Henry Keswick, of the hereditary drug-trading family which founded Jardine Matheson. Sir John Henry was attached to the British embassy in Chungking during World War 2, and was in regular contact during this period with Chou En-lai, who was running the Chinese Communist legation in Chungking. Concerning that compromise, the EIR says that both the RIIA and the State Department documents "yield the same interpretation: the creation of the PRC included an alliance between the British dope-runners and the Chinese dope-runners. This was negotiated from the British side by Sir John Henry Keswick and from the Chinese side by Chou En-lai. The Chinese team also prominently included top figures in the opium trade ... [including] elements of the so-called Green Gangs, [who] ran the opium trade not only in the Far East but throughout the far-flung Chinese expatriate community."

The EIR continues: "From both the British and the Chinese side, the alliance was explicitly against the United States. The Chinese knew it, and said so, the British knew it, and said so, and American diplomats cabled home that the United States had been shafted."

The British then replaced their "pro-colonialist" policy with the "softer" pro-Maoist policy, with the help of the pro-Maoist IPR group in the U.S. State Department centered around John S. Service and John Carter Vincent. When the Communists finally took over China, Americans were infuriated at what they thought were Communists in the IPR who had infiltrated the State Department and helped bring about the Communist victory. The fact that the IPR was a British entity serving British foreign policy objectives was a deep secret never remotely guessed at by the general public or the U.S. Congress. Concerning the IPR, the EIR summarizes: "The dead giveaway on the IPR's British character is the organization's move to Canada subsequent to the 1950 McCarran Committee investigation, which mistook pro-British treason for pro-Communist treason. With hearty British cheers, the disgraced IPR moved to Canada ... [where it] came under the official sponsorship of the Canadian Institute of International Affairs, the local RIIA subsidiary...."

And what did the British get out of their secret deal? First, the PRC granted them continued control over Hong Kong. Second, the PRC in 1949 let them move the Shanghai heroin laboratories into Hong Kong. Third, as early as 1947, the Chinese banking community in Shanghai was organizationally divided between a PRC faction which remained on the mainland and an "expatriate" faction which soon left for British-controlled Hong Kong. The two factions remained in close contact, however, thereby creating the financial ties between the PRC, the expatriate Chinese, and the British which "would later [be used to] underwrite the Far East narcotics traffic."

Around 40 million Chinese died in the post-war PRC consolidation. Americans and others of the West have since suffered vast narcotics addiction. To what bottomless depth is it possible for human corruption to fall?

Lord Humphrey Trevelyan was appointed in 1951 as British ambassador to the PRC. He is credited with laying the groundwork for the later American commercial opening to the PRC, executed by Henry Kissinger. Trevelyan today sits on the Board of the British Bank of the Middle East, and also on the board of British Petroleum, "along with John Keswick's brother Sir William Johnston Keswick, and various other members of the boards of the HongShang and the RIIA Council. Lord Trevelyan completed the circle by taking the chairmanship of the Council of the Royal Institute, while keeping an active hand in the opium business through the British Bank of the Middle East."

The EIR has included a fascinating chapter on the history of the Canadian Bronfman family, of which we can only scratch the surface. First came Yechiel Bronfman, "a grist mill owner from Bessarabia, Romania," who emigrated to Canada in 1889, sponsored by the Moses Montefiore Colonization Committee, created in 1872 by Baron Maurice de Hirsch, Baron Alfred de Rothschild, and others in the Zionist community. In Canada, says the EIR, the Bronfman family "first turned to selling wood, then to horse trading, and then most successfully to the hotel business (and prostitution)." The Bronfmans, who shortly attained multi-millionaire status, were selected by the British to import and distribute British liquor during the Canadian Prohibition period, and then to export that same liquor to the U.S. during the American Prohibition which started immediately thereafter. During the Canadian Prohibition, two of the Bronfman sons, Sam and Abe, "collaborated with the Hudson's Bay Company – in which the Keswick family of Jardine Matheson had controlling interest – to buy the Canadian Pure Drug Company," utilized to enable the legal distribution of "medicinal" alcohol. But the family's major assignment came with American Prohibition, when it was charged with selecting the American gangs which would distribute British liquor, and smuggling that liquor to them. That success led to the use of the same network to distribute opium from the Far East.

Arnold Rothstein, who had started the serious work of creating an American crime syndicate consisting of members who would cooperate instead of seeking to kill each other, was himself killed in 1928. His work was picked up by one John Torrio, "a Bronfman man" says the EIR, who was better able to work with the Italian crime elements in the U.S. than Rothstein or Bronfman himself could. Torrio was very successful, and he was later followed by Luciano and ultimately by Meyer Lansky. The crime kingpins, however, were the Bronfmans, who were beholden to the British elites, who were the Bronfmans' financiers, their political protectors, and their booze and opium suppliers.

The EIR devotes a whole chapter to the Permindex operation. Of course that entity also leads back to the British, and makes the involvement of such a person as Major Louis Bloomfield, the personal attorney of the Bronfman family, much more understandable. Bloomfield, the Chairman of the Board of Permindex, was recruited in 1938 into the British Special Operations Executive (SOE) where he worked under Sir William Stephenson to implement an agreement negotiated by Stephenson (for Winston Churchill) and President Roosevelt to allow "British intelligence to set up shop in the United States and to effectively merge its operations with those of the FBI and military intelligence.... Bloomfield, described by numerous authors and associates as a practicing homosexual, developed a deeply personal friendship with FBI Director J. Edgar Hoover. Through that relationship, Bloomfield was able to retain his powerful position in Division Five long after the end of the war. As late as 1963, when Bloomfield was case-officering the assassination plot against John F. Kennedy, he was still a top official in Division Five."

Let's pause to reconsider the Kennedy assassination. The operative elements of a plausible scenario might be as follows:

- Joe Kennedy was supplied booze by Bronfman and the British, and (like Bronfman himself) remained interested his whole life in becoming a part of, and being accepted by, the British elites.
- Upon JFK's election, Joe and his son John started doing the task assigned by the British-Bronfman combine of expunging the unwanted Mafia elements from the American crime syndicate and preserving the desired ones, including Lansky and Trafficante.

- The Kennedys did OK until their anti-Semitism got in the way, causing them to choke on Israel's covert development of nuclear weapons.
- The British, seeing *their creation*, Israel, being threatened, concurred with Israeli Prime Minister David Ben-Gurion's desire to terminate John Kennedy.
- The assassination was then ordered and executed as described by Michael Collins Piper in *Final Judgment*.

The Permindex operation is discussed in very great detail, as is its more modern replacement entity known as Resorts International, which is the real headquarters organization of the overtly criminal aspects of the drug business, including money-laundering, drug and gun-running, and assassination. A whole chapter is also devoted to the well-developed and long-planned British effort to lure American youth into drug usage, i.e., to develop their drug market, resulting in the paroxysm of the 60's with which we are all familiar. We will resist the urge to go into these matters as well, and content ourselves to discuss just two other topics covered in this uniquely valuable book.

The first has to do with the EIR's description of the organization of the family elements within the oligarchy which is attempting to control us. Some of the family names at the top go back to the 1300's. The religious and other ties that bind them together are described. Some of the family names are Bruce (from King Robert Bruce of Scotland), Russell, Villiers, Keswick, Inchcape, Pease, Matheson, Mackay, Churchill, Lloyd, Cecil, and Lytton. These folks hide their involvement in the illegal activities which afflict us by utilizing several camouflaging layers of subordinates who do their dirty work for them. Law enforcement officials call these layers "cutouts." There are three cutout layers below the elite oligarchy, says the EIR:

> "The first is a front for Jewish-surnamed criminal elements. [In the first edition of *Dope, Inc.* were the words, 'In the West, the prime cutout ... is the Zionist lobby.... In China (it was) the corrupted Soong family which carried out the day-to-day business operations of Jardine Matheson.'] This cutout begins at the top with a cohesive grouping of *Hofjuden* ('Court Jews') who have served British monarchs and Venetian doges for generations. These families have a centuries-long unbroken tradition of attaching themselves to the predominant noble houses of Europe: the Venetians and Genoese, the nobility of Amsterdam, and then when the Dutch nobility was merged with the British in the so-called Glorious Revolution of 1688, the Hofjuden centered themselves around the British and have served it to this day.
>
> "The Hofjuden have less than nothing to do with the Jewish people, their well-being and aspirations for themselves and their posterity. These families' only relation to the Jews has been to periodically call down persecution upon them, and then to excuse their own role in it by their surnames [i.e., *hide* their role by claiming to be one of the persecuted Jews]. One cannot condemn the Jewish people for the centuries of crimes committed by the

Hofjuden, whose primary victim has been that people itself.

"Among these top families are the Montefiores, servants of the Genoese nobility since the thirteenth century; ... the Goldsmids and Mocattas, leading bullion merchants for the British royal family; ... the Oppenheimers, controllers of a large proportion of the diamond and gold mining in South Africa; the Sassoons, the first Hofjuden to settle in India and devote their resources primarily to opium production; ... the Canadian de Hirsch family, bankrollers of Jewish emigration from Eastern Europe to Canada; the Rothschilds, with a long-standing special interest in subverting the American republic; and the other 'Our Crowd' banking families of Warburg, Schiff, Meyer, Loeb, Schroder, etc....

"The second major layer of cutouts [consists of] the émigré nobility and pseudo-nobility of Eastern Europe and the Mediterranean – the Jesuit / Russian Orthodox, or 'Solidarist' nobility.... Typical of these families are the Radziwills, leaders of the Polish Solidarists; the unreconstructed fascist Ferenc Nagy of Permindex; the de Menils, [involved in Permindex]; the di Spadaforas, representatives of the Italian House of Savoy in the Permindex Assassination Bureau; and of course, the families of minor nobility such as one well-known Brzezinski. The political family of William F. Buckley, Jr. and James Buckley are permanent hangers-on of the Jesuit émigré circles, and promoters of drug decriminalization.

"The third and most active 'cutout' [consists of] the Socialist International front organizations in North America. [Included are] Social Democrats U.S.A. and the League for Industrial Democracy, ... [which] are the funding sources for pro-drug and pro-terrorist organizations: the Institute for Policy Studies, the Communist Workers Party, Yippies, and the rotten American Civil Liberties Union networks epitomized by William Kunstler."

The first edition of *Dope, Inc.* was more explicit about the relationship between the Hofjuden and the Jewish people. The EIR there stated:

"The Hofjuden should not be confused with the Jewish people.... The only relation the Hofjuden have had to Jewry is that of persecutors and tormentors. As the clandestine operations bureau of the oligarchy, they quickly learned that they could augment their capabilities tremendously by subjecting Jews to waves of persecutions and then recruiting terrorized Jews into Zionist organizations that had as their ostensible aim the 'survival' of Jewry! In street parlance, the Hofjuden have run a six-century-long protection-extortion racket against the Jewish people – to the overall effect of building up a sizable 'Zionist' network at the disposal of British Secret Intelligence. This traditional relationship to Jewry was carried to its [logical] conclusion in the 20th century when the Rothschilds, Warburgs, Oppenheimers, Schroders, and other Hofjuden became the leading financial backers of Adolf Hitler.

"One of the greatest benefits that the Hofju-den gained by their complicity in Hitler's genocide of the East European population was that they could henceforth hide behind the memory of the awesome fate of millions of Jews and conduct the filthiest sorts of operations – from drug-running to terrorism to genocide against Arab and related populations – without being exposed for these crimes against humanity. Whenever any critic attempted to expose these crimes, he was quickly assaulted as a 'Nazi,' a 'fascist,' or an 'anti-Semite.'"

Our final effort will be to summarize the EIR's view of the organizational structure of Dope, Inc. as of 1986. The oligarchy, says the EIR, views the world's peoples as so many "talking beasts" to be utilized as desired in the service of the oligarchy. Narcotics serve that purpose as an efficient tool for both control and profit, since it weakens the resistance of the target populations, and also brings in several hundred *billion* dollars annually to help grow the oligarchy's various criminal projects. These projects presently include depopulation (fewer proles are needed to harvest the required food, fiber, and minerals), destruction of national sovereignty, debt collection, destruction of the Western Alliance, and the reduction of U.S. power to 25% of its post-World War 2 strength.

The effort is led by the families owning or controlling the network of major London banks and holding companies, including the HongShang, the Oppenheimer interests, Barclays Bank, the London gold pool, etc. Bronfman's Canadian enterprises are controlled by Eagle Star Insurance, a major London financial corporation, which in turn is jointly run by Barclays, Lloyds, Hill Samuel, and N.M. Rothschild and Sons. Canada itself is little more than a colonial tool in the hands of the British elites, useful in helping to bring the U.S. to heel.

A large-scale effort to "buy up" American finance was launched following Nixon's (i.e., Paul Volcker's) removal of the gold backing from the dollar. A 40% de facto devaluation occurred with respect to gold-based European capital pools, and, combined with a troubled stock market, the London and other European elites found easy pickings, particularly among the U.S. brokerage firms. One of the first to go was George Ball's Lehman Brothers, followed by Lazard Frères, Drexel Burnham Lambert, and others. Then in 1981, Salomon Brothers, investment banker to Citibank, and perhaps the most powerful investment banker on Wall Street, merged with Phibro, the Oppenheimer trading arm. An indicator of the great strength of the European financial power in the U.S. security markets, which helped to bring about these foreign takeovers, is that foreign equity investment amounted in 1980 to about 20% of the value of all U.S. stocks. Much of the money brought to bear in our markets is suspected to be "drug money," much of which otherwise disappears from the world's balance sheets.

Back in the early 60's, the First National City Bank had hired a Dutchman, Robert Meyjes, who proposed to set up a "private international banking" division of the bank. He did so, and sent some 600 bank trainees through the division in the next 10 years. Meyjes is now in Citibank's Paris office, and his "trainees" are scattered in various banks around the world, running an "old-boy" network of covert "banking," privately handling the deposits of people who are not anxious to say where their money came from. David Rockefeller's Chase Manhattan Bank quickly caught on (they referred to it internally as "looking for Mafia money"), and followed suit, not very successfully, says the EIR, until they accepted onto their board Mr. Y.K. Pao, the vice-chairman of the HongShang, prior to which they found no entry into Hong Kong's lucrative activities.

Further consolidations took place in the 80's. Lehman Brothers had been taken over by Kuhn Loeb, which was in turn taken over by American Express, on whose board Henry Kissinger was elected in 1984. American Express also absorbed Shearson Hayden Stone, which had just previously gobbled the German-Jewish investment bank Loeb Rhoades. American Express then became the monster Wall Street umbrella called Shearson Lehman American Express. The board member of American Express who managed that series of mergers was attorney Kenneth Bialkin, the then-current [1986] chairman of the ADL.

Henry Kissinger is the at least nominal head of Kissinger Associates, whose members, says the EIR, "represent a de facto board of directors for the entity we call Dope, Inc." The members include:

- Mario d'Urso, who ran the old Kuhn Loeb international department, and is now "the New York chief for the Jefferson Insurance Company," a joint arm of the two giant Italian insurance companies which control the fortunes of the ancient Venetian trading families.
- Britain's Lord Carrington, the cofounder of Kissinger Associates and a former director of both Hambro's Bank and Barclays Bank.
- Lord Eric Roll of Ipsden, the chairman of the London merchant bank S.G. Warburg.

Kissinger Associates is represented in Hong Kong by Sir Y.K. Kan, who also "represents the four overseas Chinese families which control the Hong Kong-based Bank of East Asia."

The EIR summarizes as follows: "The monster we identified in 1978 has molted, shedding such skin as the Banco Ambrosiano and Investors Overseas Service, only to multiply in extent and influence. Six years ago, the narcotics traffic menaced all future generations of youth. Now it is the center of the gravest threat to Western civilization since the fourteenth century. Slowly, belatedly, the governments of the West have acknowledged the extent of the problem, and, in their lumbering fashion, accepted parts of the analysis we offered six years ago. But effective, ruthless action has yet to be taken against the citizens and institutions who have brought the dregs of the financial underworld to the apex of power in political life." The EIR has also said, however, that the malefactors are known, and given the political will, the cleanup job can be accomplished.

Chapter 12

## "LET'S FIX AMERICA!"

(By Alan B. Jones. Pub. 1994 by ABJ Press, PO Box 2362, Paradise, CA 95967.)

Let's briefly review the strategy we outlined in our introduction. We observed that corrective actions aimed at fixing our many problems would invariably be misdirected or insufficient unless we understood reasonably well how those problems originated. We have therefore attempted to demonstrate in the preceding chapters that a secret war has been declared against us by certain monied elites, aimed at weakening us and ultimately bringing us under their dominion. It is our belief, however, that once enough of us recognize our peril, we will be successful in undertaking the drastic actions required to restore our national independence and substantially eliminate our several problems, down to and including their roots.

In *Let's Fix America!* (LFA) we listed a set of problems which are pressing hard on our society, though we made little effort to identify their origins. The solutions proposed still seem proper, but somewhat sterile until it is understood that many of the problems have been deliberately created to weaken us. We propose in this final chapter, therefore, to review the LFA proposals specifically within the context of the material reviewed in the preceding chapters, taking particular notice of alterations we might make in the light of those reviews.

LFA Chapter 2 (Currency Stability) deals with abolishing the Federal Reserve System and returning our banking system to a gold-backed system essentially free of federal government involvement, including prohibiting the banks from holding government bonds as "assets." G. Edward Griffin has clearly shown in our current Chapter 5 that: (1) the Federal Reserve System was conspiratorially created exactly by agents of the elites who are seeking to dominate us, (2) the system is nothing but a banking cartel acting for the benefit of those elites in concert with similar central banks in other countries, and (3) the system's main purpose is to enable the financing of government deficits such as to produce both the inflation which has destroyed our incentive to save and the monstrous national debt which today's and tomorrow's taxpayers must labor to pay off. Even if our generation is successful in forcing current congresses to live within balanced budgets, the Fed *must* be abolished in order to emphasize to future generations how strongly we have come to feel about never again permitting the central government to pay for whatever it wants with fiat "money" which it can create at will.

LFA Chapter 3 (Balanced Budgets) proposes measures which will facilitate the creation of balanced budgets, but will in addition absolutely prevent the federal government from running an ultimate deficit. Our purpose, of course, is to force politicians to be fiscally responsible, that seldom being their natural inclination, and not at all what the elites desire. The centerpiece of the proposal is a constitutional amendment requiring that any residual unbalance at the end of a fiscal year between receipts and expenditures (including budgeted debt retirement) be either paid to or billed to the several states in proportion to their populations. It might help to time these checks or bills sent to the states so as to be highly visible during congressional elections.

LFA Chapter 4 (The Tax Load) addresses the core issue facing our citizen taxpayers who see an ever-increasing percentage of the fruits of their labor being expropriated by various levels of government and spent on non-productive activities – what the Iron Mountain gurus prescribed as the *waste* necessary to keep us peons under control. We proposed in LFA Chapters 2 and 3 to fix up one such category of waste by gradually eliminating our national debt, on which we have spent on the order of $2 trillion in interest since the start of LBJ's Great Society. We will similarly deal with other specific issues in later chapters. In this one, however, we propose to impose a constitutional cap on the *total* of federal, state, and local taxes, defining the cap as a fixed percentage (say 30%) of a carefully defined "national income" (perhaps just personal and corporate receipts from the sale of goods and services). The federal budget cap for a given fiscal year would then be the constitutional percentage of the previous year's national income less the previous year's total tax receipts received by all state and local jurisdictions. It is to be noted that this process will give state and local jurisdictions the first call on taxpayers' money, since those entities are weaker than the federal government and more responsive to taxpayer oversight. (The same principle is proposed to be applied to state/county budgeting procedures.) We expect that this procedure will produce instant experts in the state legislatures willing and able to help out their federal legislative counterparts in their budgeting tasks, and vice versa.

LFA Chapter 5 (The Income Tax) deals with the abomination which is our federal income tax. It is to be abolished, along with the IRS and the whole tax preparation industry, and the 16th Amendment repealed, to prevent the income tax from easily reappearing. In its place we propose a federal consumption tax on the sale of services and goods-for-use. Gone will be taxes on personal income and corporate profits, and thus also on interest, dividends, and capital gains. With inflation halted (LFA Chapters 2 and 3), savings and gross capital formation should balloon, the economic stagnation brought on by regressive economic policies should stop, employment and general economic growth should blossom, and our country should enjoy renewed economic strength (rather than further elite-engendered weakness) throughout the world. We urge that state income taxes also be abolished and replaced by similar sales taxes on consumption. The states should collect the federal sales taxes and forward them to the Treasury, one check per state per fiscal quarter. Many more of the details are discussed in LFA Chapter 5.

This change is extremely important, and will strike at the root of the elites' attack on our American society. Our free society is seen by them as the only entity on earth still capable of growing strong enough economically and socially to challenge their program for dominating the earth. They are therefore attacking our ability to grow economically, their tools being waste forced upon us (by war, drugs, welfare, environmentalism, etc.) and *the taxation of our free economy's engine of growth.* We have thus been conned into taxing our incomes, which are the rewards we pay ourselves for our productive successes. We propose to reverse this perverse policy of penalizing production, and henceforth tax consumption rather than productive enterprise. Note that this will impose taxes on the *spending* of accumulated or inherited wealth, and will correspondingly reduce taxes on those working to earn incomes through productive labor.

LFA Chapter 6 (Social Security and Pensions) proposes an actuarially sound alternative to the existing Social Security system, which is now generally recognized to be nothing more or less than a pyramid scheme, a Ponzi game, illegal when practiced privately. Attractive at first, with many payers per payee, it has finally reversed, and taxes are becoming prohibitive on today's fewer number of workers supporting our retired payees. The system weakens the society by reducing individual responsibility and increasing dependence on Big Brother. The LFA replacement will phase out Social Security and all other governmental pension systems, making government employees subject to the same private pension systems as other citizens, and grossly reducing the federal government's budget.

The replacement is a private policy containing certain common minimum provisions. A worker will be required to purchase at least the minimum policy from the company of his choice. The policy shall be capable of being "rolled over" to another company, at the worker's option. The minimum policy shall provide a minimum retirement income, protecting society from large numbers of indigent retirees. Larger premiums may be paid at the worker's option to yield larger retirement income, or income for a non-working spouse. The "phase-in" process will take a number of years, and is discussed at length in LFA. The accumulated funds, however, belong to the policy owner, are earmarked for his future use, and are beyond the reach of the U.S. Treasury or Congress. These funds will add mightily to the capital accumulations available to fuel our free-enterprise capitalist economy, and should provide a major boost to our country's economic strength and our society's well-being.

LFA Chapter 7 (Medicare and Medical Issues) takes on our medical care system. It was working pretty well until Medicare came along, at which time large segments of our society began receiving benefits which no *private* entity had to find the money to pay for. Only government had to pay, and it doesn't care to economize, since infinite tax resources are always available, or the money can be created if necessary. Furthermore, the more money that is spent, the larger the bureaucracy that is justified to handle it.

LFA's hard-nosed message: *There is no free lunch!* The job is to wean ourselves off of the government teat to which we have been seduced, get the government out of the medical care business, and return to a viable, long-term, lower cost system in which the great majority of our citizens accept personal responsibility for paying for their own medical care, including premiums for private insurance covering at least those large expenses which cannot otherwise be afforded. To protect society from large numbers of medically indigent, workers will be required to purchase at least minimum basic policies. The policies will be actuarially sound, will belong to individuals, and will travel with them wherever employed. They will contain annuity elements to enable continuation of coverage during periods of unemployment and to build up funds adequate for the larger medical expenses statistically expected after retirement. Welfare recipients may be granted minimum basic policies, as state welfare agencies may find appropriate.

Many other details are covered in LFA Chapter 7, with special attention given to the FDA, the AMA, and malpractice litigation issues. The primary results to be expected, however, are (1) a huge intractable item will be removed from the federal budget, (2) individuals will regain a substantial measure of independence from Big Brother government, and (3) medical costs will stop their upward spiral as consumers realize that they must pay for their medical purchases, as they do for any other service, and as they return to shopping for the lowest cost treatments adequate to their needs. That is, the *waste* associated with accepting marginally useful expensive services that someone else has to pay for will be severely reduced, to the ultimate benefit of us all.

LFA Chapter 8 (The Four-Graybeard Criteria) digresses long enough to present a philosophical foundation for "good law" to which we have tried to adhere. We briefly present these thoughts here to whet the appetite and encourage further study. First is the Tenth Amendment to the Constitution, which expressed the intent of our founders that the states yield to the federal government those powers *and only those powers* that were listed in the Constitution. Second is Frederic Bastiat, who says that man's fatal flaw is to satisfy his desires with the least pain, including the possible use of plunder, especially legal plunder. The test for legal plunder is to ask whether a given law takes away something belonging to one person and gives it to someone else to whom it did not belong. Third is Albert Jay Nock, who declares that a corrupt government does not seek to abolish crime, but rather to maintain a monopoly over it. His test for a good law is to ask whether it tends to increase or decrease the government's capacity to exploit its citizens. Fourth and last is Ayn Rand, who declares that the only legitimate function of government is to protect individuals from attempts by others to violate their individual natural rights (to life, liberty, and property) by force. The test for a good law is therefore to ask whether it prevents or punishes the infringement by physical force of an individual's inalienable rights.

How we wish these several criteria might be carved in stone within the halls of Congress!

LFA Chapter 9 (Welfare) addresses welfare. This money hog is so blatant that most people have caught on. Since LBJ declared his War on Poverty, we have spent, i.e., *wasted*, about $5 trillion on federal welfare, an amount about equal to our present national debt. About the same number of citizens are in "poverty" now as were in 1964. As this is written (1996), Congress has just managed to pass a law sending block grants to the states to administer these programs with somewhat more freedom than before. What is needed, of course, is to remove welfare from the federal budget, reduce federal taxes by that amount, and announce to the states that they may keep any or all parts of the program that they wish provided they pay for it, and otherwise take on the total responsibility for welfare within their own states. As we all know by now, the federal welfare system has produced generational cycles of dependence on government, with single-parent families producing male juveniles headed for gangs, crime, and jail, and females headed for prostitution and the next generation of single-parent families. The LFA proposal will eliminate this monster of waste and societal damage which the Iron Mountain folks specifically recommended, will vastly reduce the federal budget, and will put the responsibility for welfare all the way back to the county level, where it might be effectively monitored and locally paid for.

LFA Chapter 10 (Bailout Surprises) proposes in one fell swoop to eliminate another host of unwise, unconstitutional, and fiscally unsound government programs capable of causing major taxpayer pain, including the federal deposit insurance program that has recently caused taxpayer losses on the order of $500 billion (the S&L bailout). We propose, simply, that essentially *all* federal insurance, price guarantee, loan, and loan guarantee programs be abolished, over an appropriate transitional time period, but while always honoring existing contracts. Bank loan guarantees, mortgage guarantees, farm loans and price supports, small business loans, and myriad other similar programs will be a thing of the past. Such programs inevitably produce widespread economic *waste*, i.e., they transfer their losses to taxpayers, precisely as a result of government being conned (or bribed) into assuming responsibility for the rightful obligations of various private individuals, groups, or companies.

LFA Chapter 11 (Drugs) seeks to deal with the issue at the prime focus of the EIR's *Dope, Inc.* which we reviewed above. The program of addicting Americans to narcotic drugs is clearly the mother of all efforts to produce waste, perhaps second only to a good, healthy war. We needn't go again into the monstrous social and economic costs, as they are now well known. We labeled the proposed LFA solution "legalization," but are now led to alter that to "medicalization," to conform more closely to labels coming into more common public use. In a word, we would continue to prohibit the illicit importation and sale of narcotic drugs, but would enable the low-cost sale of such drugs by state or state-licensed agencies to medically certified addicts, as may be provided by state law. This is our effort to eliminate the repeat "hooked addict" market, which will take the bulk of the profit out of the illicit trade, and essentially eliminate drug-pushing as a viable occupation.

Two other major areas may be attacked, as suggested by the EIR. One is money laundering, though we believe that as street distribution declines following drug "medicalization," fewer dollars will require laundering, making detection that much more difficult. Special attention should be given, however, to "private international banking" adjuncts to domestic banks, as described by the EIR, and laws aimed at preventing illicit funds from being deposited should be strengthened.

The last major area to be attacked, if we really wish to get serious, involves an attack on the overall drug system, utilizing laws presently on the books against criminal syndicalism. We should bring to clear public attention the roles being played by the Golden Triangle countries, Afghanistan, Communist China, the Hong Kong heroin labs, the HongShang, the RIIA and CFR, Mexico, the Cali Cartel, the Bronfmans, the U.S. mobs in their employ, the "rogue" British financial institutions controlling these elements, and their American subsidiaries. Americans suspected of being involved in the syndicate, whether overtly engaged in banking, government (e.g., the CIA), or local crime, should be publicly charged and tried. Without such public exposure, the American public is unlikely to rouse itself sufficiently to even support the "medicalization" program discussed above.

We will next discuss LFA Chapter 13 (Education), and then back up to Chapter 12. As William McIlhany described in his *The Tax-Exempt Foundations*, the secret minutes of the Carnegie Endowment for International Peace requested the Rockefeller Foundation to take on the "responsibility" for controlling education regarding domestic matters, while Carnegie would do the same for international matters. They so agreed. The education was to produce socialization, which would in turn enable a "comfortable merger" into a whole which could readily be controlled by the elites at the top. "Comfortable merging" required the prior "dumbing down" of American society, and socialization required suppression of individual initiative and responsibility. We see such suppression and dumbing down both being advanced in our public schools, and frozen there by the monopolistic straitjacket of labor law supportive of the personnel and programs of America's biggest labor union, the National Education Association.

The LFA Chapter 13 solution is to empower parents with state vouchers, presentable to any school of the parents' choice, which, if the school agrees to accept the student, will be presented by the school to the state in payment or partial payment for the tuition charges for that child. The state is to be denied authority to interfere with the educational policies, methods, materials, or teacher qualifications of such voucher schools, except perhaps to deny voucher schools the right to hire convicted felons as teachers. New schools of various kinds should sprout like weeds, particularly in our crime-ridden city slums. Public schools will lose revenue as their enrollments drop, and they can be expected to either reform in a hurry or go out of business. Good teachers can be expected to drift into the rejuvenated private schooling system with little difficulty. It took a long time for the elites to capture the public schools as effectively as they have, and it will take a similarly long time to rebuild an honest system. As it gradually takes hold, however, with no centralized "authority" running it, we can expect to look forward to a strengthened national backbone and an enhanced ability of our body politic to uncover relevant historical truths, learn from them, and further strengthen and improve the societal heritage to be passed on to our children.

LFA Chapter 12 (Crime) examines "how to avoid growing criminals." Frederic Bastiat, as we noted a few paragraphs earlier, assigned the source of crime to man's fatal flaw of seeking to satisfy his desires with the least possible pain, including, for example, stealing instead of earning. While it seems that human society will always include some residual number of predators, it should certainly strive to reduce that number to a tolerable minimum. We have instead, in recent years, built up three major industries which have been exactly counterproductive in that regard, namely, the welfare, drug, and public education industries.

Our proposed solutions are to tear down those existing industries, and rebuild them where appropriate, taking care to protect their impacted victims in the process. Welfare will be managed locally, with welfare recipients given incentives to help them shed their dependency and acquire skills leading to self-sufficiency and self-esteem. Two-parent families will again become "normal," with adult role models to help guide children toward healthy adult lives. The drug scourge will be stopped, and the kingpins identified, prosecuted, and incarcerated where possible. The greatest single cause of societal waste operative today will thus be stopped, in the process enabling us to substantially reduce our prison populations. Education reform will enable new paths to be opened to young people as viable alternatives to gangs and street crime. An additional supportive change would be to permit states to lower or abolish the minimum wage for minors, to enable employers to give them a temporary boost into the adult job market.

LFA Chapter 12 also contains several proposals for reforms within the criminal justice system. It proposes: enabling adult court access to juvenile crime records, escalating sentences steeply for repeat offenses, repealing parole board authority to reduce sentences, mandating restitution for valuable losses in criminal sentences, and enabling convicts to work during incarceration to help pay restitution, incarceration costs, and any other debts.

LFA Chapter 14 (Liability Litigation) concerns our growing litigiousness. In this arena, one special interest group (trial lawyers) has acquired a cash cow for its members by creating law which encourages anyone to sue any deep pocket in sight for any alleged slight, shortcoming, or injury, at no cost to oneself. Juries can impose arbitrarily large judgments, frequently in proportion to the thespian abilities of the trial lawyer, and a percentage of which the lawyer will take as his fee. Doctors and other medical personnel and institutions are thus forced to pay huge premiums for malpractice insurance, we all are forced into purchasing huge automobile liability coverage, companies fear class action judgments which can bankrupt them, etc. It all amounts to another source of monstrous waste – Bastiatian plunder – which must be paid for by taxpayers and other hard-working victims of that plunder everywhere.

The LFA's proposed solution is to confine the authority of juries in liability suits to establishing the percentage of fault among all the litigants, including the appellants, with percentages assigned as appropriate for "no one" (e.g., "acts of God") or "unknown" or "non-litigant(s)." Monetary losses will be determined by accountants and appraisers selected by the litigants or appointed by the court, and shall exclude "pain and suffering" and punitive fines. Awards in liability suits will then be taken as the percent fault of each defendant times that professionally determined monetary loss.

LFA Chapter 15 (Abortion) involves an issue which is tearing our society apart and getting in the way of electing legislators equipped to help solve our many other problems. The issue arose from our Supreme Court's decision (Roe vs Wade) to tell the states what they could and could not do with respect to abortion. The Constitution, however, does not give either the Supreme Court, the Congress, or any other element of the federal government the power to legislate or adjudicate with respect to the medical procedure of abortion. (The Supreme Court, of course, should refrain from *legislating* on *any* matter.) The LFA's proposed fix is simply for the Congress to exercise its constitutional authority to enact a resolution denying the Supreme Court jurisdiction over suits concerning abortion, such matters being reserved to the states by the Tenth Amendment. The issue would then properly go back to the individual states, which can be expected to legislate as each sees fit.

LFA Chapter 16 (AIDS) considers what to do about the "Acquired Immune Deficiency Syndrome." The second sentence in that chapter reads, "It is a disease which present scientific knowledge attributes to a virus commonly labeled the HIV, which stands for Human Immunodeficiency Virus." Since those words were written in 1994, new scientific knowledge has come into existence which directly challenges the HIV hypothesis. Evidence has been presented that AIDS is instead a set of opportunistic diseases contracted as a result of a person's immune system being weakened by the long-term use of drugs. Its only tie to homosexuality is that drug use by homosexuals is common to heighten their sexual response. (See *Inventing the AIDS Virus* by Dr. Peter H. Duesberg, pub. 1996 by

Regnery Publishing, Inc., 422 First St. SE, Suite 300, Washington, DC 20003.)

This development seems unlikely to gain common public currency in the immediate future, as federal health agencies and private researchers on the public dole seem determined to bury it. This public corruption seems a small matter compared to our other major aggravations, but the publication of Duesberg's research is sufficient for us to warn readers off of the severe corrective actions to the AIDS "epidemic" which we wrote into LFA Chapter 16. Congressional hearings on the matter should clearly be held.

LFA Chapter 17 (Illegal Immigration) addresses a problem of growing concern. There are perhaps two major aspects to this problem which are damaging to our society. First, large numbers of illegals flowing across our borders are unlikely to be assimilated into our society, not having had to go through the legally required processes of learning our language and the basics of our society's political institutions. They remain, instead, fodder for revolutionary demagogues. Second, the illegals have found it easy to apply for and receive public assistance benefits without having their illegal status challenged. They therefore continue to come, drawn by readily available taxpayer-supplied benefits. A third specific problem is that pregnant women illegally enter the U.S. just before their babies are due and present themselves to hospitals to have their babies, who then become legal U.S. citizens, enabling the later entry of the baby's whole family. LFA proposals to correct these matters include (1) authorizing agencies delivering taxpayer-financed services to deny those services to anyone who cannot tender proof of citizenship or of permanent resident status, (2) authorizing such local agencies, including law enforcement agencies, to assist in identifying, apprehending, holding, and delivering such illegal immigrants to the INS for deportation proceedings, and (3) enacting a constitutional amendment denying citizenship to babies born in the U.S. to non-citizen parents.

LFA Chapter 18 (Foreign Policy) gets back to the heart of the several programs created by the elites to subdue and control us and all the other countries of the world that are to come under their dominion. The best-known instruments of control which they are using are the United Nations, the International Monetary Fund, the World Bank, and most recently the NAFTA and GATT control organizations, in particular the World Trade Organization. The LFA proposed that we opt out of the UN, the IMF, and the World Bank, and we would presently extend that to rescinding our membership in NAFTA and GATT and the WTO. The defense of Europe should be left to Europeans, and U.S. troops billeted around the world should be returned to the U.S. Our foreign aid program should be terminated. The "Bricker Amendment" should be revived and enacted, providing that no treaty containing any unconstitutional provision shall be effective as internal law, thus forcing treaties, like other law, to adhere to the provisions of the U.S. Constitution. We would now also add that the Council on Foreign Relations (CFR) should be identified as a subsidiary of the

Royal Institute of International Affairs (RIIA), and should be required to register as a foreign lobby, i.e., of Britain.

The LFA dealt sparsely with trade issues, and corrective actions should be beefed up. (1) As we attempt to separate our country from the financial power of the European banking families, we can expect our new gold-backed dollar to come under attack. We must therefore be meticulous in assuring that the gold conversion rate be set such as to avoid disastrous gold loss upon presentation of accumulated stores of foreign dollars and short-term claims on dollars. (2) Trade treaties between the U.S. and other countries shall always require constitutional approval by the Senate, and should always contain provisions for automatically correcting trade imbalances, for example, by adjusting tariffs in agreed-upon ways to compensate for any significant monetary imbalances which develop. (3) An Interest Equalization Tax of the kind proposed by John Kennedy, as we discussed in our Chapter 1, should be reimposed, but this time without loopholes. The tax would be due on any loan to, or investment in, any foreign entity by any domestic person, bank, company, or other U.S. entity, including foreign branches of any such entity. This is aimed at encouraging the channeling of domestic capital and corporate profits back into the growth and maintenance of domestic corporations and domestic infrastructure. Without such a tax, the profits available to domestic companies who move their production abroad has now been proven to be so large as to cause extreme damage to our own working force and indeed to our national independence. The size of the tax can be adjusted to balance our domestic well-being with our desire˙ to help others improve theirs.

LFA Chapter 19 (Congress) seeks first to generalize what Congress has done wrong to get us into so much trouble. (Even though various of the elites' tax-free foundations may have proposed bad legislation, Congress passed it.) Simply, they ignored the Tenth Amendment and legislated on matters which the Constitution prohibited. The Supreme Court, in all the years after having been packed by FDR, went along. The LFA proposes two categories of corrective actions – one dealing with reducing the corrupting motivations acting on our legislators, and one with reducing the field of opportunity for exploitive legislation.

In the first category we recommend term limits, adequate salaries and maintenance while in office, equal and adequate election financing for both incumbents and challengers, expulsion from office for receiving gifts or failing to report proffered gifts from PACs or others, and criminalizing the offering of gifts to legislators. LFA discusses these several matters at length.

In the second category, since the Tenth Amendment was so easy to ignore, we recommend that the Bill of Rights be beefed up by adding another amendment specifically prohibiting the Congress from making any law respecting: (a) any activity or project not impacting substantially equally the citizens of all the states; (b) the health, education, welfare, feeding, housing, clothing, or fiscal support of the citizens; (c) benefits granted to one entity at the expense of a competing entity of the same kind; and (d) the economic regulation of any business. Item a will return local projects to local jurisdictions and halt the practice of logrolling. Item b will move great hunks of the federal budget back to the states. Item c will remove from corruptible legislators the ability to decide which enterprise will prosper and which will not. Item d will free the country's farms and businesses from federal meddling.

These are measures aimed at clearing the decks for the really important measures which Congress and the other branches of our federal government must pursue if we are to regain and preserve for future generations our middle class freedom and our national vitality. Most sorely needed is the public exposure, by our own federal government, of the *fact* that an undeclared war has been initiated against our free middle-class society, plus the identification of the combatants and the various battlegrounds on which that war is being fought. Our final contribution toward this last need is contained in our epilogue – a remarkable 1974 article by novelist Taylor Caldwell who eloquently summarized the problem and appealed to Americans to hear and to act. We can find no better words to conclude our own presentation.

Epilogue

# "THE MIDDLE CLASS MUST NOT FAIL"

(By Taylor Caldwell. First published May 29, 1974 in *The Review of the News*, and reprinted in the May 1, 1995 issue of *The New American*, PO Box 8040, Appleton, WI 54913. Reprinted here by permission.)

"With the rise of the Industrial Civilization in the world, about 200 years ago, there also arose a social body which we know as the middle class. Before that, most of the world suffered under a feudal system in which the people were truly slaves of their governments in all things. There was no strong buffer between them and their despotic rulers, no assurance of freedom to pursue commerce and to live decently, to keep the fruits of their labor and hold the paying of tribute at a minimum. The middle class made the dream of liberty a possibility, set limits on the government, fought for its constitutions, removed much of government privilege and tyranny, demanded that rulers obey the just laws as closely as the people, and enforced a general civic morality.

"Sound leaders looked to the experience of Rome, the first to encourage a middle class, noting that Rome had been a strong and prosperous republic, with much public virtue, a large degree of freedom for every citizen, and a constitution (the Twelve Tables of Law) on which our own is based. After the fall of Rome, governments had everywhere destroyed the middle class, returned to despotism, and entered the Dark Ages. It had been centuries since a rising middle class resolved to keep government at a minimum and to force respect for the people and eschew tribute except for such absolute necessities as armed forces, street protection, and the guarantee of the authority of contracts and commerce.

"Those who for centuries had ruled their nations, from father to son, in total despotism, realized that they were threatened. Were they not the elite, by divine right? Were they not by birth and money entitled to rule a nation of docile slaves? Did the people not understand that they were truly inferior dogs who needed a strong hand to rule them, and should they not be meek before their government?

"Little wonder that the elite hated the middle class which challenged them in the name of God-given liberty. And little wonder that this hatred grew deeper as the middle class became stronger and imposed restrictions through which all people, including the most humble, had the right to rule their own lives and keep the greater part of what they earned for themselves.

"Clearly, if the elite were to rule again, the middle class had to be destroyed. It had to be destroyed so despotism and the system of tribute could be returned, and grandeur and honor and immense riches for the elite – assuring their monopoly rule of all the world. For you see the elite of all nations, then as now, were not divided. They were one international class, and worked together and protected each other. But the middle class laughed and said "we will bind you with the chains of our Constitution, which you must obey also, lest we depose you, for we are now powerful and we are human beings and we wish to be free from your old despotism."

"The elite did not give up. While it profited from the Industrial Revolution, which under liberty of enterprise freed the people from the feudal and despotic systems, and which gave a new birth to the middle class, it also hated the threat to its own authority. It did not wish to destroy the Industrial Revolution; it wished to use it for its exclusive purposes. In the early 19th century this elite looked for a way, once and for all, to regain its power and extort tribute from the people and so destroy the burgeoning middle class which stood in its way, and to subdue the populace again to their proper role as slaves of government by the elite.

"Through the "League of Just Men," elitist conspirators sought a fanatic to cloak the point of their purpose in slogans and cant. The man they hired was Karl Marx. Certainly Marx was no worker; he had never soiled his hands with labor. He hated the middle class, which he contemptuously called the bourgeoisie, for he considered himself superior in mentality and breeding to what he called "the gross merchants of commerce and exploitation." He did not attack the waiting despots, no indeed. They were of one mind with him. Rather he proposed in his books and pam-

phlets the return to government of the total power to
exact tribute from the people in order that the government might better direct every phase of the people's
lives, as he asserted, "for their own welfare."  The
elite, in turn, would control the governments.

"Marx began to accuse the middle class of
heinous crimes and aroused the workers against their
benefactors.  He labored to create envy and malice
among the workers – all aimed at the entrepreneurial
middle class which had raised them from serfdom,
restored their human dignity, and given them liberty
for the first time in nearly 2,000 years.

"Karl Marx was made to order by the self-styled
elite.  They financed the propagation of his sedition all
over Europe and America.   They bled France and
Germany with it.   They financed sedition in Russia.
And the plan began to succeed.  By 1910 the Scandi-
navian countries had already fallen to the socialism of
Karl Marx.  Only three nations stood between the elite
and their ambitions – the British Empire, Czarist
Russia, and the United States of America.

"Much is now made of supposed Czarist tyranny.  But the fact is that the Czar of Russia had already granted his people a greater measure of freedom.
A constitution had been established, and a parliamen-
tary system.   Russia, too, was well on her way to
nourishing and encouraging a middle class.

"The elitists were anxious to promote the
Marxist notion of demanding tribute from the people,

for only through forced tribute could freedom be destroyed and the people reduced again to forced labor for the benefit of the elite. Only thus could the middle class be eliminated. So, we have Karl Marx's infamous notion: "To each according to his needs, from each according to his ability." That is a foundation for slavery and tribute. Marx and the elite had a juicy bait for the workers, who were deluded to envy and hate the middle class which had freed them. If the riches were taken away from the middle class, then the workers would become their equals. Marx called this redistribution of wealth. Not wealth from the elite, with their vast fortunes in every country of the world – inherited fortunes which would not be taxed as income – but wealth from the strong middle class, which would be robbed in the name of the people. Only *earned* income would be vulnerable to seizure.

"But in the way of all this happiness for the conspiring international elite, and the slavery of the people, stood the United States, the British Empire, and Czarist Russia. They would have to be destroyed. Britain had only a small income tax, used for the armed forces, for roads, for the maintenance of law and order, and for the payment of a tiny body of bureaucrats.

"Over and over, in America, the elite tried to establish their federal income tax, but they did not succeed. The people were too vigilant, too jealous of their freedom, too proud, too respectful of themselves. They embraced the ancient proverb, "To work is to pray," and they guarded the fruits of their labors. No,

America had no graduated income tax to drain the capital of the hard-working middle class, and so she became strong and rich and powerful, the envy of nations which exacted tribute and forced labor from their people. Attempts were made to exact such tribute from Americans during the Civil War and the war with Spain, but each time the Supreme Court declared that our Constitution prohibited it. As late as 1902 the graduated income tax was again declared unconstitutional, and the Chief Justice observed: "It is a method to enslave our people, and deprive them of their liberty and right to the fruit of their labors."

"The conspiratorial elite fumed. How best, now, to institute their system of tribute and slavery? The solution was *war*. During wartime, governments were better able to tax the people, harnessing their patriotism to maintain enlarged armed services.

"And so the elite began to prepare America for war, and conspirators of the French and German and Russian and English elite worked with them – for the destruction of their own nationals and the elimination, once and for all, of the defiant middle class. The American elite, under advice of their brother conspirators in other nations, proposed an amendment to the American Constitution – a graduated income tax, just as Karl Marx had proposed. To support this the elite were very busy, through their henchmen, the socialists and the populists, and through their secret communists, in arousing the envy of the workers against the middle class. They told the workers that they would never be taxed, "only the rich," and even then the highest rate would be only two to three percent.   And the taxes would go to "our exploited workers," through all sorts of governmental benefits.  The unthinking, the envious, the stupid, and the malicious thought this was wonderful.  They supported the 16th Amendment – the federal income tax – and it was passed into law in 1913.

"Now the stage was set for war, the attack on the British Empire, Czarist Russia, and the German Empire.  The major thrust of the effort to destroy the freedom of the whole world, and reduce it to total control by the elite, had begun.

"The rest is sad contemporary history.  Few in America heeded what Thomas Jefferson had said long ago, that when we are taxed on our earned incomes, in our food and our drink, in our coming and going, in our property, we would face the return of slavery and the reestablishment of an all-powerful and despotic elite.  So it is that we of the middle class are being destroyed through the exaction of tribute, resulting in an ever-increasing power and despotism of a central government controlled by a conspiratorial elite, and everlasting wars to subdue us and drive us to our knees.

"Do not believe for an instant that the world's conspiring elite in every nation have so much as a serious quarrel among them.   They have just one object: control through tribute.  Your slavery, through tribute, and mine.  And they use wars for their purposes just as they use the inequities, harassments, bullying, capriciousness, and extortion of their graduated income tax. The system of taxation with which they have yoked us is really forced tribute from the hard-working, and especially from the middle class, who are slowly being eliminated.

"Behind this attack are the self-styled elite, secure in their own power and riches. Most of them have huge fortunes which are tax-exempt. But every man and woman of us – we of the middle class – are taxed in our food and drink, in our property, in our incomes, in our comings and goings. The harder we work, the more tribute we have to pay, for the elite are determined that never again will the middle class challenge them, and never again will we be able to save money and so rise to power, and never again will we protest the slavery they have planned for us.

"But many of us still dare to protest, and will continue to do so while God gives us breath. To be effective we know we must direct our attacks on the real criminals, the wealthy and powerful and secret elite of all the world – the conspirators laboring night and day to enslave us. Even our own government is now their victim, for it is the conspiratorial elite who choose our rulers, nominate them, and remove them by assassination or smear.

"I have fought these enemies of liberty in every book I have written. But too few have listened to me, as too few have listened to others who have warned of these conspirators. The hour is late. Americans must soon listen and act – or endure the black night of slavery that is worse than death."

\*     \*     \*

We hope that in writing this book we have supplied enough details, and pointed to sources for many more, to answer the question "What is happening to us?" thus adding to the efforts of Miss Caldwell to expose the malefactors who are assaulting us.  Our earlier effort, *Let's Fix America!*, was aimed at answering the consequential question "What can we do about it?", a question which becomes much more urgent given the context we have presented in the preceding chapters.

We urge readers who have gotten this far to take the following action.  Identify at least one person who is active in public life who you can contact and talk with personally.  *Hand* him (or her) a copy of this book, tell him that even though you thought you already knew everything, you learned things that *everyone* in public life should know much more about.  Ask him to read it also, call you when he's done so, and then pass on copies to others who should in turn become a part of the knowledge chain.  Out of this effort should emerge a good number of new candidates for public office who can help us regain our country.

Note that carte blanche permission has been granted to reproduce this book in whole or part in order to further its distribution.  The text is available on floppy disk, and several such disks have already been distributed.

Alan B. Jones
October, 1996

# INDEX

-------------------------------------------------------------------